Balanchine and the Lost Muse

Balanchine and the Lost Muse

REVOLUTION AND THE MAKING OF
A CHOREOGRAPHER

Elizabeth Kendall

OXFORD
UNIVERSITY PRESS

OXFORD
UNIVERSITY PRESS

Oxford University Press is a department of the University of Oxford.
It furthers the University's objective of excellence in research,
scholarship, and education by publishing worldwide.

Oxford   New York

Auckland   Cape Town   Dar es Salaam   Hong Kong   Karachi
Kuala Lumpur   Madrid   Melbourne   Mexico City   Nairobi
New Delhi   Shanghai   Taipei   Toronto

With offices in

Argentina   Austria   Brazil   Chile   Czech Republic   France   Greece
Guatemala   Hungary   Italy   Japan   Poland   Portugal   Singapore
South Korea   Switzerland   Thailand   Turkey   Ukraine   Vietnam

Oxford is a registered trade mark of Oxford University Press
in the UK and certain other countries.

Published in the United States of America by
Oxford University Press
198 Madison Avenue, New York, NY 10016

Library of Congress Cataloging-in-Publication Data
Kendall, Elizabeth, 1947–
Balanchine and the lost muse : revolution and the making of a choreographer / Elizabeth Kendall.
pages cm
Includes bibliographical references and index.
ISBN 978-0-19-995934-1 (alk. paper)
1. Balanchine, George. 2. Choreographers—United States—Biography.
3. Ivanova, Lidiia, d.1924. I. Title.
GV1785.B32K46   2013
792.8'2092—dc23   2012042482

Frontispiece: Georges and Lidochka, 1921
Courtesy, Bernard Taper

1 3 5 7 9 8 6 4 2

Printed in the United States of America
on acid-free paper

For

Tsiskari Balanchivadze and Keti Machavariani Balanchivadze

And in memory of Djarji Balanchivadze,
1941–2011
Pianist, composer, painter

Contents

Balanchine

Preface

This book had its beginnings in two revelatory moments. The first came in 1981 when I interviewed George Balanchine, founder of the New York City Ballet and virtual inventor of ballet in America, in his office in Lincoln Center's New York State Theater. I was a young dance critic sent by the Ford Foundation. He was seventy-seven, slim and dapper, white hair brushed back from a high forehead. "Is boring, questions we must talk about," said Balanchine as he rose to meet me. I agreed and prepared to leave—I had no right to his time. "So, we do questions, then we talk," he said briskly but mischievously. Indeed, after we discussed Foundation business he began telling me tales about his life back in 1920s revolutionary Petrograd, maybe because he liked young women: tales about starving, and sewing saddles and playing battered pianos in movie houses just to get food. How far away—like the distance to a star—was this past from the complacent America where we sat now. I put myself in his shoes, and as him despaired of conveying the real nature of his youthful experience. My patchy Russian history was causing him to serve up traumatic memories as careful fairy tales.

I'd fallen in love with Balanchine's company, the New York City Ballet, right after I'd arrived in New York in 1973. Actually, "falling in love" isn't right. I'd come to write about avant-garde modern dance; I'd sampled the whole dance scene, and I'd fallen *into* the New York City Ballet. I'd found myself responding to City Ballet's dancing with emotions almost religious in nature: exaltation, wonder, and a sharp gratitude for the beauty and longing being enacted onstage, especially by the ballerinas. This was a time when all the young women I knew were waking up to feminism. Where in our culture were the spaces, the works of art, where women's inner lives could be explored and dramatized?

They were here. Balanchine was allowing—expecting—female inner lives to surface in his choreography. The women on his stage danced intimately and daringly with partners. But they also danced alone, unsupported, "speaking" with the audience. Central to Balanchine's work was always the ballerina, the figure who holds all eyes, who takes the music into her body and makes it physical, human. And City Ballet's 1970s ballerinas (especially Allegra Kent, and then Suzanne Farrell and Patricia McBride) did something more. Each seemed to become, in flashes, a mythic heroine of one of the worlds ballet had traveled through to get here today. They embodied, in quick glimpses, the innocent cruelty of French *romantisme*, the mischievousness of *commedia dell'arte*, the melancholy of Russian novels, the hauteur of tsarist St. Petersburg. Yet they remained themselves, contemporary women. These dancers would hit a vein deep inside the music where they could time-travel. They would dive down and come up with some kind of elegaic radiance, cathartic to a young woman watching from the darkened theater.

The second revelation came much later, in the early 2000s. I was in the museum inside St. Petersburg's fabled Vaganova Academy of Russian Ballet, the school where young Balanchine and so many other dancer greats had trained—Nijinsky, Nijinska, Nureyev, Makarova,

Lidochka in *The Magic Flute*
Author's collection.

Baryshnikov. An oil painting hung above the museum curator's desk: a dark-haired young dancer with a mournful face, seated, hands clasped over a frilly white ballet costume. Why hadn't I seen it before? I moved closer and read the label: Lidia Ivanova, costumed as Lise in *The Magic Flute.*

Here was that classmate and friend of Balanchine's who should have come out with him to the West, but didn't, because she'd drowned on the eve of their departure, possibly a murder. She'd shown up in the Balanchine biographies, but without pictures or explanation. The story of her death—and life—remained a blank in *his* story. This dancer eyeing me from the wall would have been the first young girl Balanchine watched becoming a ballerina, maybe the first to be transformed from friend to muse.

I was alone in the spacious ground-floor museum waiting for a curator. Everywhere hung photos and paintings of dancer greats. Were their ghosts here too in the images? If so, Lidia's ghost was definitely unquiet. No one knew why or how she'd died. But her portrait offered a possible new approach to Balanchine himself. It wasn't hanging here because she was a footnote to the story we already knew. She had her own story in this anti-world of Russian and then Soviet ballet, hidden from us so long by the Iron Curtain and by Russian émigrés' own mythologizing.* If I could learn that story . . . maybe I could see Balanchine's young life more clearly and know better where those miraculous ballets had come from.

It's been a fascinating journey, through archives, libraries, museums, city streets, cluttered apartments, even architectural ruins buried in the woods—in Russia, Georgia, Finland, and the United States. I've deciphered Russian handwriting, studied Soviet memos, measured Finnish typographical maps, admired the squatly ornate Georgian script I couldn't read but which friends translated for me. I've come out of this book believing that the keepers of libraries, archives, and museums are the under-sung heroes of our lives. They guard the past; they watch over the pieces that have made it to the present; they show us the way to go back inside that past and try to understand it, from its own point of view. Without them the story of these two young people could not have come to light.

---

* It was hanging there, I learned later, because the museum's 1959 founder, Marietta Frangopulo, had belonged to Balanchine's Young Ballet, had loved Lidochka and stubbornly put her portrait here, even if Lida's mysterious death was a quasi-forbidden topic in Soviet times.

Acknowledgments

I have been helped by generous fellowships from The Dorothy and Lewis B. Cullman Center at the New York Public Library; the Fulbright Foundation; the Likhachev Foundation in St. Petersburg, Russia; and the Leon Levy Center for Biography at CUNY, in New York City. Without any of these I couldn't have written this book. A huge thank-you to directors and fellow fellows, especially Madison Smartt Bell, Adam Begley, Gary Giddins, Linda Gordon, Alexander Kobak, Stephen Kotkin, Jonathan Levi, Daniel Max, Anna Shulgat, Jean Strouse, Elena Vitenberg, and Brenda Wineapple.

Thank you to the Balanchine Foundation and the Balanchine Trust for generous and crucial belief and support, and to Eugene Lang College of New School for flexibility.

Thanks to staff helpers of the Russian State Historical Archives (especially Vladimir Bersenev) the Archive of Literature and Art of St. Petersburg; the two History of St. Petersburg Archives; the Military History Archive in Moscow; the Provincial Archives of Mikkeli, Finland; the New York Public Library; the National Archives of Georgia; the Georgia Theater, Music and Film Museum; the Vaganova Ballet Academy, especially its Rector Alexei Fomkin; the wonderful staff of the St. Petersburg State Museum of Theater and Music: Chief Curator Tatiana Vlasova and Elena Fedosova, Elena Grushvitskaya, Elena Ampelogova, Galina Pogodina, and Sergei Laletin, and my "home" archive, the National Library of Finland, especially Maire Aho, Irma Reijonen and Irina Lukka.

Many thanks to researchers Irina Anisimova in Petersburg, Ramaz Oboladze and Rusiko Labadze in Tbilisi, and Cosmo Bjorkenheim, Gleb Boudin, Max Kuhn, and Nathan Thrower in New York.

For keeping me healthy, many thanks to Pio Cabada, Debbi Fuhrman, Don Philpott, Lisa Spaeth, and everyone at the late Good and Plenty.

Thanks to generous friends and colleagues: Polina Barskova, Thomas Bender, Judy Bernstein Bunzl, Alexandra Chasin, Arlene Croce, Leila Dediashvili, Pavel Dmitriev, Tamara Fedotova-Gershova, Jamey Gambrell, Lynn Garafola, Wendy Gimbel, Valery Golovitzer, Elena Gracheva, Charlotte Henze, Jennifer Homans, Marvin Hoshino, Jussi Iltanen, Laura Jacobs, Alexander Kapliuk, Irina Klyagin, Paul Kolnik, Irina Kolpakova, Gabriela Komleva, Lucy Kostelanetz, Tamriko Kvachadze, Joel Lobenthal, Stephen Lovell, Nina Matushevskaya and the SPb balletomanes, the late Stanislav Maximov, Alexei Nedviga, Jerry and Helen Polynsky, Vadim Rykhliakov, Timothy Scholl, Vladlen Semenov, Tatiana Semenova, Lewis Siegelbaum, Irina Sitnikova, Arkady Sokolov-Kaminsky, Ellen Sorrin, the late Richard Stites, Yevgenya Tikotski, Yuri Tsivian, Solomon Volkov, Karin von Aroldingen, and Wendy Walters.

Thanks to all the dancers who've lent their imagination and courage to Balanchine ballets: the older pantheon, and the younger NYCB generation now dancing so gallantly.

Thank you so very much to my agent, Lane Zachary, and to my editor Norman Hirschy and the brilliant Oxford University Press crew, especially assistant editor Lisbeth Redfield, production editor Joellyn Ausanka, and copy editor *extraordinaire* Steve Dodson.

My deepest thanks go to the people who have been this book's family: Keti Balanchivadze and Tsiskari Balanchivadze (the book's dedicatees), Stathis Eust, Barbara Horgan, Zippora Karz, Daria Khitrova, Elena Kunikova, Manana Kvachadze, Irina Lukka, Leena Pallari, Daria Pavlova—and to the two who helped more than they can ever know, Ulrika Hallberg and Margo Jefferson.

Cast of Characters

Almedingen, Edith Martha (Alexandrovna), 1898–1971—Russian-born British novelist & memoirist; possible first cousin of Maria Balanchinvadze

Almedingen-Chumbadze, Sophia Nikolaevna, 1885–195?—Kazakhstan-born St. Petersburg dentist, possible half-sister of Maria Balanchivadze

Andrianov, Samuil Konstantinovich, 1884–1917—Mariinsky *danseur noble*, minor choreographer; Georges' first teacher

Balanchivadze, Maria Nikolaevna (Vasilieva), 1873–1959—consort/wife of Meliton, Georges' mother

Balanchivadze, Meliton Antonovich, 1862–1937—composer, Georges' father

Benois, Alexander Nikolaevich, 1870–1960—artist, art critic, GATOB advisor

Chekrygin, Alexander Ivanovich, 1884–1942—Mariinsky *caractère* dancer, dance reformer, Georges' last teacher

Danilova, Alexandra Dionysievna (Choura), 1902–1997—Georges and Lidochka's schoolmate, Ballets Russes ballerina, SAB teacher

Dmitriev, Vladimir Pavlovich, 1884?–19??—opera baritone, Leningrad croupier, 1924 tour organizer of Young Soviet Dancers

Dmitriev, Vladimir Vladimirovich, 1900–1948—painter, scenic artist, Young Ballet circle

Erbstein, Boris Mikhailovich, 1901–1963—scenic artist, Young Ballet circle

Findeizen, Nikolai Fedorovich, 1868–1928—Russian musicologist, journalist, publisher, Meliton's friend

Fokine, Mikhail Mikhailovich, 1880–1942—dancer, groundbreaking choreographer

Gerdt, Elizaveta Pavlovna, 1891–1975—Mariinsky ballerina, teacher

Goleizovsky, Kasyan Yaroslavich, 1892–1970—Moscow experimental choreographer

Gvozdev, Alexei Alexandrovich, 1888–1939—theater critic, teacher

Isaenko, Grigory Grigorievich, 1865?–1923?—boys' caretaker at Imperial Theater School 1888–1917, Theater School Inspector (2nd in command) 1919–1923

Ivanov Alexander Alexandrovich, 1872–1929—Lidochka's father, Russian army *shtabs-kapitan*, Red Army officer, Svetlana factory chief of repairs

Ivanova, Alexandra Ivanovna, 1867–1942?—Lidochka's mother

Kostrovitskaya, Vera Sergeevna, 1906–1979—Young Ballet member, Mariinsky dancer, Theater School teacher, writer

Kshesinskaya, Matilda Felixovna, 1872–1971—Mariinsky prima ballerina, lover of Tsarevich Nikolai (later Nikolai II), Paris ballet teacher

Likhosherstova, Varvara Ivanovna, 1854–1937—Theater School Inspectress 1884–1924

Lopukhov, Fedor Vasilievich, 1886–1973—dancer, choreographer, GATOB ballet master

Lunacharsky, Anatoly Vasilievich, 1875–1933—arts critic, revolutionary, first Soviet People's Commissar of Enlightenment, responsible for culture and education

Mayakovsky, Vladimir Vladimirovich, 1893–1930—Futurist poet, playwright, Bolshevik propagandist

Meyerhold, Vsevolod Emilievich, 1874–1940—actor, experimental theater director and producer

Mikhailov, Mikhail Mikhailovich, 1903–1979—Georges' classmate, Mariinsky soloist, pedagogue, memoirist

Muretova, Maria Grigorievna, 186?–19??—Vasily Velichko's cousin and co-writer, Georgi's godmother

Oblakov, Andrei Alexandrovich, 1874–?—Mariinsky dancer, Theater School director 1919–?

Preobrazhenskaya, Olga Osipovna, 1871–1962—Mariinsky prima ballerina, Lidochka's teacher, Paris ballet teacher

Semenov, Viktor Alexandrovich, 1892–1944—Mariinsky *danseur noble*; Georges' middle teacher, later Theater School director

Stefanovich, Konstantin Konstantinovich—Interior Ministry official, Georgi's godfather

Vaganova, Agrippina Yakovlevna, 1879–1951—Mariinsky ballerina, master pedagogue, Lidochka's last teacher

Velichko, Vasily Lvovich, 1860–1904—poet, playwright, Georgiaphile, Russian nationalist, Tamara Balanchivadze's godfather

Zheverzheev, Levkii Ivanovich, 1881–1942—St. Petersburg merchant and arts collector, founder of avant-garde Union of Youth, Tamara Geva's father

Zheverzheeva, Tamara (Tamara Geva), 1905–1997—dancer, actress, Georges' first wife

Balanchine and the Lost Muse

Памяти Лидии Ивановой

Завет, воспоминание, испуг?
Зачем опять трепещут тополя?
В безветрии истаял томный звук,
Тепло и жизнь покинули поля.

А грезилась волшебная страна,
Фонтаны скрипок, серебристый тюль.
И не гадала милая весна,
Что встретить ей не суждено июль.

Исчезла. Пауза. Безмолвна гладь.
Лишь эхо отвечает на вопрос
И в легком духе можем отгадать
Мы веянье уже нездешних рос . . .

М. Кузмин

In Memory of Lidia Ivanova

A covenant, a memory, a fear?
Why do the poplars tremble again?
A sound has faded in windlessness,
Warmth and life have left the fields.

In the dream a magic land.
Fountains of violins, silvery tulle.
And she didn't guess, dear Spring,
That she was not to meet July.

She's gone. A pause. Smooth still water.
To the question comes only an echo.
And in the light air we can sense
Unearthly roses stirring . . .

Mikhail Kuzmin
April 1927 (translation, EK)

Introduction

1. Lidochka Childhood apartment
2. Lidochka 1920s apartment
3. Balanchivadzes' neighborhood
4. Theater School
5. Aunt Nadia's apartment
6. Mariinsky/State Theater
7. Alexandrinskii Drama Theater
8. Mikhailovsky/Maly Theater
9. Uritskii Square (Palace Square)
10. Motorboat accident (Lidochka's death)
11. Field of Mars (revolutionary victims buried)
12. Summer Garden
13. To Smolny (off map)
14. Kshessinskaya's Mansion

Petrograd Map, 1923.

Author's collection.

On May 20, 1920, in Petrograd, Russia, in the chamber theater of the Petrograd State Ballet School, formerly the Imperial Theater School, the senior students presented an old bucolic ballet, *The Magic Flute*. It was about a peasant girl, Lise, whose mother wants her to marry a marquis instead of her true love, the peasant lad Luc. In the audience, teachers and younger students sat up eagerly on their curved birch chairs (left over from tsarist times): the two sixteen-year-olds playing the leads were not only the school's stars but everybody's favorites off the stage too.

In the role of Luc was Georgi Balanchivadze, the future Balanchine, called Georges by his schoolmates, a slim, intense, dark-haired boy with a keen profile from his Georgian father, who was kind to the younger students and who revealed onstage that night a gift for witty and exuberant dance-acting. Playing Lise was Lidia Ivanova, whom everyone affectionately called Lida or Lidochka. She was of middle height, with black hair, big slanted black eyes, and what one classmate called "a sunlit smile," and she had as much exuberance as her partner as well as surprising strength. Her jump was high, like a man's. All through this comic *Magic Flute*, "village peasants" filled the stage—the mayor, the marquis, the "friends" and "families" of the two leads—miming joy or indignation, hipping and hopping to the melodies of a dance-inducing magic flute given to Luc by a sorcerer. In front of them, lit by the stage lights, playing off each other, were Balanchivadze and Ivanova in the first big roles of their lives. They seemed, as one classmate wrote, "not so much to dance the steps as to *live* the ballet, sincerely and spontaneously."[1]

With this ballet the two classmates began their dancing careers—in what was the most perilous time in Russian ballet history. The Russian revolution was not even three years old. When Lenin's Bolshevik Party had seized control in November of 1917 (October in Russia), no one believed it could govern a country the size of a continent. World War I was still raging; Russian soldiers were still fighting German and other enemy soldiers on the empire's western edges. Even after Lenin concluded a separate peace with Germany in March of 1918, the fragile new state had to face invasion by allied forces landing from outside the country—British, Americans, Japanese—and remnants of the tsarist army massing inside under the White Russian generals. Petrograd, so close to Europe, was its most menaced city. In 1918, Lenin and the governing Bolsheviks abandoned it for the relative safety of Moscow. Moscow's symbolic aura drew them too: it was Russia's ancient capital, a city of the folk, not of the hated Europeanized court. By 1920, when Georges and Lidochka appeared in the idyllic *Magic Flute*, their abandoned Petrograd had been on the severest of war footings for two years. Resources were dwindling in the face of an Allied blockade. No inhabitant got food without ration tickets, and most were starving anyway.

In fact, Petrograd in 1920 was dying on a scale that had never been seen in the West, even in the worst of wars. This once great imperial capital of palaces and canals that Peter the Great had decreed into being at the wide swampy mouth of the Neva River in 1703—this sprawling seaport that in 1914, according to Baedeker's *Russia*, had combined "the character of a great modern centre of trade and industry with that of a political city swarming with officials"—was reversing itself, shrinking, disintegrating, receding back into swampland.[2] Electricity and transport had broken down. Water mains had burst. Toilets had frozen. Stores were boarded up. Nothing was for sale except precious household possessions offered on street corners by tattered souls. The population had turned into cave dwellers. "It was an ominous, primitive time," wrote the critic Viktor Shklovsky. "People slept in their coats, covered with rugs. . . . They froze to death—whole apartments of them."[3] Whoever had managed to get out had fled abroad, or to the countryside in search of food. Or else they'd died of starvation, cholera, or tuberculosis. At the start of World War I, more than two million people had lived in the imperial capital; in 1920, only a third as many were left.

In such conditions, why worry about training dancers? The fate of all the city's arts institutions hung by a thread, and ballet's thread—that of the monarchy's favorite art—was thinnest of all. Even the once-splendid sea-green ballet and opera theater, the former Imperial Mariinsky, was in a shambles, unheated, its pipes long burst. Gone was its bemedaled and bejeweled audience: dead, disappeared, or reclassified as "former persons." Its new audience of soldiers and workers wore ragged greatcoats, spit sunflower seed shells, and stamped their feet to show approval. In the ballet school across town, finding food for the students and wood for the great tile stoves became a daily struggle. The school's directors bombarded the government with telegrams, pleading for food and fuel for the students, but not because they were artists—because they were something even more crucial to the new ideological landscape: "physical laborers," like factory workers.[4]

Despite such efforts, the *Magic Flute's* happy peasant "laborers" hadn't had a good meal or a new piece of clothing in three years. They'd done their ballet training in unheated studios, bundled in too-small winter coats, wearing boots of carpet shreds. Some still walked miles every day to forage for food and wood; many, including young Balanchivadze, were sick with incipient tuberculosis. They'd improvised their *Magic Flute* costumes from what they'd found in the school's storage. Not even a printed program was possible; someone wrote out the cast list in pencil, in cramped, elegant handwriting.

Yet they managed to delight their audience. A few days later, they delighted another audience in a workers' auditorium, then another in a textile factory. The half-starved workers received the old comic tale with wild applause. What they saw onstage was not just students but young theater artists on a mission. Georges's and Lidochka's generation had received a uniquely bifurcated education. As children they'd been trained in the antiquated imperial system, with its half-luxurious, half-Spartan routines. As adolescents they'd absorbed revolutionary idealism from the teachers and directors installed by the Bolshevik government. They'd been invited, in effect, to turn a revolutionary gaze onto their own bodies, inscribed already with imperial airs and graces. Could such bodies find their way to a new ballet?

The two classmates Georges and Lidochka were leaders in this search. Already in *The Magic Flute*, Lidochka challenged the music, playing with tempi as she thought a modern ballerina should. Even her looks were new: she wasn't "sickly-thin" like older ballerinas but womanly, said one classmate—"as if she had been made by nature not to play illusory sylphs, nymphs, and ghosts, but rather to create, on the ballet stage, real, living creatures."[5] Georges too examined ballet's relation to music. He'd enrolled four months earlier as a piano student in the Petrograd Conservatory. And he'd just started to choreograph: he'd made his first pas de deux, *Night*, for another student concert that same spring. The two students who danced it interacted not through classical pirouettes and lifts, but in half-poses, half-arabesques, and melting gestures. The steps even hinted explicitly at sex in modern guise, not the exotic

"Orientale" sex on earlier reformist choreographer Mikhail Fokine's stage.

Georges, Lidochka, and their classmates weren't alone in their excitement. In Petrograd's grim postrevolutionary years, a belief in the arts burned surprisingly bright. Giant revolutionary pageants with constructivist scenery periodically took over city streets, often with the Academic ("Ak") Theaters' participation, including its student dancers. Classic plays by Shakespeare, Moliere, Lermontov were spiced up with circus improvisations. A new kind of political theater emerged; its blueprint was *Mystery-Bouffe*, created on the revolution's first birthday by three great arts pioneers, Mayakovsky, Meyerhold, and Malevich. Other writers found refuge in the Maxim Gorky–sponsored House of the Arts, a former palace on the Moika Canal, where they composed literary responses to a surreal time. "We created a scientific school and rolled a rock up the mountain," wrote sometime resident Viktor Shklovsky.[6] Musicians flourished too. Scriabin's hallucinatory piano études were played everywhere. Glazunov, the Conservatory's chief, was a god to the city. His student Shostakovich was already exploring musical dissonance.

The aristocratic art of ballet had a special place in citizens' hearts, despite Proletkult, a semi-autonomous group of avant-garde artists, sworn to expunge the decadent-bourgeois innuendos left in the arts. Petrograders gathered anyway at the former Mariinsky on ballet nights to watch the charming old spectacles, still subsidized by the state. In the city's desperate struggle to survive, those half-starved dancers seemed to offer physical courage from the stage. But less than a year after *The Magic Flute*'s 1920 success, the relation between the state and the arts changed drastically. Lenin, faced with peasant rebellions across the land, decreed the New Economic Policy, or NEP—a semi-return to capitalism. The NEP turned the Bolshevik classless utopia on its head. A new breed of Nepmen and Nepwomen sprang up, in spats and fur coats, sequined dresses and cloche hats. The city revived, but the arts confronted chaos. State support almost disappeared. Making money was suddenly the order of the day.

And ballet was in a special bind. NEP audiences clamored for a new-style dancing, bold and jazzy, that could serve the new-style *estrada* (popular) stages in cabarets, casinos, summer parks. The former Mariinsky with its old fairy-tale repertory stood alone and isolated. It almost closed twice in 1922. The whole art seemed inside out: its center, the grand old ballet theater, was atrophied; its periphery was alive with frenzied invention. It was in this fractured moment that Georges,

Lidochka, and their classmates began their careers. They finished school; they joined the ex-Mariinsky State Theater and danced the old sylphs, peasants, and jesters of its repertory, but they also strutted their popular "numbers" on the *estrada* stages. Lidochka was a phenomenon in both worlds, attracting fans who followed her from theater to theater. Georges was a sought-after young experimenter, creating many of the new numbers himself. With their peers they formed a bold new company, the Young Ballet.

Offstage, Lida was courted by the bigwigs of the day, Chekists (secret police) and Nepmen. Georges turned courtier himself, romancing younger dancers and marrying one, the dance student Tamara Geva. Georges and Lida were not a romantic couple. But even without romance, they were a pair. They'd been each other's first dancing partners; they remained an informal king and queen of their generation. Lidochka was impulsive, headstrong, brimming with vitality. Georges was detached, dreamy, mysterious. These differences only intensified as they grew older. Lidochka lived at full tilt, offstage and on. Georges hid his feelings, pouring them into his work. One can almost see these two dramatizing themselves in a city that had been theater-crazy from 1890 on. Before the Revolution, Petrograd had seemed like one big Venetian-flavored carnival, with everyone in it masked and costumed. After the Revolution, the carnival continued for a surprising number of years, till Stalin squelched it. Georges and Lidochka grew up with this Russian-ized vision of *commedia*—in the plays of Meyerhold, the poetry of Blok and Akhmatova, the music of Stravinsky, and the ballets of Fokine. It makes sense that they would don their own *commedia* masks as they emerged from ballet school into the rich milieu of the Russian theater. Georges was the gifted young man apart, the loner, the revolutionary Pierrot. He even used smoky lines around his eyes to accentuate his "mask." Lida, if we peer back in time, seems to be flaunting her boldness onstage and off, like a flapper edition of Columbine.

At the peak of the NEP, in the spring of 1924, these two vivid young people, along with Georges's young wife and two other dancer friends, got the chance to travel out of the revolution they'd been shut in since 1917. A mysterious Nepman wanted to fund them on a summer tour to Europe. The five made excited plans, but on the eve of departure, disaster struck. Lidochka went with fans on a summer boating trip on the canals. She never came back. The newspapers said she was thrown from the boat and drowned. Her body wasn't found. Given the time and place and the art she practiced, this death seems like the last ghastly revelation of one of those theatrical masked balls. Or else like a modern version of the old nineteenth-century ballets that Georges and Lidochka knew by heart—*Giselle, Swan Lake, The Sleeping Beauty*—whose ballerina heroines were innocent girls menaced or destroyed by the worldliness around them.

Echoes of these ballet classics abound in Balanchine's own later work. Is Lidochka there too? Is it her fate played out in such tragic ballets as *Serenade* and *La Valse*? Even before she died, she and Georges had created a macabre solo together, a portrait of a girl in the grip of terror called *Valse Triste*. There is no doubt that her death affected her companions, not just their lives but their art. Did it play a part too in their decision not to return to Russia, as Balanchine and Danilova strongly implied later?

This book finds affirmative answers to these questions. Lidochka was only twenty when she died, but already a dance pioneer. "A gorgeous ballerina, extremely talented," Balanchine said of her decades later. Balanchine was a young choreographer just beginning a body of work centered on pioneering ballerinas. The two friends were hugely important to each other, even if Lidochka wasn't Georges's personal muse. He already had one of those, his young wife Tamara Geva, and he would go on to have a string of them, with whom he fell in love, around whom he shaped wonderful ballets. Lidochka wasn't anybody's personal muse. She'd invented herself. Even so young, she was muse to her age. Using only intuition and talent, she'd divined new ways to move, new ways to use ballet. Georges absorbed her discoveries.

The two stories told in this book are parallel stories, intertwining at many points. Lida and Georges were trained side by side in imperial times. Side by side, they reinvented themselves in the grueling civil war years. Then they plunged into the violent social currents of the NEP— only to be spewed out again, one into death, one into a journey that took him halfway across the globe. Both their stories began, though, as separate strands, in a lost time and place before there was a revolution, in the winter of 1903–1904, when both were born. Their ballet training began too in the ancien régime, in 1913 and 1914 respectively. To understand these two childhoods, readers must peer back through the frenetic NEP Petrograd and the ragged revolutionary Petrograd, back to the submerged imperial capital, St. Petersburg, raised again to life, the great, bustling, modern yet antiquated city as it was at the start of the twentieth century, its canals clogged with barges; its streets crowded with horse-drawn carriages, trams, and horse-driven *izvoshchik* cabs; its population a patchwork of uniformed officers and civil servants, ladies in big hats, and peasants everywhere—servant peasants, workers, peasant food vendors, workers fresh from peasant villages. The population of not just the cities but the whole Russian Empire was supposed to be neatly grouped and regulated: the masses in their assigned social "estates" (worker, peasant, merchant, *meshchanin* [petty bourgeois]), and the elite ranged up and down the fourteen rungs of Peter the Great's surreal Table of Ranks, which still bestowed hierarchical status on army, civil, and court officials. But Russian life in the early twentieth century was anything but ordered, especially in the cities. Urban citizens were skating all over the social scale, ambitious peasants flooding into universities, impoverished nobles retreating to garrets, merchants and artists amassing fortunes and prestige—just as in Chekhov plays.

The Balanchivadzes and Ivanovs eluded the pattern even more dramatically than most families. Balanchine's parents won a savings-bond lottery; the family shot up the social scale, only to fall down it abruptly when the money disappeared in bad investments. Lidochka's army officer father, with humble origins and a will to rise, grew obsessed with the arts and with fame for his daughter. Neither family resembled the families who were sending children to the Imperial Theater School to be trained as private entertainers for the monarchy and its circles. Most Theater School parents were theater people already, or else they were high officials with bohemian mistresses. Neither the Balanchivadzes nor the Ivanovs fit that profile, although both families interacted at times with the glittering St. Petersburg alternative society, the demimonde (in Russian *polusvet*, "half-world") that everywhere permeated the surface of respectable life.

More of this narrative will belong to Georges than to Lidochka. He lived until 1983, sixty years longer than she. He fulfilled his youthful promise to become the greatest ballet choreographer of the twentieth century. She did not get the chance to fulfill hers. He left descendents who've kept family papers and a mighty institution, the New York City Ballet, guarding his archives. She was an only child whose distant relatives couldn't keep her personal effects intact. As the narrative unfolds, Lidochka will make her appearance at the moment she appeared in Balanchine's life, in the Imperial Theater School. But she will also open this book to the female version of imperial ballet training, whose intimate features were veiled to the young Balanchine in their gender-segregated school years. Through Lidochka, we see inside the girls' floor of the School, and meet female classmates and contemporaries important to both her and Georges, especially their friend Alexandra Danilova, known as Choura. Lidochka's short life told alongside

Balanchine's brings into focus the figure of the ballerina who would define his career.

This book begins, though, even before their births, with the lives of their parents, especially Balanchine's parents, who exemplify the social and geographical reach of the Russian empire's last years. The hopes and desires of his Georgian father, and the sometimes very different ones of his Russian mother, would determine what kind of a small being would enter so young the secluded, demanding, yet magical world of the Russian ballet. The same is true of Lidochka. Her parents carved a special place for themselves in volatile Petersburg society and passed on *their* acute if inchoate hopes to their child. The families and early childhoods of Georges and Lidochka are the starting point and, in a sense, the ending point. "Childhood is the fiery furnace in which we are melted down to essentials," wrote Katherine Anne Porter. Family and childhood laid the groundwork for the life, and the death, that each of these children would be handed in the maelstrom of the early twentieth century.

ONE

Maria and Meliton

Meliton Balanchivadze, early 1890s.

BALANCHINE is a Trademark of The George Balanchine Trust. Photo by Rafael. Courtesy
of New York City Ballet Archives, Ballet Society Collection.

In the late summer of 1889, Meliton Antonovich Balanchivadze, a young man of twenty-seven, dressed as a gentleman, stepped off the train at St. Petersburg's central Nikolaevsky station, carrying most of his worldly belongings. He was small, with a neat brown mustache and goatee and an impish smile. He had never been to the Russian empire's imperial capital. He'd never been out of his home country, Georgia, at the southern rim of the vast Russian Empire. He'd spent his childhood in a place smaller than a town, Banoja, just a piece of farmland in Western Georgia. But he didn't have to face the bustling metropolis alone. His younger brother of nineteen, Vasily (Vaso), had been here for two years, studying art with the great realist painter Ilya Repin. Vaso met his big brother at the station and took him back to his fourth-floor bohemian room in one of St. Petersburg's poorest districts, at the intersection of Gorokhovaya Street and the Fontanka River.[1]

Meliton had come with the bold intention of studying music at the St. Petersburg Conservatory, the finest music academy in the empire. He was already famous at home, though largely self-taught. He'd sung in the Tbilisi opera chorus. He'd become a specialist in Georgian folk songs—he'd even composed new songs. To acquire real European musical training was the dream of his life, and a necessary step for bigger plans. He wanted credibility as a musician, not just at home but in the wider world. He wanted to write an opera. Yet he'd paid a price for his ambitions. He'd essentially abandoned a young wife and two children, a girl of seven and a boy of three. He'd left a father behind too, a rural priest, who was deeply doubtful about the human cost of his eldest son's Meliton's Petersburg plans.

Yet it was that father, Anton Balanchivadze, who'd implanted the ambitions in all three of his sons. As a young man, Anton himself had risen from rural roots. His family were Banoja "church peasants," peasants who worked lands owned by the church, though his mother, née Koridze, was one of those key rural elders who keep ancient wisdom alive: she sang the old Georgian songs for neighbors and guests, accompanying herself on the stringed *chonguri*.[2] Anton, born Amiran, had gotten himself to the seminary in nearby Kutaisi, the main city of western Georgia. Rising up the social scale in Georgia was done through the orthodox priesthood. He'd become a deacon (*diakon*, one step below priest) in the township of Puti, where he'd married a local noble-born girl, Evelita Assatiani—they'd eloped in the face of her father's opposition—then returned to Banoja as a full-fledged priest. As a priest, he'd had to change his name: Amiran was the Prometheus character of Georgia's pre-Christian mythology. He became the Christian Anton (a variation of Anthony).[3]

By the time he had children, Anton's ambitions had widened, and he'd grasped the key to advancement in the greater Russian Empire: education, especially Russian-language education. His eldest, Meliton, especially dear to him, would be pushed. At the start of their marriage, he and Evelita had endured four stillbirths before Meliton was born in 1862.[4] In 1868, when the child was six, Anton opened a school that rotated among pupils' houses, with himself as teacher.[5] In return, his parishioners built him the steep-roofed gray stone church of St. George that still stands on Banoja's highest hill, overlooking mountains and valleys.[6] At eight, the boy was sent away to school at his father's Kutaisi seminary. The whole family moved there shortly thereafter, so that the younger siblings, Ivan (born 1867), Vasily (1870), and Anna (1875), could attend real schools. Anton even opened several *dukanis* (workingmen's taverns) in Kutaisi—to insure money for schooling.[7]

At twelve, Meliton graduated from the Kutaisi Seminary and entered the city's elite Provincial Gymnasium. Two years later, Anton moved him a rung higher, to the seminary in the country's capital. The Tbilisi Seminary was the finest school in Georgia, founded in 1850 to prepare young men of property to be imperial officials. Nominally controlled by the Georgian church, though staffed by Russian schoolmasters who'd gone to seed or drink, it still offered a thorough education. Meliton would later write better Russian than his Russian wife. Yet more was happening in the seminary than education by the book. The school was also a hotbed of opposition to Georgia's Russian colonizers.[8] The passionate search for a Georgian identity had begun around the time of Meliton's birth. Its leaders were the literary "men of the '60s" dominated by two great poet-journalists, Akaki Tsereteli (1840–1915) and

Ilya Chavchavadze (1837–1905), known even today in Georgia by their first names. When this pair had relocated from separate provinces to Tbilisi, journals sprang up around them, theater flourished, and the ancient Georgian language came into its own. By this time, the 1860s, Georgia, land of craggy mountains, green valleys, and churning muddy rivers on the southern rim of the Caucasus, lying between the Black and Caspian Seas (and so between Europe and Asia), had been part of the Russian Empire for roughly two generations.[9] The Russians had long since reunited its western and eastern parts, separated for centuries by the jagged Likhi mountain range and by conflicting cultures deposited during invasions by Byzantines, Mongols, Turks, Persians, and Ottomans.

And yet, this very imperial context had pushed educated Georgians into a crisis about their own identity. Should Georgia become its own nation, and if so, what were its defining characteristics? The passionate search for that identity, played out underground in the Tbilisi Seminary, changed Meliton's thinking about his future. Or rather, the Georgian identity quest got wired somehow into the youth's own love of music, as well as wine, women, and the secular delights of the Georgian capital. Meliton had a likeable personality, a ready wit, a penchant for song and story. But school was not his natural habitat, except for its music. In Kutaisi his "silver soprano" had graced a church choir.[10] At his Tbilisi seminary he also sang in the choir. But in 1878, Meliton dropped out of the seminary without a diploma. Small, with alert brown eyes and a humorous irony that made him both charming and elusive, this sixteen-year-old was as ambitious as his father, but in a different sphere.

That sphere was music, an art central to the Georgian psyche, but one which hadn't yet made its contribution to the search for national roots. And not just church music. The gracious tree-lined Tbilisi, informal capital of the Russian Caucasus, surrounded by mountains, bisected by the muddy Mtkvari River, contained a unique and flourishing secular musical scene. Fewer Georgians inhabited it than Armenian merchants, Persian and Jewish craftsmen, and Russian officers (Georgians lived on the land), so musical synthesizing had gone on here for decades. Georgia's religious polyphony had mingled with Russian romances, Neapolitan airs that came through the ports, and the local *estrada* ballads. Old instruments like the stringed *chonguri* and the clarinet-like *duduk* doubled the newer guitar and accordion. Italian opera was added to the mix by Count Mikhail Vorontsov, the forceful Russian governor-general from 1845 to 1855, who built a "Moorish" theater on the town's main boulevard.[11]

Maria and Meliton

Newly free of school, Meliton sang in the famous Exarch's Church Choir, becoming its director's assistant—"Meliton, give the tone!" But soon, a distant cousin, Filimon Koridze, a celebrity opera basso who'd returned from Europe, helped him make the leap into secular music. Now a baritone, Meliton joined the Tbilisi opera chorus, singing small roles in *Evgeny Onegin* and *Faust*. Outside the opera he mastered the guitar and the violin, learned city ballads, and became a favorite song-ster in Tiflis *and* Kutais. His musical mission grew: to give Georgian music a place in world music. Neither sacred nor secular Georgian music was known outside its borders. No Georgian music had been written down in Western notation. Yet Georgia has what ethnomusicol-ogists have called the oldest polyphonic tradition in the world: compli-cated blends of voices and stringed and wind instruments, articulated differently in each mountainous hamlet.

Leaving the Opera, Meliton assembled an ethnographic choir, taught it a repertory, and gave a concert on March 13, 1883, seen as "a progressive event in the life of the nation."[12] Over the next few years, he ventured into remote mountain corners, collecting and transcribing his country's songs. He joined Vladimir (Lado) Agniashvili's Tbilisi chorus and became its di-rector in 1887, adding to its repertoire. At twenty-six, he'd filtered these sounds and traditions into a potpourri song collection of his own, scored for orchestra and set mainly to the words of Ilya and Akaki. A few songs landed in Russia, making Meliton the first Georgian to add to the European lieder tradition. He was a frequent guest at Tbilisi and Kutaisi "musical-literary evenings," which functioned as laboratories of national identity.

Yet despite his growing fame, Meliton had kept a foot in the upright rural culture of his father. At eighteen, he'd taken time out to go home and marry a local girl, Gayane Eristavi, from a poor rural branch of one of Georgia's ancient noble families, based in the nearby hamlet of Sachino. Anton himself had officiated at the Banoja wedding. The pair settled in Kutaisi, and Gayane warmly supported her husband's musical mission.[13] A daughter, Nino, was born in 1882 and a son, Apollon, in 1886, both christened by Anton.

But Meliton's very success had made him ashamed of his musical "backwardness." He knew he needed formal training in Russia, but despaired of getting it. He lacked the resources of better-born *intel-ligents*. And Gayane, rural Georgian to the core, didn't want to live in St. Petersburg. Yet when cognac manufacturer David Sarajishvili stepped forward and offered the young musician a stipend for Russian study (fifty rubles a month, a factory worker's salary), Meliton seized his chance. He and Gayane agreed to a painful separation, possibly a divorce, though it's doubtful whether Anton would have permitted one (and divorces can't be tracked, since they weren't added to Georgian marriage records as they were to Russian ones). She took her children back to her home village, a shameful step for a young Georgian wife. In August of 1889, Meliton set off alone, at twenty-seven, to seek his fortune in the imperial capital.[14]

He enrolled first in a singing class with Vasily Samus, trainer of renowned singers like Tchaikovsky's favorite lyric tenor, Nikolai Figner. Or that's what his biographer, Khuchua, reports. Khuchua conveys the apocryphal story of Meliton's singing in his midyear exams for the Conservatory's director, the piano virtuoso Anton Rubinstein, and the great man replying, "My dear *kavkazets* [person from the Caucasus], you're not going to be an opera singer—you'd be lost onstage because of your small size." Rubinstein advised him to study composition—"It will be of great use to your country"—and sent him a piano the next day—up to the fourth floor![15] But Meliton's petition to join Rimsky Korsakov's composition class, lodged in St. Petersburg's historical archive (CSHA SPb), with assent scribbled on it, suggests that he intended to study composition from the beginning. At any rate, the Conservatory was interested in the young Georgian, one of the few from his country enrolled at a Russian conservatory as well as the first to study composition, counterpoint, harmony, and orchestration.

It seemed at this point that Anton's dream for his sons had been realized. Vaso and Meliton were studying at the empire's highest level, even if they'd chosen the arts instead of predictable professions. Their middle brother, Ivan, had gone the predictable route: he'd joined the Russian army. He was in Odessa in the junker officers' school. Yet back home in Georgia, a crisis was brewing. Anton's health began to fail in the fall of 1889. He'd written often and warmly to Ivan and Vaso, mostly in Georgian but sometimes in halting Russian, apologizing for his "country Russian." He wrote less often to Meliton. One last-will-and-testament-style letter to Meliton exists from late 1889—it's undated, but Anton died on December 27, 1889—informing his son of his illness, cautioning him not to be "proud if you have success," even accusing him of neglecting his responsibilities. "If you don't love me and don't write me, at least write to your children."[16] With Anton's death the funds stopped, and Vaso was forced to leave Petersburg and go home to teach art in a Kutaisi school (to the young Mayakovsky, among others). Later he would put his skills briefly to the service of money counterfeiting, and still later would become a beloved character actor in Georgian movies.

But Meliton, with stipend secure, chose to stay on in the imperial capital. It was a wonderful time for a young musician. In 1889, the city was just beginning the spurt of growth that would make it one of the great cities of the world, the eighth largest by 1900, with a million and a half inhabitants, just under Tokyo in size, and just ahead of Manchester, England. Russian music, only a generation old, was flourishing. At midcentury, the imperial capital had lacked both concert hall and conservatory; composing wasn't a respectable profession, and opera was in the grip of "Italomania." In 1862, Rubinstein had founded the Conservatory as a bastion of the German counterpoint tradition. Another group of early Russian composers, the Mighty Five (in Russian, *kuchkists*—Balakirev, Mussorgsky, Cui, Borodin, and Rimsky-Korsakov) had objected, believing that European pedagogy would suppress the folk roots they drew on.

But by the time Meliton arrived, all was resolved. The lush orchestral music of the nineteenth century was the art par excellence of the new bourgeois Petersburg. Poet Osip Mandelstam put music on the first page of his memoir of turn-of-the-century Petersburg, *The Noise of Time*. All of life seemed to revolve, he wrote, "around the glass railroad station in Pavlovsk [exurban concert hall with wildly popular summer orchestral concerts] and Galkin, the conductor, stands at the center of the world."[17] Nikolai Galkin held weekly soirees, helping to popularize the Russian composers like Mussorgsky and Rimsky-Korsakov. In January of 1890, Tchaikovsky's dramatic-lyrical ballet *The Sleeping Beauty* premiered in the Imperial Mariinsky Theater, marking the start of the late-imperial flowering of music, poetry, painting, and theater called the Silver Age. And one of the former Kuchkists, Rimsky-Korsakov, had been ensconced for two decades as a beloved propagator of European pedagogy at the Conservatory itself. He told students each fall that "he would speak and they would listen. Then he would speak less and they would start to work, and finally he would not speak at all and they would work."[18]

But Meliton couldn't quite grasp the work gospel. As a Georgian, he faced a double bind: how to hold onto Georgian sounds within Russian music, even as the Russian students struggled to find Russianness in a thicket of European counterpoint. And school didn't bring out his best traits. One can imagine him, trudging grimly upriver along the frozen Fontanka River to the classical allée called Theater Street, then the site of the Conservatory—the same street where twenty-three years later his son Georgi would enroll in the Imperial Theater School. He stuck it out for six years, but in 1895 he left the Conservatory, again without a diploma.

Meliton was now thirty-three. He'd composed little in his student years. But instead of leaving the imperial capital, he invented a Petersburg profession: impresario of all things Georgian. He organized glamorous "Georgian evenings" for the benefit of Georgian student societies. He'd rejoined his homeland, though in diasporic miniature, and broadened his mission as well. His evenings were meant to "correct" Russia's cartoon ideas of Georgia, offering something besides daggers, wine horns, shashliks, and shaggy hats. Celebrities donated their services, including star dancers like Tamara Karsavina. Now Meliton began at last to write the music he'd dreamed of writing, an opera, *Wily Tamara*, based on an epic poem by Akaki. He'd chosen this tale over others because, as he told a writer friend, "opera needs a strong woman at its center."[19] *Wily Tamara* tells of a depraved medieval queen of Imereti (Meliton's home province) who loves, then destroys, one Grigol, a "people's poet."

Meliton showcased his work in one of his own grandest evenings, held in the St. Petersburg Hall of Nobles (the present-day Petersburg Philharmonia) in December 1897. It featured a student chorus under his baton, plus dance, poetry, and the premiere of *Wily Tamara*'s third act, conducted by star conductor Johann Decker-Schenk.[20] A Russian critic was agog at "the special beauty of the Georgian women in evening clothes," the Georgian champagne, the men's Georgian national costume (boots and belted tunic), and "the wild acclaim that met the opera fragments." A Georgian critic noted the opera's weakness "from a professional-technical point of view," but celebrated the birth of "a Georgian body of music."[21]

By coupling that plushest of musical genres with his own brand of romantic patriotism, Meliton was imitating earlier opera greats, Wagner, Glinka, Mussorgsky, and Rimsky—and joining contemporaries like the Czech Smetana, the Finnish Sibelius, and the American Scott Joplin. And yet he premiered his *Wily Tamara* fragments not in Tbilisi but in St. Petersburg, not in the Georgian language but in Russian, in a translation by the Russian Georgiophile Vasily Velichko. Empire-wide exposure was crucial to him. Nor did Meliton revert to an all-Georgian private life. He began keeping company in the late 1890s with a young Russian woman eleven years his junior, born in 1873.

Little is known even now about Maria Nikolaevna Vasilieva, Balanchine's mother. Some say she'd been Meliton's housekeeper or his landlady's daughter, but early photos show her as a cool beauty in beautiful clothes. Was she a courtesan, dressed by patrons? She had a classical profile and a distant air. She'd had minimal schooling. In family letters she writes a simple roundish hand and makes some grammatical

Maria Vasilieva.
BALANCHINE is a Trademark of The George Balanchine Trust. Courtesy of New York City Ballet Archives, Ballet Society Collection.

mistakes. Her children's baptismal certificates list her as a former *remeslennitsa* (craftswoman), urban equivalent of peasant. Some say she worked in a bank. She'd had at least some culture in her background: she played the piano well.

Maria was probably illegitimate. Her son Andrei claimed later that her father was Nicholas von Almedingen, a German who started a business and a family in Russia and then left, causing his daughter to take her mother's name, Vasilieva. The story sounds dubious. If Maria's father was an Almedingen, the name's rarity makes it more likely that he belonged to the St. Petersburg Almedingens, late-eighteenth-century Austro-German émigrés, some of whom now edited a St. Petersburg illustrated children's journal called *Rodnik*. (The name's origins could lie in an old Baden-Wurttemberg town or with an old noble family of Ulm.[22]) In terms of age, either of two Petersburg Nikolai Almedingens, a gentleman-farmer father or his army officer son, could have fathered her.[23] Other persistent rumors hold that Maria's mother was Jewish on *her* mother's side. There was a Babusia in Maria's life: in family letters she bore the affectionate nickname for grandmother, *babushka*. But this Babusia (or Babulia as she's sometimes called) was not a grandmotherly force for the Balanchivadze children. Balanchine never mentioned her; his brother Andrei merely commented once in a 1921 letter that he was sorry to hear about her death. Then, too, the godmother whom Meliton and Maria chose for their first child, Tamara, Elizaveta Grigorievna Khazanovich, had a Jewish surname, but it belonged to her deceased husband. Maria's origins are so elusive that a suppressed Jewish part seems plausible, even if next-generation Balanchivadzes in Tbilisi believe their grandmother's "Germanic" temperament precludes this.[24] To them as children she seemed neither warm nor humorous, therefore not Jewish: a responsible caretaker, but emotionally detached.

In short, Maria Nikolaevna was one of those many Petersburg young women of uncertain parentage, surviving by her wits in the dynamic capital. What did she have in common with a thirty-seven-year-old impoverished but charming composer from Georgia, who was possibly not divorced? Did he deceive her about that? Did she accept him anyway? These are some of the compelling questions about Balanchine's parents. Maria didn't harbor a love for all things Georgian. When she emigrated to Tbilisi after the Revolution, she refused to learn the language. But in the years Meliton courted her, she was on her own, grateful perhaps for his attention. She loved music: Meliton sang and played wonderfully. She was religious: he was a priest's son. And he had that Georgian wit and love of good times.

Or was it simply the age-old illogic of sex that governed their union? In 1900, Maria Vasilieva gave birth to Meliton's child, a girl, Nina, who died in infancy.[25] Perhaps grief and guilt tightened the couple's bonds. But some have suggested another reason for Meliton's and Maria's staying together. Maria held a lottery number attached to a savings bond which turned up lucky in 1901, yielding 200,000 gold rubles, an immense sum in the days when factory workers made 500 rubles a year.[26] Did Meliton stay with Maria because of the money? Just before the lottery win, he was desperate enough to seek funds from the Georgian-Russian arts patron Count K. I. Bagration-Mukhranskii, who agreed to help if Meliton promised to work on his opera. That unfinished opera—already the bane of his existence. Meliton sent the opera fragments; the count sent the money. But by then—miraculously, alarmingly—its recipient was rich enough to patronize the arts himself.

Becoming rich wrought a profound change in Meliton and Maria, as individuals and as a pair. The money distracted Meliton from his musical mission: he would write only two more of his opera's acts between 1907 and 1912 and wouldn't finish it until the 1930s (when Stalin himself asked where was the rest of the "first Georgian opera"). For Maria, a fortune seemed to intensify what must have been deep yearnings for family and stability. In the aftermath of the lottery, the couple moved to the prosperous Rozhdestvensky (Birth of Christ) neighborhood, named after its church in Petersburg's northeast near Smolny Cathedral,[27] a bourgeois neighborhood of newly built *dokhodnye doma* (rental apartment buildings), designed in a riot of art nouveau styles. Meliton set himself up as an importer of Kakheti Georgian wines with an office on fashionable Liteiny Prospekt,[28] though it was Maria Balanchivadze who moved officially up the commercial hierarchy in 1902, from craftswoman to member of the Second Merchants' Guild of Tsarskoe Selo.[29] To join such a guild required a substantial investment.

The year 1902 also saw the event that mattered most to Maria: the arrival of healthy baby Tamara. She was born July 31 and christened September 3 in the Birth of Christ Church, known locally as the Church on the Sands.[30] Christening documents attest that Tamara was born "to the unmarried Maria Nikolaevna Vasilieva, merchant's daughter of the Second Merchants' Guild, etc." Meliton hadn't married Maria. Yet standing as godfather was Meliton's friend Vasily Lvovich Velichko, translator-adapter of his opera libretto and a State Councilor (5th rank). Elizaveta Grigorievna Khazanovich, widow of a Titular Councilor (9th rank), was godmother.[31] Tamara was photographed a month before her first birthday in the fashionable photography studio R. Charles on Nevsky Prospekt. In one image, a bewildered baby in lace looks up from a velvet-covered armchair. In another, Maria, in a tight-waisted gown, looks fondly down at her baby as she supports her on a balustrade.

Summer 1903 was a monumental time in St. Petersburg history. The city had celebrated its two-hundredth birthday in May with the grand opening of the newly built Troitsky Bridge across the Neva. The celebration brought the tsar and tsarina out of seclusion in nearby Tsarskoe Selo and set church bells ringing, cannons firing, and seventeenth-century-clad actors declaiming in the Summer Garden and the other parks. Maria and Meliton must have celebrated in private. The young mother showing off her daughter in the photo was a month pregnant with her next child, Georgi: the future Balanchine.

TWO

Georgi

Georgi, about age five.

BALANCHINE Is a Trademark of The George Balanchine Trust. Photo by R. Charles.
Courtesy of New York City Ballet Archives, Ballet Society Collection.

Georgi Melitonovich Balanchivadze came into the world on January 9, 1904 (January 22 by the Western calendar Russia would adopt in 1918). His earliest picture, taken at the family's favorite R. Charles studio, shows a barefoot baby in a frilly bonnet, in the lap of a young peasant wet nurse. The tiny face displays that arched-eyebrow haughtiness of the grown Balanchine, as if his character were already set. But the picture underscores just how ancient and country-bound were child-rearing rituals in 1904 St. Petersburg. The nurse, hardly more than sixteen, wears the elaborate satin *sarafan* pinafore and pearl-embroidered *kokoshnik* headdress of wet-nurse uniforms. Hiring the traditional peasant-like figure to nurse an urban baby, dressing her like a queen ... Even if several city agencies now regulated the wet-nurse business, it's hard to place such a picture in the twentieth century.[1]

Balanchine was born in what could be called the last stable moment of the 300-year-old Romanov dynasty. Two weeks after his birth, the Japanese navy attacked Port Arthur, Russia's distant port in Manchuria, provoking a savage war with Japan that would turn disastrous for the Russian military in the Far East and the monarchy at home—and would lead to the first Russian revolution of 1905. On the intimate level, the family too seemed in a state of uncertainty. Georgi's christening was delayed three months until April 1, though Tamara had been christened a month after her birth and little brother Andrei would be christened three days after his. Christening delays weren't uncommon, especially in winter, but one is tempted to read a struggle into this one, a campaign by Maria to get Meliton to marry her before their first son met the world. If so, she lost. The christening document from the Birth of Christ Church lists Georgi too as the child of the unmarried Maria Nikolaevna Vasilieva. That his father was present we know from the godparents:

Georgi's godmother was Maria Grigorievna Muretova, cousin and cowriter of Meliton's opera-translator friend Vasily Velichko; his godfather was another friend of Velichko's, Konstantin Konstantinovich Stefanovich, former vice-governor of Georgia, now an Interior Ministry official, 4th rank in the Table of Ranks, who would serve in 1908 on Prime Minister Pyotr Stolypin's 1908 agricultural reform commission.[2] These were high personages indeed, but connected not with Maria but with Meliton.

The little family settled gradually into a wealthy life against the backdrop of the Russo-Japanese War and its aftermath: the strikes, riots, assassinations, and fractious formations and dissolutions of three Duma parliaments that accompanied that first revolution of 1905. When Georgi was still an infant, the family suddenly grew. Meliton's brother Ivan and his Polish-born wife Emilia Karlovna (Balanchivadze) arrived in St. Petersburg and moved in. Ivan, now a veteran of the Warsaw Gendarmerie, where he'd risen to *shtabs-kapitan* (staff-captain, between lieutenant and captain), was waiting for his next army assignment. A year and a half later, on June 1, 1905, baby Andrei arrived, born like sister and brother "to the unmarried Maria Vasilieva." A few months later, an older brother for Georgi turned up too: Meliton's first son, Apollon, left behind in Georgia in 1889. He'd been raised by his mother Gayane with help from paternal grandparents and uncles. Inspired by his uncle Ivan's military career, Apollon at nineteen had volunteered for the Russo-Japanese War. He'd survived, and here he was, ready to enter St. Petersburg's Vladimir Junker High School, and meet the father he barely knew.[3] It might have been legal complications linked to Apollon that pushed Meliton to marry Maria, an event that may have happened, or not—documents can be falsified—in the nine months between Andrei's June 1905 birth and March 1906, when Meliton legally recognized (*priznal*) all three children.[4] Perhaps it was these family shifts that prompted the Balanchivadzes to change apartments so often (though changing apartments was a Petersburg custom). By the time Georgi was one and a half, they'd had three addresses, all within the upscale Rozhde-stvensky neighborhood.[5] Two years later, in 1907, they moved again to the palatial twelve rooms Balanchine remembered best, on the neighborhood's main artery, Suvorovsky Prospekt, 47 (striking in a city starved for living space).

The three small Balanchivadzes began their lives in a city enchanting for children. Servants took care of them as in any haute-bourgeois family, foreigners or quasi-foreigners as fashion demanded; if small Petersburgers got breast milk from Russians, they were schooled by French or Germans.[6] A German nursemaid or bonne took them for walks in the

Tauride Gardens, to the zoo on the Petersburg Side, or to the Neva Embankment to hear the cannons fire at noon from the Peter and Paul Fortress across the water. A tutor figured in the Balanchivadze picture, as did a piano teacher with a German name, Alisa Frantsevna Kiuntsel (Küntzel). Balanchine's own memories focused on the sounds and smells of the "big, noisy city" of his birth—"the rattle of droshkies' wheels on the wooden pavements, the cries of street vendors, the pealing of the church bells on High Easter; the mingled . . . aromas of coffee beans, spices, and rope tar at a merchant's shop his mother sometimes took him to . . ."[7] Petersburg native Osip Mandelstam, thirteen years older, remembered the city's sounds too, and the ubiquitous music. Vladimir Nabokov, five years older, concentrated on sights and smells—the elegant shop windows, the private sleighs and carriages. "I would moreover submit," he wrote in *Speak, Memory*, "that, in regard to the power of hoarding up impressions, Russian children of my generation passed through a period of genius, as if destiny were loyally trying what it could for them by giving them more than their share, in view of the cataclysm that was to remove completely the world they had known."[8]

Balanchine's descriptions of his own childhood convey not just sensory wonder but melancholy.[9] He talked about a special attachment to the German nursemaid, Varvara (Barbara), who might have instinctively favored a less-favored child.[10] "My family . . . had a German *bonne*, whom I liked very much," he told Volkov. "I was very small then. And then she left."[11] Here is a hint of the resentment at not having his wishes honored that flashed out sometimes when Balanchine remembered. Maybe the sudden appearance of a younger brother *and* a long-lost older brother was disorienting. Georgi was probably eclipsed too in his mother's eyes by his demonstrative siblings. Tamara was cheerful, pretty, and amusing, the light of her mother's life, and would remain so until her death.[12] Andrei the baby, round-faced, blond, and smiling, was close to his mother too into adulthood. Georgi, keener-featured and darker-complexioned than Andrei, prouder and pricklier than Tamara, was not the kind of child who demanded attention. His earliest memories are of events outside his parents' range: he got lost in a theater and was held up to be found; he practiced a Beethoven sonata and realized it was beautiful; he encountered female charm in the person of his dentist; he played at being a priest.[13] It seems that this proud little boy got sidelined in the family's early years, that his character didn't click with the others' agendas. "Everyone wants to be the favorite child in a family, but not everyone has the luck," Balanchine told Volkov in the 1980s.[14]

But any child might have escaped notice in what was essentially an apartment-salon. "A huge number of guests always came to our apartment," remembered Andrei, "and (later) to the dacha in Finland: one big ongoing feast at the table. And the Christmas parties were especially lavish."[15] Most of the guests were Meliton's, starting with the Georgian students who flocked to the apartment, whose musical projects he encouraged.[16] He assembled them in an informal Georgian chorus that sang in the Balanchivadzes' drawing room. Prominent Russian musicians came too, composers like Vasily Safonov, Liverii Saketti, and Anatoly Lyadov, along with Meliton's closest musical friend, a Wagner enthusiast and Russia's first ethnomusicologist, Nikolai Findeizen. Meliton developed a real friendship with Findeizen, writing articles in his *Russian Musical Gazette*, joining his Friends of Music Society, serving as juror for his First All-Russian Exhibition of Musical Instruments of 1907, for which he brought his own *chonguri* from home. Meliton paid for a Findeizen-edited collection of the complete letters of Mikhail Glinka, the "father of Russian music," on the fifty-year anniversary (1907) of his death, and was warmly thanked in the preface.[17] The small Balanchivadzes were surrounded by music, not just in their own lessons but at the parties too. All three would go on to be connected with music, Tamara as a theater decor artist, Andrei as a major Georgian composer, Georgi as the musical choreographer he was.[18]

To the parties also came the high-placed godparents and their circle, whose presence needs some examining. Many Westerners have assumed that the cultured part of St. Petersburg, described by the all-purpose term "intelligentsia," uniformly opposed the Romanovs' antiquated monarchy and favored a parliamentary government. But a different wing of this intelligentsia passionately supported the monarchy and its God-given right to rule, together with the Orthodox religion. The Balanchivadze children's godparents belonged to it, the key figure here being Meliton's opera librettist (and Tamara's godfather) Vasily Lvovich Velichko. Velichko was a Ukrainian-born nobleman, poet, playwright, essayist, high-ranking state councilor, organizer of a nationalist literary circle in the 1880s and '90s (frequented by Vladimir Soloviov, Nikolai Leskov, and Ilya Repin), and one of the founders of the Russian Assembly, a precursor of the mostly anti-Semitic "Black Hundreds" groups of 1905–6, dedicated to rekindling the patriotism of the upper classes.[19] Three of the other five Balanchivadze godparents, Maria Georgievna Muretova, Stefanovich, and Stefanovich's wife Margarita Valerianovna (Andrei's godmother), were Velichko's friends or relatives. One can imagine these mustachioed and bejeweled types patting the children on the head—Velichko had a mustache waxed out to fine points. This group approved of Georgians, whom they naively saw as happy feudals living in timeless social harmony, as opposed to Georgia's Armenians, whom they demonized like Jews—Armenians controlled commerce in the Caucasus.[20] Around 1902, Velichko dedicated a poem to Meliton called "In Imereti." "How wonderful! How like heaven on earth!" go the opening lines of his ode to the unsullied wilderness and people of western Georgia. These godparents were also devout. Georgi's godfather Konstantin Stefanovich came from the religious elite: his father, also Konstantin, was the dean of St. Petersburg's Kazan Cathedral.

Georgi, the most private of the Balanchivadze siblings, took religion to heart. He made up games in which he was a priest, with two chairs serving as altar. He blessed small objects. He imagined himself as a holy figure in church robes. But this is not the usual set of memories for a privileged Petersburg child. One wouldn't catch Nabokov playing at the priesthood; what he remembered of parental convictions was a servant sharpening pencils for liberal political meetings. Nor did Mandelstam or another Petersburg memoirist, Viktor Shklovsky, take delight in synagogue ceremonies—they didn't go to the synagogue. In all these homes, a polite religious skepticism prevailed. In the Balanchivadzes, religion was revered, not only by the godparents but by the church-going Maria too. And Meliton, though secular to the core, had had a seminary education. Around 1910, when Georgi was six, a Balanchivadze relative,[21] the Archbishop of Tbilisi, underwent the ritual conversion to Orthodox monk in St. Petersburg's Kazan Cathedral (only the highest Georgian church figures were summoned to the capital). He prostrated himself on the great cathedral's stone floor as the cloth of black crepe was thrown over him to mark his worldly death, then rose, a new being. Georgi remembered this earthly-heavenly drama all his life and took it into his private mythology. In his ballets, not a few mock corpses ascend to a new life.[22]

Hardly any of these family friends came from Maria Balanchivadze's side. Two maternal Petersburg relations, Aunt Nadia and Aunt Anya, show up in family letters.[23] They, or at least Nadia, lived at 1–3 Bolshaya Moskovskaya St. next to the yellow and gold Vladimir Cathedral. Nadia, like the German bonne, had a soft spot for Georgi; it's she to whom he ran away at the start of his ballet education. Both aunts later helped Andrei too, in 1926, when he returned to Leningrad from Georgia to study at the Conservatory. There was also the shadowy Babusia, the possible grandmother. And one more apparent relative joined the mix around 1909, twenty-four-year-old Sofia Nikolaevna Almedingen, who'd grown up in Central Asia with her army-officer father, the younger of the two Almedingens who could have been Maria's father. Sofia provides the only link between Maria and her rumored paternity. She was already a dentist when she arrived in the capital, where she set up an office. Perhaps she was that dentist whom young Georgi told Taper he found so beautiful.[24] In a few years, like her possible half-sister, Sofia would marry a Georgian, a financial colleague of Meliton's, Silovan Antonovich Chumbadze—another proof that she and the Balanchivadzes were connected. After the revolution, Sofia Almedingen-Chumbadze would emigrate with her daughter Nino to Tbilisi, where she and Maria Balanchivadze were close friends.[25]

Whether or not all these groups mingled at parties or visited separately, the dressed-up Balanchivadze children were always on display. Already veterans of early music lessons, they performed for guests on their instruments. One of Andrei's favorite memories has the two little boys at the piano playing pieces by ear they'd heard at the Mariinsky Theater, where they sometimes went to the opera and ballet (their first opera, *The Tale of Tsar Saltan*, by their father's old teacher Rimsky, thrilled them). They'd arranged these pieces for four hands, and made what they called a "menu" of selections. "We asked guests to choose what they wanted to hear," remembered Andrei.[26] Tamara entertained with the violin, her instrument. They performed in other ways too, sitting yearly for formal photos—in sailor suits, then in white Cossack-like shirts (Tamara in a sailor-collared frilly dress), and once, when they were nine, seven, and five, in "motley" court-jester costumes, as befitted the city's prerevolutionary craze for *commedia dell'arte*. If these pictures are proof, Maria Balanchivadze had a passion for theater. Why else would she dress her children as Harlequins? They were also taken yearly to the city's children's *yolka* (Christmas tree) party held in the Grand Hall of Nobles, where Meliton's opera fragments had premiered, and where they played the usual children's games, but were careful not to muss up their velvet clothes.[27] In another R. Charles photo, Georgi can be seen alone at five, still long-haired, sitting mournfully on some studio rocks in a velvet suit, holding a single rose.

Such a family life might have seemed stuffy. But in private, without guests, affection and high spirits entered the picture. Meliton called Maria *Gogosha*, fusing the Georgian word for girl with the Russian diminutive. The children called their parents *papenka* and *mamenka*. They had nicknames too: Andrei was Liolia; Georgi was Zholia, or Gogi.[28] Meliton sometimes shared his own culture with his children, even if he was distracted with money matters. He played Georgian dances and taught them songs. "He would sit us at the piano with him and we sang all together—Papa, Georgi, my sister Tamara, and me," remembered

Tamara, Georgi, and Andrei dressed as Harlequins.

Andrei. "Papa loved 'people's songs' most—from Imereti (his home province in Western Georgia) . . . and Kutaisi city songs. We both, me and Georgi, loved these songs. Also, from childhood we loved games, and everything about music."[29] Georgi's earliest childhood contained a soundtrack of those intricate Georgian rhythms and haunting melodies bubbling up from under the more metrical surface of Czerny and Beethoven.

Georgi

But overall, the place of Georgia in Meliton's Petersburg children's lives is something of a mystery. Meliton may have been held back from fully sharing his country, from guilt about his neglected first wife and children, and parents. Both parents were dead (his mother had died in 1895) by the time Meliton turned fifty in 1912, when he traveled "home" to an elaborate birthday celebration for himself in Kutaisi, during which various Balanchivadzes gave speeches and toasts in the Georgian manner. In Georgia, Meliton was a celebrity—for his opera, not his money, though Vaso in his birthday speech cited the old Georgian proverb about two brothers splitting a single nut, and proposed that Meliton split with him the gifts and money he was getting for the occasion. "I hope you live another forty years and write another opera," Vaso added affectionately, "because another opera will take another forty years."[30]

Reading about such Balanchivadze occasions, it's hard not to feel resentment on behalf of the small Petersburg siblings and their mother. Why didn't Meliton take them with him for his Georgian celebration and show them to relatives? Was he still hesitant about merging his two lives, or simply inattentive? Even if his Russian children had received Georgian-flavored first names, they weren't taught the language, with its clotted guttural sounds and exotic alphabet. The children didn't sing their Georgian songs for the guests; they played classical music. For photographs, they wore every costume *but* Georgian, though buying a Georgian costume for one's children was almost de rigueur for Russian tourists in Tbilisi.[31] Balanchine sometimes said he was Georgian, but when pressed he claimed "Petersburg nationality." Perhaps a silent struggle was going on between the parents, with Meliton trying to explain his country to his children and Maria regularly objecting, wanting them to grow up as regular elite little Petersburgers.

Even if Maria's origins are obscure, her character comes clearly through history: she was a woman of social ambition, building a mini personal empire in and around the imperial capital. The family vacation home (dacha) in Finland—then part of the Russian Empire—was one of the first things bought with the lottery money. It was registered in her name. Dachas, symbols of the bourgeoisie's longing for country estates, even if tiny, had by the early twentieth century become all but necessary for middle-class Russians. Cholera, gone from European capitals, was still a danger here: a major outbreak came in 1908.[32] When Maria went looking for theirs, she chose the newest, grandest dacha settlement around, called Lounatjoki, a made-up Finnish name meaning either "southwest river" or "lunch river."[33]

Lounatjoki was laid out in 1900 by the Léovilla financial association, on a tract of lakes and pinewoods bordering the St. Petersburg-Helsinki railway line, between the Russian capital and the Finnish port of Vyborg. It featured a hundred-odd numbered land plots, a post office, a bakery, roads leading out from a new wooden railway station (with pretentious names like Count Tolstoy Prospekt and Prince Trubetskoi Prospekt), plus an Orthodox monastery and a summer theater for fairly elaborate summer productions. A horse tram ran on Beloselsky Prospekt. A miniature train waited evenings for the Petersburg train, then dropped off the *dachniks* on its way through the woods. Maria bought her first Lounatjoki plot in 1906, when Georgi was two.[34] In 1908 she bought two more, probably as investments.[35] On one of these, the family built a two-story wooden house in olde-Russian art nouveau style, with cupola, two gabled porches and balustraded steps leading to the ground.[36] Lounatjoki's other smart dachas also sported such extravagant elements from architectural pattern books. None resembled the "house in the woods, our nearest neighbors far away" of Balanchine's memory—though in the end he spent more time there in isolated winters than crowded summers.[37]

In 1909, the Balanchivadzes reached their social peak. They had a prestigious dacha, an apartment in town, and three nicely dressed children who behaved as they should, except for five-year-old Georgi, who sometimes hung back and displayed a temper. Meliton had joined the board of the Fourth St. Petersburg Mutual Credit Association, a group of wealthy entrepreneurs who lent each other money.[38] Petersburg, the banking capital of the empire, contained, along with banks and stock exchanges, about forty mutual credit associations. But early in 1910, the web of risky investments Meliton had made with the lottery fortune began to unravel. In November of that year, he wrote Maria an agitated letter from somewhere outside Petersburg, reassuring her about financial ventures, even as he confessed his guilt. "I feel as if I'm throwing away my most precious thing—my family," he writes, begging Maria not to worry, because he thinks he can sell a piece of land in Yalta, possibly an earlier investment, to an old wine-merchant colleague, a Major General Vitmer. The emotional turmoil in the letter is so palpable the children must have felt it, especially a sensitive six-year-old like Georgi. Five months later, in May 1911, Meliton wrote Maria again, reassuring her this time about a roof-tile factory he'd bought near Moscow. Its materials, graphite and sand, he wrote, would be in place in ten days; the money was guaranteed; he would do as she said and use the money "only for the factory"; Stefanovich (Georgi's godfather) might bring more money from Minsk; and he, Meliton, once home in Lounatjoki, would "get back on the rails" and do his music again.[39]

But things went badly wrong. Money was lost. The apartment in town was let go. One of the Lounatjoki plots was sold. Maria and the children, nine, seven, and five, had already moved year-round to the dacha, a radical disruption for city kids. Meliton was made to answer for his misdeeds and sent away. Balanchine thought he went to debtors' prison; Andrei says it was house arrest—his father was given rooms in the city that he couldn't leave.[40] It's hard to reconcile the children's memory of a father away in disgrace with Meliton's fiftieth birthday celebration the following year in Georgia. But Meliton kept the different parts of his life hidden from each other. Sometimes it seems as if he were living two, possibly more, lives. And even if partial recovery ensued later, an era had ended for the children, the city era, with Father home.

Act II of the family's life began: Finland in the woods. Short summers full of dazzling light, long dark winters full of snow and cold. How precious for a child in those crystalline-dark winters would be the warmth and light of the wooden dacha, the smells of cooking, the sounds of piano music, the not quite embraceable Mama framed in the doorway. In this rustic setting, we find Maria Balanchivadze coping as bravely and vigorously, if impersonally, as she'd coped with life in town. "We had an enormous garden (in Finland), a city block long," Balanchine told Tanaquil

Lounatjoki Station, Finnish Railroad.
From the collection of Matti Etäsalo.

LeClerc, his then wife, in 1966, when she wrote *The Ballet Cook Book.*[41] "Not for fun, but to eat. We cultivated potatoes, carrots, beets, green beans, little sweet peas (the kind you eat pod and all), eggplants, cucumbers, tomatoes, lettuce, parsley, roots, and, naturally, cabbages." He described his mother making sauerkraut "in a big pot," managing massive pickling operations on mushrooms and cucumbers, cooking everything herself. There was a Finnish sauna too for bathing (like a Russian *banya*), which Georgi didn't like. "As soon as someone would yell, 'C'mon, more steam,' I'd get out of there."[42]

For three, possibly four years, till he was nine, young Balanchivadze lived this country life in Finland, a woman-centered life with mother, "auntie," siblings, possibly a servant, and possibly a periodic piano teacher, except for the times when Meliton was there. Then guests appeared again. A photo from circa 1913 shows the house and family: Maria and another woman (the servant?) on the porch; Andrei and Georgi perched on opposite balustrades; Tamara on the bottom step; a young man in a student cap, probably Apollon, on a nearby rock. Balanchine said almost nothing about these years so crucial to his growing up—they may have lodged too deep in his psyche. Contrasted with Andrei's memories of communal Christmases, Balanchine's quintessential Christmas featured "only the family at home [but which home?]: mother, auntie, and the children. And, of course, the Christmas tree . . . decorated with gold paper angels and stars, tangled up in silver 'rain,' or tinsel."[43] Mother and children sometimes took the three-hour train ride to town to "Auntie's" on Bolshaya Moskovskaya St., next to the Vladimir Cathedral.[44] But the young Balanchine missed his father, distant anyway for much of his life, a man whose musical mission had been swallowed by a fortune. He always kept his picture near. Tamara was close enough to Maria to feel cosseted even without a father; Andrei was still a little boy, who would later grow close to his father in Georgia. Georgi, the "quiet child" (in his own words), grew quieter in Finland.[45] On one of his solitary walks around Lounatjoki, he squirmed through a trapdoor into the empty summer theater, stood on the stage, and felt "strangely excited."[46] A portent of his future life, he told Taper years later, though he said almost nothing else about this theater, or his life as a country child. By the time Balanchine talked to Volkov near the end of his life, he'd even "forgotten" that Tamara was older; he said *he* was the older one.[47]

But Maria's ambitions for her children had not dimmed, even as they grew up wild in Finland, throwing snowballs at the local Finnish children who taunted them.[48] Starting with Tamara, Maria set to work on a mother-daughter dream. The pretty, demonstrative little girl would go to the Imperial Theater School and become a dancer. The school was part of the tsar's own household, and education was fully subsidized after a trial year of nominal payments from a student's family. Romanovs visited the school; students danced often in ballets at the Mariinsky Theater. "My sister wanted to be a ballerina," said Andrei, "she even dreamed of that." But in 1912, when Maria took her to the Theater School to audition, to their sorrow she wasn't accepted.

For Georgi, a career in the army seemed the answer. His uncle Ivan and half-brother Apollon were army men. Ivan had recently returned again to Petersburg from the Crimean capital Simferopol, where he'd commanded the prison from 1904 to 1908. He was now an officer in the Petersburg Gendarmes.[49] Apollon had finished military school and was serving in the twentieth Selstrom Rifle Regiment. Ivan pulled serious strings to get Georgi "seen" for the city's prestigious *Kadetskii Korpus*, the Cadet Corps. And Georgi, "even if he wasn't consulted, was already used to that idea, and not even against it," remembered Andrei. "He knew that the Cadet Corps was a tsar's school, and that officers came from there."[50]

With hindsight, we recognize the old-fashioned flavor of such ambitions. War was about to break out, then revolution, and such hierarchical distinctions would be swept away. But Maria's dreams for her children were so insistent that she showed a willingness to shortcut respectability, or ignore the child's possible wishes, just to get him or her up the social ladder, closer to the court. That was the old collective dream of Petersburgers—up the ladder towards the court. In their charming book *From the Life of Petersburg, 1890s–1910s*, authors D.A. Zasosov and V. I. Pyzin describe a typical Petersburg merchant family, "whose children already went to universities, to institutes, learned music and languages . . . The parents tried to marry their daughters to *chinovniki* [bureaucrats with rank] or officers, in this way getting themselves related to the nobility."[51] The ballet offered another way up for daughters, maybe not through marriage, but through training for a world that didn't need marriage to be glorious—the Petersburg demimonde with its parties, restaurants, hothouse flowers in winter, *chinovniki*, and officers entertaining mistresses and setting them up with children in apartments. The demimonde was an alternate, semi-hidden social world, to which ballet was firmly linked. And it was probably Maria's own home turf too. As for Cadet Corps schools like the one envisioned for Georgi, they bred the other half of the demimonde social equation: the patrons for the ballerinas. Graduates were catapulted into the officer category. And in the tsarist army in the early twentieth century, even after reformist leveling, the officers were mainly aristocrats.

The half-Japanese, half-American sculptor Isamu Noguchi, Balanchine's exact contemporary and colleague, once called himself "the product of an American woman's imagination." Balanchine on his side was the product of a Russian-Petersburg woman's imagination, except that the gender wires got unexpectedly crossed in her plans. It happened in August of 1913, when Tamara was eleven and Georgi nine. The family traveled to town to audition Tamara a second time for ballet and enroll Georgi in the military school. But the military school rolls were full for that year, so they proceeded to the Theater School. It must have looked forbidding already from the outside, with a *shveitsar* porter in imperial livery guarding its central door. The School occupied an entire façade of the famous Theater Street, a symmetrical allée of twin neoclassical imperial yellow facades extending back from the Roman-flavored Alexandrinsky Theater, designed by architect Carlo Rossi in the late 1820s. It embodied in miniature the utopian symmetry that the Romanovs kept trying to impose on their once-swampy capital—and on their vast chaotic land.[52] And the training that went on behind the Theater School facade was just as utopian, imposing on students' bodies a three-centuries-old European theatrical-classical ideal.

Inside, that August morning, the children were separated into small groups. Each group was marched in twos through the wide dancing halls to be inspected in turn by dancing masters, medical doctors, music masters, and academic teachers. The proceedings lasted two days. Along the way, children not approved by any one of the commissions were eliminated. Tamara was again not taken.[53] But Georgi, whose naturally proud bearing had attracted notice, had been put into the proceedings too. On the judging panel sat the shrewd senior ballerina Olga Preobra-zhenskaya, who singled him out from a line of boys walking and made him walk separately.[54]

At the end of the second day the school offered Maria a place for him. This must have startled her, since Georgi notoriously hated to dance. At Christmas parties, brother Andrei sometimes danced a waltz. "I loved to dance," he said. "Georgi did not like to dance, and hid himself in a corner. If somebody wanted to pair him with somebody, he began to cry and wave his arms and legs—he completely did not agree to that."[55]

Nevertheless, Maria accepted the school's offer and made special arrangements for Georgi to become a boarder on the spot, since the family lived too far to bring him back when school started. When she told her son he would be staying, he "cried and screamed horribly," remembered Andrei. "But who heard him? Then they cut his hair, dressed him in a uniform with a lyre on the breast and put him in the pension." Balanchine himself used strong words when he told Taper about this moment when his childhood broke in two. "Was accepted for school," say Taper's notes paraphrasing him, "and then the mother and sister went back to Finland and left him—all happened on the same day. Felt like a dog that had just been taken out and abandoned. Was shortly after that that he ran away."[56]

"The amazing fate of a person," is what Andrei says about his brother's abrupt entry into the life envisioned for his sister. Fate, maybe, but Balanchine's being put in the school against his own wishes probably constituted the greatest trauma of his life, greater even than revolution, emigration, and the later financial and emotional ups and downs of a roving choreographer. It seems to have darkened his memories of pre-ballet years and sealed over whatever longings—for love, rescue, father, *mother*—already lodged in his child's psyche, longings that would surface perhaps only in the great brokenhearted ballets of his mature years.

No one witnessed the goodbye between mother and son in the school's stone hall. It must have been especially devastating for this proud little boy, choking back his tears while his mother called on him to submit to his fate.[57] The *vospitatel* (schoolmaster) in charge of the thirty boy boarders came down the stone stairs to fetch the newest recruit. Did he pause tactfully to let the mother detach the child from her embrace? Did Georgi glance down one last time as he climbed the stairs to the boys' quarters? Did she turn back to look up at him?

THREE

Theater School: Boys

Theater Street.
Courtesy Saint-Petersburg State Museum of Theater and Music.

The Imperial Theater School was founded in 1738 during the reign of Anna Ioannovna (1730–40), Peter the Great's portly half-niece.[1] In the prolonged chaos following Peter's 1725 death, she'd been chosen over Peter's daughter Elizabeth and brought to the throne from East Prussia (where she'd married the prince) by powerful Moscow nobles who thought they could control her and so reverse Peter's Europeanization of Russian court life. Instead, upon being crowned, Anna tore up this agreement and removed her court back to Peter's almost abandoned settlement of St. Petersburg. There she founded, among other institutions, a *Pazheskii Korpus* (Corps des Pages) military school for the sons of the nobility faithful to *her*,[2] and imported a French dancing master, Jean Batiste Landé, to civilize them. It was the bewigged, lace-fronted Landé who decided to make real dancers on the side. He asked the empress for six sons and six daughters of palace staff; he got twelve of each. After a year, some were ready to go into the plays of the Italian troupe resident in Russia's first imperial theater.

So was born not only the flagship academy of this most Russian-identified of arts, but ballet's close relations with court and army. Over the next century, the school occupied a succession of palace rooms and private houses. Then, in 1825, came Nicholas I, the stern tsar, who would give it its permanent home. On his first day in office, Nicholas had stared down the revolt of the liberal army officers called Decembrists. For the rest of his long reign he made a fetish of order, or rather the appearance of order. This may explain his love of theater. He collected Russia's various theatrical entities under a newly created Ministry of the Imperial Court. In his reign, three new major theaters opened in St. Petersburg, the Alexandrinsky (drama), Mikhailovsky (French-speaking), and Kamennoostrovsky (summer).

But of all the theatrical genres, Nicholas preferred the ballet. He never missed a ballet performance, or so it was claimed. He sometimes deserted the tsar's box to sit closer to the artists in the front row. He came backstage in intermissions and talked to them; he sponsored the weddings of several; he made up ballet deficits from the royal purse. "We actors should be especially grateful to Nicholas I," wrote venerable dancer T. A. Stukolkin, "who did such generous things for us, who loved us and treated us like his own children."[3] In 1836, Nicholas had the Theater School moved next to the Imperial Theater's office on Theater St., at the very center of his newly Romanized capital of straight avenues and imperial vistas.[4]

Perhaps because of Nicholas, the Imperial Theater School's atmosphere congealed at mid-nineteenth century, its students relegated to a perpetual acting out of his military-utopian vision for his empire. Girls' uniforms, even in the early twentieth century, were long blue serge dresses with old-fashioned tight bodices and low waists, covered by starched pinafore aprons, black for weekdays, white for Sundays. The boys' military-style dress—black pants, light-blue jacket—displayed the "regimental insignia," a lyre, on the collar. All Russian boarding schools had old-fashioned uniforms, but these were extreme. Other barracks-like features marked the schedules: cold baths in early morning; regimental walks around the block; strict and rapid meals, with older students serving younger; dormitories with straight rows of beds, girls' on the first floor, boys' on the second. The sealed-in nature of school life remained almost unchanged until 1917. But it wasn't cramped: three high-ceilinged floors offered students imperial space to move around in.[5]

Young Georgi Balanchivadze entered this half-sumptuous, half-Spartan domain in its last intact moment, before World War I would begin to erode the antiquated routines. He'd been brought back from country to city, but not to the noisy carnival city he'd known in childhood. This was an isolated central pocket of it, cut off from all sounds except the muffled music from rehearsal halls, purged of random sights and even of spontaneous talk. Upon reaching the boys' second-floor quarters, the nine-year-old was taken down again to the courtyard bathhouse to have his long hair shorn and his miniature uniform issued, along with a formal black coat, short dance pants, and a regulation bathrobe for Friday night *banya* steambaths. He probably donned this uniform on the spot—new clothes for a new person. Upstairs, he was shown the dormitory hall with its two rows of beds and the carpet runner laid between on the parquet floor. As the youngest, he received a bed at the end, with a polished wood bed-stand beside it, a tin plaque with his name above it, and a light fixture above that.

His whole being reacted in a spasm of rage—and he ran away. We know this not just because he said so, but because his brother too remembered the escape.[6] As an instant boarder, Georgi was there before the other boys. He'd lain awake among the empty beds, listening to the horrible jangling of the tin nametags.[7] This is when he must have made his desperate plans and put them in action, since the episode doesn't show up in the official logbook.[8] Probably it happened on a supervised walk outside, with the boy darting out of his keeper's sight and racing through the crowds, trying to find his Aunt Nadia's building. This wasn't as crazy as it seems. While in town for the audition, Maria and the children stayed at this aunt's apartment, within walking distance—though a long walk—from Theater Street. Maria would have reassured her son that "Auntie" was right over there, across the Fontanka.

Still, most nine-year-olds don't make a point of noticing where their mother is leading them, especially if they don't think they need to. Georgi would have run to the Fontanka at the southern end of Theater Street, crossed it on the Chernyshev Bridge (now Lomonosov Bridge), continued straight ahead on Lomonosov Street to the bustling "Five Corners" intersection, and turned left up the biggest of its five streets, Zagorodny Prospekt, from where he could see the gold-domed Vladimir Cathedral next to Aunt Nadia's apartment. Did the real streets conform to the ones in his memory? Did he have to ask his way from passersby?

To escape alone at age nine in a virtually unknown city is to be driven by furious despair. But to get somewhere, one needs a quick wit. Georgi found not just Aunt Nadia's apartment building, but the lady herself. She took him in but insisted he go back. A school official came knocking at her door looking for little Balanchivadze.[9] The address was the one on file in the school's logbook, though the family's Finland address was also noted, "Lounatjoki, Finnish Railway." The boy was brought back, and allowed, surprisingly, to remain. His escape could have been judged the fault of the attending master. But his own family blamed him too. They wished him to be in the school, and there he would stay.

Soon the other thirty-one boarders, ages eleven to seventeen, all older and bigger than Georgi, filled up the dormitory beds.[10] Nine younger boys like him had been admitted too, but they lived at home. First-years were usually day students on probation; only a few were asked back for a second year. How did the older boarders react to the newest small recruit making a show of haughty indifference? It might have been they who rechristened him *Georges*—a French name for the smallest, unhappiest among them. They also called him "Rat," because of compulsive sniffing that showed his front teeth (a habit that never left him). But Georgi/ Georges could do nothing about the bullying: he had to fall into the school routine too and learn by imitating.

Mornings early, a servant walked among the beds shaking a bell. The just-awakened boys were washed all together in cold water by attendants, assigned to several at once, at what classmate Mikhail remembers was a "large round copper tank, with a mass of faucets sticking out of it."[11] "We were all the tsar's dependents," said Balanchine later. "We had servants and lackeys at the school: all handsome men in uniform, buttoned from top to bottom . . . We didn't make the beds, we left everything. The servants took care of it."[12] After a quick breakfast of tea and bread came the fabled morning walk outside. They put on their formal black coats and spilled out of the front door. This would be their only chance in the day to glimpse the outside world. The master on duty restrained them until the column of girls was out of sight, then assembled them by height in pairs—Georges, the smallest, at the front—and paraded them along a triangular route that reversed the little boy's earlier escape: up Theater Street (not down), around the Alexandrinsky Theater to the Nevsky Prospekt; right turn along the Nevsky past the Anichkov Palace and gardens; right again at the Fontanka River's Anichkov Bridge (with its four giant bronze horses being restrained by four naked bronze men); down along the Fontanka's granite embankment to the Chernyshev bridge; sharp right onto Theater Street, and back to the Theater School's door. And then to ballet class—to work!

Everything about the days and nights would have been a shock. It wasn't just that Georges hadn't known such a rigid routine. He'd never been in school at all. Despite passionate empire-wide debates about schooling, especially after the 1905 revolution, no elementary education had yet been made compulsory for Russian children.[13] A tutor had figured in the Balanchivadze family's first years, but neither Georgi nor Andrei remembered his name; the nursemaids were more important. From age five, Georgi had lived in the women's world of the Finnish dacha, helping his mother in the garden, reading, writing, playing piano, walking alone in the woods. Now he'd landed in an all-male society where every move was clocked. Solitude was impossible, except evenings at the piano. But the littlest probably couldn't risk playing alone. Excellence was impossible too, at least at first. The older boys were more experienced at every aspect of his new life, especially in the morning ballet classes.

Six days a week, from 10:00 to 11:30 or noon (shorter classes for younger students), the whole school studied the rudiments of their art, girls below and boys above. Georgi was sent with the other youngest to the smallest of his floor's three rehearsal halls. The Theater School in tsarist years didn't separate pupils into levels by year. Instead, eight years were compressed into three levels: Junior, Middle, and Senior. Georgi's Junior class contained mostly ten- and eleven-year-olds, but some, such as Mikhail Dudko and Kiril Zhuralev, had already studied for two years. The newest and youngest, like him, learned by watching the others, as all performed the exercises prescribed for ballet students: *pliés* and *tendus*, *ronds de jambe, dévelopés, battements*, and the rest of the procedures with their French names, first with the left hand holding the barre, then with the right. Center exercises followed with more complicated steps, then jumps and bigger steps that moved across the floor. But all the rehearsal halls had been designed to facilitate such moves. Ceilings were high; windows were huge. The floors were "slightly sloping . . . like a stage surface," wrote Georges's classmate Mikhailov, "specially made so the foot wouldn't slip." One wall was covered with mirrors so the boys could check their positions; the other walls had thick ballet barres attached with brackets at two levels, so students of different heights could hold onto them for the first part of the class.[14]

With the boys in their places, in came their teacher, Samuil Konstantinovich Andrianov, dressed in smart street clothes. Andrianov was a tall and beautifully proportioned twenty-nine-year-old who was kind to all in his charge, even the littlest. He'd been a student of the great Pavel Gerdt, the Mariinsky's lead *danseur noble* for half a century. He must have loved teaching; he'd begun at age twenty at the start of his Mariinsky career. When Georges landed in his class, Andrianov was at the peak of his powers. Mornings he schooled students in his own light, pure way of dancing. Afternoons he put on his own dancing clothes to rehearse in the school's biggest hall, where Mariinsky artists readied performances. Wednesday and Sunday evenings he partnered the great ballerinas of the day on the Mariinsky stage, including his wife, Elizaveta Gerdt, daughter of his teacher. Maybe Andrianov's choice to give class in street clothes was meant to impress his charges. The boys worked it out that if he showed up in the morning in a gray suit, he was in a good mood. If he wore a black one—watch out.[15] "Andrianov," said Balanchine later, "made our generation."[16]

Morning technique class was followed by another quick wash, a change of clothes, a breakneck lunch, and an afternoon of academic classes on the "girls'" floor below—Russian, French, math, religion—where boys and

Samuil Andrianov.
Courtesy Saint-Petersburg State Museum of Theater and Music.

girls studied together, but on separate sides of the room. Dinner came at
4:30, upstairs again in the boys' dining room, where an icon with red-
glass-enclosed candle hung in the corner facing five long tables with white
tablecloths.[17] The *vospitatel* (caretaker) on duty sat at the head of one; an
older boy passed out food and made sure the youngest minded their manners. The food was good, or that's what Balanchine's generation remembered. It probably got even better in hindsight after the hungry civil war
years. "We . . . had borsch and bitki (ground meat patties)," Balanchine

said later, "and kasha [cereal] on Thursday. The bitki were served in sour cream sauce, delicious! And the borsch was a work of genius!"[18]

A second round of classes started after dinner: pantomime, posture, and fencing for the older boys, ballroom for everyone, even the youngest. Ballroom was taught by a colorful ex-Mariinsky dancer, Nikolai Gavlikovsky, now forty-two, said to be the first male dancer to do a double *tour en l'air*.[19] Here the boys and girls of the school got their only glimpse of each other in those early years. Among the girls was one almost as small as Balanchivadze, though a year older: Alexandra Danilova, Choura for short.[20] Choura had been stuck in the school in 1911 at eight and a half, even younger than Georges. In 1913, she was still the smallest girl, and so would have been paired with Georges in waltzes and schottisches. But according to Mikhailov, the little boys were so tired by evening that girls were soon forgotten. After ballroom classes, all returned to their dormitories, where homework and music lessons awaited. They could choose piano or violin. Balanchivadze chose piano and worked hard: it was the only bridge between his new life and his old. Many older boys were absent evenings, rehearsing or performing the Mariinsky's ballets or operas. But first-years did not get stage roles, so Georges was in bed by 9 PM. "We could read before going to sleep," he remembered later. "I liked reading Jules Verne—*Twenty Thousand Leagues Under the Sea, The Mysterious Island*. I still remember the captions under the pictures: 'If we hear bells at night in the open sea, that means the ship has sunk.'"[21]

On Saturdays, those not needed by the Theater were allowed to go out overnight, to whichever family was registered in the logbook. Young Balanchivadze didn't get this privilege for more than a month after he became a student. Perhaps it was his punishment for running away. Finally, on September 28 he got permission with sixteen other boys and was "signed out" to his listed family. But here the mystery of Maria Balanchivadze's identity only deepens. The name listed in the logbook for Balanchivadze isn't any Nadezhda, the formal version of Aunt Nadia's name, but someone named Agrippina Ivanovna Zernyshkova, also labeled "aunt" in the logbook, also residing at Aunt Nadia's address, 1–3 Bolshaya Moskovskaya St.[22] The city directory has Agrippina, daughter of a Titular Counselor (9th rank), living with her sister Alexandra and her Interior Ministry official brother Georgi (5th rank).[23] The Zernyshkovs might have been relatives too, or neighbors or employers. Or perhaps they had a telephone and Nadia hadn't. "On Sundays my aunt sometimes came over and picked me up at school and took me home for the day. She lived in Petersburg," said Balanchine later.[24] Aunt Nadia was the only aunt he ever mentioned by name. But only the mysterious Agrippina was allowed to fetch him from school.

After his first weekend out, Georgi went to the Zernyshkovs or Aunt Nadia on Bolshaya Moskovskaya a week later, and again on six more weekends that fall of 1913.[25] On December 29, (the logbook says) he traveled to his immediate family in Finland for the winter holidays. All the boys went home then for eight days, returning January 6, 1914. The logbook is a specially formatted thick tome, each calendar day claiming a double-page spread separated into squares, within which were noted those sick in the infirmary, those called to rehearsal, those out for weekend furloughs, and those affected by "special occurrences."[26] The 1913–14 logbook is also the only one of those years to make it into the central RGIA Archives. No corresponding girls' logbook survives. It tells us that Balanchivadze saw his relatives even more the next spring: he was logged out on sixteen different Saturdays. Not only that, but sometime before Christmas 1913, the school administration asked Meliton Balanchivadze to host a country holiday party for the boys' division. Meliton, after all, was an impresario, who made it his business to know everyone. He agreed, which suggests he'd partially recovered his money. All the boys, plus caretakers, teachers and staff—about fifty in all—came by train for a winter day in Lounatjoki, to be shown the Balanchivadzes' lavish hospitality.[27]

Even with such an event, which mixed school and family, and even if Georges saw family often during his first school year, those initial solitary weekends set the tone for later memories. "It was sad and lonely to be left," Balanchine said much later. "You'd go to church and stand there for some time. The school had a chapel. The master would be there with maybe two or three other students. You had to kill time before dinner. I would go to the reception hall and play the piano. There was no one there, total emptiness. Then came dinner, and after dinner, bed."[28] The experience was so melancholy that the grown Balanchine never lost his dread of weekends and holidays. "On holidays [weekend days] you feel so lonely, so abandoned," he said. "On weekdays everything goes by schedule, people work, go here and there, the stores are open, everyone's fine. When it's a holiday, you get the feeling that you've suddenly been transported somewhere else, as if you're in a movie; something alien, unfamiliar is happening, and you're watching from the outside. You don't even want to participate in it."[29]

Gradually, though, the school began to turn a human face towards its youngest boarder. Georges got sick three times, in October, January, and March (less than some of the other boys), but he landed each time in the eight-bed *lazaret* (infirmary) behind the dormitory, a caring place to rest and get well in.[30] In the spring, the logbook indicates a further recovery. Balanchivadze and a classmate named Slavianinov did something naughty in ballet class—twice, on March 11 and April 22. Their punishment was the lightest of the three possible: they were deprived of sweets, by order of Andrianov, rather than made to stand in the hall under a clock or forgo weekend privileges.[31] They must have been joking around. But boys in a depression are unlikely to joke.

Even if he punished them sometimes, Andrianov was adored by his pupils. They also liked at least three of the four *vospitatel* masters who rotated as overall caretakers and also taught school. One of them, Ivan Petrov, taught Russian; he was frail, generous, and eccentric—he would say things three times and slap the table for emphasis.[32] Another *vospitatel*, Piotr Lauberg, was an older man with a Ukrainian accent who doubled as math teacher—an "excellent" teacher, said Balanchine later, though others, like Natalia Lisovskaya, thought him lazy. "He was forty-five (at the time I thought he was ancient), a good, kind man," said Balanchine. "In the upper classes they teased him, they liked doing it.... The mathematician wept at this, and we felt sorry for him. We younger boys never mocked him, we were well disciplined."[33]

The other favorite was Grigory Grigorievich Isaenko, short, big-nosed, pot-bellied. Isaenko would become after the revolution the school's inspector, second-in-command, and would take extra care of Balanchivadze in the disastrous civil war years. Many students remembered Isaenko's compulsive teasing. Some said too, later, that the amiable servant-educator had fallen in love with the teenaged Balanchivadze. All trusted and liked him anyway—the civil war made everyone mutually dependent. Still, this idea of a *vospitatel* in love with a student raises questions. Was Isaenko careful to keep this hidden? Would the school have noticed such a thing? Did Georges trust the schoolmaster?[34] Whatever was true, Isaenko was a witness to Balanchivadze's entire school career: he was there at the start; he encouraged his talent.

Finally, comfort came from the chapel on the school's top (third) floor,[35] called the Holy Trinity Church. Students went there on the twelve yearly religious holidays and on royal family birthdays, they confessed there during the Lenten fast, and those left behind on weekends found refuge in its sparse services. The presiding priest too offered a symbolic link with home, in services and religion classes ("The Laws of God"), especially to a student who'd played at the priesthood. The Theater School priest, serving so close to the court, was traditionally an aristocrat. In Georges's time, he was Father Vasily Faustovich Pigulevsky, who'd received his job thirty-one years before. In 1913, Father Vasily still had a full beard and intelligent eyes. Outside the school he dressed like a gentleman. Inside, with only the students as witnesses, he took it easy. He allowed climbing onto windowsills and jumping under desks. Students knew the best way to waste time was to ask about his dinner. "Batiushka" (Father) would describe the delicious food being cooked in his school apartment a floor below by his wife and seven children. "Such meals wouldn't be available to children like you," he said, "children of poor parents, who are fed pretty much on anything." Before the Revolution, Father Vasily couldn't help his boasting, or so said former students in Soviet times. He even showed them the banknotes in his wallet.[36]

But the jokey old priest was liked too. He was not a strict believer. He chided students gaily when they confessed to him. He called them "little fool," "little black grouse" (the bird), or in a more bombastic mood, simply "idiot" (*bolvan*). His easy irony might have reminded small Balanchivadze of his own father. Father Vasily kept a bottle of communion wine on the side for himself and his favorites. He even had the grace to submit to teasing. One graduating girls' class made up a ditty: "Goodbye, our Father Pigulevsky/You who love to go to the theater/You would have been happier being in the Horse Guards/Not conducting church services for the likes of us."[37] When he was older Georges would serve as his altar boy, and watch over that wine.

Gradually, not just the priest's jokes but everything about the school grew familiar to Georges, and he began to grasp too its main purpose: to make theater. Ballets were rehearsed afternoons right on the premises, in the biggest dance hall, ringed by a viewing balcony. A striking number of them were listed in the 1913–14 logbook: the stock fairy tales by the nineteenth-century master Marius Petipa—*Swan Lake, The Sleeping Beauty, Don Quixote, Paquita, The Little Humpbacked Horse*—and works now less known or partially lost, like Petipa's *Le Talisman, Esmeralda,* and *The Seasons,* the Legat brothers' *Fairy Doll,* and Mikhail Fokine's *Le Pavillon d'Armide.* Older students were called to these rehearsals if child parts were indicated, and to opera and theater rehearsals too.

Younger students weren't supposed to watch, but all Theater School memoirists remember peeking through the rehearsal hall keyhole. The little boys had favorites among the ballerinas. Georges liked Tamara Karsavina for her dark-eyed beauty and worldly charm. But he liked all the imperial ballerinas, their regal femininity glimpsed in keyhole pieces—a leg here, an arm there. Even if the Mariinsky artists used a separate entrance from the school's courtyard, the swish of fur coats could be heard, and the whiff of expensive French perfumes wafted from the rehearsal studio—the smell and aura of the theater and theater folk. Even the fabled Matilda Kshesinskaya, chic and businesslike in a blur of fur and silk, would come here to rehearse. So would Georgi's favorite Karsavina in her smart Parisian clothes, and all the other dressed-up male and female dancers of the corps de ballet. Even shut up in Theater Street, a child could see ahead to the glamorous world waiting outside.

The ballet played a central role in the imperial capital's gay society life, especially during the "season," which fell not in spring, as in London, but in winter leading up to Lent, when "it is bitterly cold . . . and the contrast between a hot, brilliantly lit-up ballroom [or theater] . . . and the snow, cold and darkness without has a peculiar charm for the senses." So wrote the anonymous author of *Russian Court Memoirs 1914–16*, published in 1917 in England, who called himself "A Russian." If not at a party, the gay crowd was at the ballet. Or else the parties followed performances. The French restaurant of the Hotel Astoria was a favorite venue. Kshesinskaya would arrive late in sleighs, with dancer and grand duke friends—"the men in uniform, the women swathed in expensive furs"[38]—and celebrate all night, especially in the winter of 1913–14. "Even the dowagers do not remember such a brilliant season as that of 1913–1914," wrote A Russian. "Balls and receptions followed each other, each more resplendent than the last. . . . It was a continual rush, as if there were an undefined presentiment current that this particular season was the last for many a gallant officer joyfully taking his part in the vortex of worldly gaiety."[39]

War was in the air, according to the newspapers: "The hour is coming," said St. Petersburg's *Novoe Vremya*. On May 6, the end of the school year, Balanchivadze, now ten, was released back into the idyll of the countryside, back to his mother, aunt, sister, little brother, older half-brother, and perhaps his father, though it seems Meliton had begun touring again with a new group of Georgian singers. He went home lucky, one of the few invited to return. But how could Georgi, now Georges, resume his old carefree life in Lounatjoki? How could he tell the family about school affairs when his sister Tamara was still pining to get in? What had been true in August of 1913 was now reversed: he was not a stranger in school, but a stranger in his own family.

In the imperial capital, great diplomatic events unfolded over that summer of 1914. A squadron of British ships arrived; its officers were feted. The Saxon king came on a state visit in August, followed by the French president. Then, abruptly, negotiations between Russia and Germany faltered over the Austria-Serbia standoff, sparked by a Serb's murder of the Austrian crown prince. The opposing sides—and their allies—readied for war. News of a war hit St. Petersburg, said a Russian, "as if a thunderbolt had suddenly fallen from a sunny sky." A wave of patriotism and anti-German feeling swept over the capital. Portraits of Nicholas II graced all the shop windows. The city's Germanic name was Russified: St. Petersburg became Petrograd. On July 20, when the tsar read the declaration of war from the Winter Palace balcony, a great throng of subjects knelt beneath, on the stones of Palace Square, and sang the national anthem.

Three hours away, in Lounatjoki dacha country, the fathers from the Petersburg train talked of nothing else. Many were reserve officers whose regiments were mobilizing. War for the Balanchivadzes meant that half-brother Apollon was reposted to the Finnish border.[40] Was Georgi excited for Apollon? In the late summer of 1914, war in Russia, as in England, France, and Germany, still had the feel of a glorious adventure. Was the boy thinking about the war as he prepared to end his Finnish summer and become again Georges, the small poseur? Was he eager to talk war with the returning older boys? An extra confusion arose: this time his sister Tamara was coming, too. Meliton had written once more to the school's administrator on August 13, with palpable results.[41]

"In view of the fact that my daughter, Tamara, turned twelve on July 31," began the letter, "I am writing to the Imperial Theater School to request that they accept her into the student body. For this reason I address Your Excellency with this humble request, to allow my daughter to be seen again in the school audition." This rather desperate letter says much about the parents' responsiveness to the sister's hopes, as opposed to those of the brother, who hadn't wanted the ballet school in the first place. Meliton was essentially begging for his daughter's admittance, even if she'd exceeded the official age. "I allow myself to remind your Excellency," he continued, "that last year my daughter attracted to herself the special attention of the ballet master Fokine [the prestigious Ballets Russes choreographer, now back in Petersburg]. My insistent request is volunteered because of the success of my son, who received after his first year at the school in ballet class an invitation to return, which happens rarely. My daughter shows no less inclination to this art."

Maria's desire for the girl to dance, and Tamara's own, must have been acute. But once Georges and Tamara entered the school on August 10, 1914, the boy would have met his sister only rarely. Lidochka must have known her—she came that year too. But Tamara didn't stay long. She might have been dismissed for high spirits and a sharp tongue (her specialties at home). Choura Danilova says Tamara didn't last in the school because she was a tomboy.[42] Probably she left before the year's end, since no fellow students mention her in a memoir. But a later photograph shows her at about age fifteen, performing in a sailor's costume. She hadn't stopped dreaming of dance.

When Tamara left the school, she effectively ceased to play a role in her brother's life. But among the twenty-nine students accepted that fall, others would come to matter a lot to the future Balanchine. Most of them were ten years old, like him. At last, some contemporaries! In two years, he would be kept back to join them and graduate with them. The new group included Mikhail Mikhailov, already eleven, son of an impoverished Mariinsky seamstress and an unknown father, refused already twice by the auditioning board but finally accepted in 1914. He went on to have a long later career as a dancer, then as an acting teacher to dancers. And he became the class scribe, writing two valuable memoirs: *A Life in Ballet* and *The Young Years of the Leningrad Ballet*.[43]

Also in the group was a girl who'd been accepted, like Mikhailov, apparently without the *protektsia* (patronage) that usually ensured a child's place in the school: Lidia Ivanova. As far as we know, the Ivanovs didn't have friends in high places (a member of the royal family was best for this) or acquaintances who were senior ballerinas (second-best). Their daughter won entry purely on the basis of her potential abilities. That Lidochka already stood out from the other little girls we learn from Mikhailov himself, who left a word portrait of her and her parents on the chaotic first day of the new school year.

"Fall, 1914. An animated crowd of parents and children at the school's entrance stairs on the usually empty Theater Street. A torrent of them had poured through the tall open doors, filling the spacious vestibule, all the way up the stairs to the third floor, where the grand hall for lessons (our future) could be glimpsed, lined with jumbled benches. I was waiting on such a bench with my mother, when my eye fell on a girl sitting nearby, between a man in military uniform and a lady in black. Unlike the other girls with their curled and beribboned hair, she wore a modest little dress. A pretty face, dark smooth hair parted in the center, a tightly braided plait showing over one shoulder, her legs tucked under the bench, her hands folded on her knees, her head inclined to one side . . . it all gave an impression of an unpretentious calm in the face of a challenging first day. That focused glance and secretive smile made me think that *this* little girl had an inner life that concerned her alone."[44]

FOUR

Lidochka

Lidochka in Pskov, age five.

Courtesy Carl Taggersell.

Finding out about Lidochka's family was one of the challenges of this book. Mikhailov's description makes it clear her father was an army officer, but he says nothing more. An encyclopedia entry on Lidia offers his full name: Alexander Alexandrovich Ivanov. Was he one of those ex-soldiers who'd been pensioned out to serve in the imperial theaters? Often fathers of Theater School students were old or injured soldiers employed in the imperial theaters as a kind of charity. The father of ballerina turned seminal teacher Agrippina Vaganova was a lowly NCO who became a Mariinsky usher.[1] But in 1914, Lida's father wasn't at the end of his army career—he was a young officer on his way up. The question was, which young officer? The surname Ivanov is the most common one in Russia. Alexander Alexandroviches are everywhere. In 1910, eleven Alexander Alexandrovich Ivanovs were Imperial Russian army officers, serving from Warsaw to Vladivostok.[2] How to find this one?

A photo offered a clue, the earliest among the Ivanov family photos sold by Lidochka's relatives in two batches, in 1961 and 1972, to St. Petersburg's Theater Museum. It says "Ivanova parents" on the back. A blondish, mustachioed young man in a high-collared military uniform sits on a chair, holding a bushy army hat and looking distractedly down. A dark-haired youngish woman in a mutton-sleeved linen dress and a saucer hat (wife? wife-to-be?) stands beside him, half-smiling at the camera. Matched with information from several St. Petersburg archives and the redoubtable Military History Archive of Moscow, the photo's story starts to emerge.[3] This particular Alexander Alexandrovich Ivanov was still a young father when his daughter Lidia was born in 1903. But he'd made a social leap as dramatic as Meliton Balanchivadze's, thanks to that massive, volatile, and internally contradictory institution of late tsarist years, the Russian army.

He was born on December 12, 1877, in the St. Petersburg *guberniya,* one of fifty Russian regions. His family status on documents was *meshchanin,* meaning the urban bourgeoisie lower than merchants.[4] But his parents probably died young. He attended a special school in St. Petersburg founded in 1860 as a charity house for orphan children of craftspeople (even lower than *meshchanin*), named later for its original patron, Tsesarevich Nikolai Alexandrovich, the oldest son of Alexander II who'd died young of meningitis.[5] At the Tsesarevich Nikolai School, poor children studied academics along with skills such as clock repair, metalworking, and blacksmithing; girls in a separate building studied "handiwork." By Ivanov's time, industrialization had brought an influx of metalworking and textile factories to the imperial capital, so the curriculum had swelled to include engineering subjects connected to railroad building and machinery production. In the school's courtyard, real metalworking shops allowed students access to their future trades. They graduated with the title of master or submaster. Young Ivanov finished in 1896, with the skills that would not only make his career but save it, and his family too, in the chaotic time after the Revolution.[6]

At first he may have tried factory engineering like his schoolmates. But three years after leaving the Tsesarevich Nikolai School, Ivanov did something unexpected for a craft school graduate: he volunteered for the army. His skills would have suited the army's push for modernization; perhaps he was recruited. But the army wasn't uniformly focused on modernizing. As a social body, it was archaically class-bound, mired in old beliefs and routines. To join it at the bottom, even as late as 1899, meant encountering a world where the mechanics of war almost disappeared in the aesthetics of class. Young recruits like Ivanov were taught, through dress, body language, and other subtle means, how to behave at work and play, what to worship, and what to think about themselves and everybody else, including women. With the exceptions of regimental wives and daughters, protected by chivalric codes, women were to be approached with a mixture of sentimentality and disdain.[7] Embracing such an ethos was crucial for rising in the ranks. And rising up was important to this self-created young man, first for himself, later for his daughter.

Ivanov entered as a cannoneer in an artillery training command—more precisely, as a "younger bombardier gunner" of the 10th Company—and was sent to Kronstadt, the military island off Petersburg's coast. This posting may have opened his mind not just to army procedures but to the pleasures of the capital, unknowable to a charity student. Young Kronstadt officers were near enough to take boats in to theaters in town and return the same evening.[8] They favored the ballet at the Imperial Mariinsky Theater, where dancers could be applauded and adored, though at a distance. Only the higher-up officers could court them. The army and the ballet seemed to act as magnets to each other. Was Ivanov brought along by his artillery mates to the Mariinsky's top gallery? His blondish looks, especially in uniform, would have pleased his fellows. Did he stare down on society women in the boxes, and beyond them to the dancers in tutus and décolleté bodices, displayed onstage as if on a chessboard? Did he note the central place of the ballerina with her cavalier, framed by circles and lines of her sisters? Was this the moment Ivanov first gravitated toward the arts?

Whatever the young officer did in his spare time, on duty he proved useful. In 1900, a year after enlisting, he was promoted to corporal. A few months after this, he was sent to the army's summer encampment at Krasnoe Selo, to take the arduous field and written exams for the next rank up, sublieutenant. He passed with the required grade of "successful." And how grand it must have been for a young orphan volunteer not just to pass the exam but to see, even take part in, the outdoor spectacle of the army massed for maneuvers, and to glimpse at its head the emperor himself on horseback, wearing his crimson cape and red cap! From the reign of Tsar Paul I (1796–1801), the Russian army had been steeped in a patriotic ethos of pageantry with religious overtones, since in Russia the person of the monarch had never been separated (by a parliament, for instance, or a prime minister) from the body of the state. This fusion of love for emperor and native land only intensified in the early years of Nicholas II, at least in the army. It reached a high pitch just before the disastrous 1904 Russo-Japanese War began to erode all such sentiments.

Several times a summer, Nicholas reviewed his troops on horseback on a vast green field in Krasnoe Selo bordered by woods, while select dress-suited and parasol-wielding guests watched from a tent. The regimental bands played national hymns, the cavalry wheeled in unison on matched horses, the troops ran in tight formation (red-clad hussars, blue-clad Cossacks, imperial guards in white elk-skin breeches), the tsar arrived on his prancing grey Arab horse followed by the imperial entourage in carriages, the mass of men shouted "hurrah" as they approached: all this was part of a mass celebration of the emperor as quasi-divinity, anointed by the Almighty to bring mystical power and unity to his country. Even when war games took over the surrounding countryside, a splendid outcome was preordained for the tsar's benefit. No muddy figures came staggering out of woods and fields.[9]

Such army displays were, in their way, the summer counterparts of the "winter maneuvers" that dancers executed on the ballet stage. Only in summer, the scale was even huger, and soldiers, not dancers, were the performers. But the dancers of the Imperial Ballet were there too during summers at Krasnoe Selo, "to entertain the gentlemen officers" (*gospod ofitserov*) in the town's famous rustic wooden theater. "And a not small role," wrote then young corps de ballet dancer Fedor Lopukhov, "was played by the restaurant nearby, with its private rooms, where Chevalier Guards celebrated and invited young male and female dancers."[10]

Perhaps young Alexander Ivanov glimpsed such illicit celebrations from afar, and longed to be part of them. After he'd passed his exams, the army privileged the young man still further by selecting him as a candidate for a rigorous two-year officer training course at one of its progressive "junker" (cadet) schools, the schools that had emerged during Alexander II's "Great Reforms" of the 1860s and '70s that accompanied the 1861 emancipation of serfs.[11] The army reforms had been pushed through by the farsighted war minister Dmitry Miliutin, who understood that the gentry's exclusive hold on the officer cadre would lead to a future deficit of qualified leaders. He believed the army should draw from a wider talent pool, especially since Russia was now competing with Prussia's rising might, and with other nations arming against Prussia. But his dream of creating junker schools had showed Miliutin the empire's woeful education levels. As late as 1869, only 10 percent of army recruits were literate, compared to 96 percent in Prussia and 85 percent in England.[12] Miliutin worked first with the minister of education to bolster primary and gymnasium levels, then focused on military education, dividing existing military schools into two: military gymnasia for early general education,[13] junker schools for officer training—and these would accept all social classes. By the time Ivanov found his way to his own junker school, Miliutin had long since retired to the countryside. But for the old reformer, a young engineer from "the people" would have been the just the type he'd searched for.[14]

Despite Miliutin's efforts, though, the army in Ivanov's junker days was still locked in a slow-motion struggle between the modernizers planning for twentieth-century war and the aristocracy resisting it. Elite officers who hadn't earned their ranks wanted an army of beautiful formations, with themselves as ornaments—and beneficiaries. Though non-aristocrats were flooding into the officers' ranks, old biases held, encouraged by the thirty-three-year-old Tsar Nicholas II, who'd done a youthful stint in the Horse Guards and never forgot the joys of elite camaraderie.[15] The Horse

Guard cavalry units were still the most prestigious in the army, notwith-standing broad advances in guns and explosives. Even the technology-savvy artillery was looked down on as plebeian, and the infantry more so. Young Ivanov, with his own social ambitions, would have been aware of the dreariness at the bottom of the scale, and yet he chose the Infantry Junker School over the artillery.[16] Perhaps he'd already figured out his spe-cial army niche: cars, or rather *avtomobili*, which in Russian meant any-thing that moved by means of a motor, including trucks and armored cars (precursors of tanks).[17] In the pre–World War I years, *avtomobili* were at the forefront of technology, and the infantry was the place to study them.

Strict military discipline reminded student junkers that they were soldiers instead of the military gymnasia's carefree cadets. They prac-ticed drills and field exercises to bugle calls; they studied religion, me-chanics, mathematics, chemistry, tactics, and foreign languages. They were forbidden to marry until graduation. Of course, St. Petersburg junkers frequented the theater on weekends and courted girls; the plea-sure-loving capital made sure of that. Many went into debt to keep their boots shined and uniforms spruce, and to pay for the champagne and *zakuski* needed to entertain their fellows and a courtesan or two.[18] Once they graduated, junkers were sent as officer candidates to regiments that needed them. But Ivanov didn't go into active service when he gradu-ated; he was posted instead, in the spring of 1903, back to Petersburg, to the reserve infantry, probably at his own request. His private life, as cap-tured in the wedding photo, required his urgent attention.

Ivanov's wife-to-be, smiling at the camera, was Alexandra Ivanovna Bal-ashova (or something like that—the handwriting on the relevant docu-ment is blurred). She was three years older than he; she'd possibly grown up in Kronstadt, which would mean in a military family.[19] The two might have met on Ivanov's first posting. One wonders what was in their minds as they prepared for the future. Had Ivanov already sowed his junker oats? Regimental wives and daughters were sacred, but all other women in this predominantly male city of soldiers and workers—working girls, students, servants, prostitutes, courtesans, ballet dancers—were fair game. Ivanov, though, had not followed the code: his wife was pregnant when this picture was taken. Their daughter Lidia was born on October 4, 1903, a few months after his junker school graduation. He might have rushed into marriage so the baby would get his name, or simply waited for the diploma and married late. Whatever the timing, husband, wife, and baby became a family, and for Ivanov a family, if he was in fact an orphan, would be essential.

In March 1904, when Lidochka was six months old, Ivanov was transferred to the 96th Omsk Infantry Division, quartered in the ancient

Alexander and Alexandra Ivanov.
Courtesy Saint-Petersburg State Museum of Theater and Music.

city of Pskov. He left his family in Petersburg, finding them an apartment in the Vasilievsky Ostrov district, on busy Srednii Prospekt, which "brushed close to slumminess" but had a neighborly esprit de corps.[20] A friend later compared Lidochka's first home to the quaint dwelling of Parasha, the humble heroine of Pushkin's 1833 Petersburg narrative, *The Bronze Horseman.* In this out-of-the-way place Lidochka grew from baby to girl. She had her mother's dark hair and eyes and a charm all her own, or so it seemed to her doting father. A little information has come from one of two surviving cousins, granddaughters of Lidiia's mother's sister. The younger, who lives in Munich, says the family mourned Lidia for years. The older cousin, in Leningrad, declines to revisit any part of the past. She was traumatized as a child in the Leningrad blockade of World War II, when Lidia's mother, her great-aunt, died of starvation in their shared apartment.

But a profusion of childhood images and later comments by class-mates[21] suggest that Ivanov began to worship his daughter already when she was little, even if he was away fighting the Russo-Japanese War in her toddler years. A studio photo of the two-year-old might have been taken to send to him in faraway Manchuria. She stands on a wooden platform in a white starched dress and little white boots, dark hair cut in short bangs, head inquisitively tilted, clutching a rustic twig fence. A young mother would have taken a small child to the nearby Neva River bank to see the big ships. There was more bustle here than in the Bal-anchivadzes' chic neighborhood to the east, because of the port, thronged with foreign ships, brothels, taverns, rooming houses, and roaming sailors. When Ivanov did come back as a sublieutenant in his old Pskov-based regiment, he turned an obsessive eye on his family stashed in the capital.[22] He visited often; Pskov was just a few hours away. A snapshot shows five-year-old Lidochka playing outdoors in winter coat and hat as uniformed dad stands nearby. Wife and daughter visited him too in the old city of churches. Both were photographed there ("Elizarov's Artistic Photographs, Pskov"), Alexandra Ivanova solo in a fur coat with puffed sleeves and matching fez and muff. Lidochka posed solo too, a little mournfully, in front of a painted lake, in her Pskov tourist regalia, a small peasant costume with a big cross and brass shield around her neck, her little polished black city shoes looking incongruous in the setting.

But Ivanov wasn't content with mere photos of Lidochka. He com-missioned a large oil portrait from a society painter named Steinberg, not the kind of artist who usually worked for a mid-rank officer.[23] Ivanov must have begun already to cultivate his contacts in the art world. Lida, still about five, looks out of the painting with shining black eyes and a mischievous smile, black bangs peeping out from a red hat. This better-than-average portrait may have marked another stage in Alexander Iva-nov's shift from army worship to arts reverence. Maybe he'd been wounded in the Russo-Japanese war or embittered by the carnage.[24] Maybe the shift was prompted by a growing personal ambition. What-ever its source, his young daughter was part of it.

One day, on a father-daughter walk, the little girl noticed a poster showing the wildly popular Czech violinist Jan Kubelik, and asked her father if he could "make it so I could be like that!'"[25] Ivanov was overjoyed at this sign of his daughter's future métier. He took Lidochka for violin lessons. He bought her an expensive instrument. With an engineer's zeal and a father's shamelessness, he knocked on famous violinists' doors, studied the history of the violin, read up on the violins of the past, each with its own name (the one he'd bought Lida was called "Psyche"). He found out how violin varnishes changed the instrument's color and tone. He took his daughter to music concerts around the city, and in summer resorts too. When he and Lidochka heard an organist play in the Lutheran art nouveau church of Terijoki (on the way to Lounatjoki), he left her there briefly to learn "ennobling music." He bought her musical scores and noticed her preferences: she liked Grieg's Sonata in E minor, Sibelius's *Swan of Tuonela*, and all of Tchaikovsky.

The source for this information is not a family document or a work of history, but a 1931 novel, *Bambochada*, by poet-turned-novelist Konstantin Vaginov.[26] Vaginov was one of those clear-eyed, tragic Leningrad *intelligents* of the 1920s who tried to describe the death of the city's old cosmopolitan life as a stark new one came into view.[27] In this novel, his third, he "collected" a group of characters who were themselves collectors—of jazz tunes, rococo candy wrappers, obsolete recipes, and morbid tales of early deaths. The death-tale collector is an old tsarist army officer, Vasily Vasilievich Yermilov, whose name parallels Ivanov's and whose daughter in the book is a famous young ballerina who has died, called Varenka. Readers of the time would have recognized Lidochka instantly. It was known among her friends that in real life, Lidochka had made up an imaginary twin for herself and called her Varochka (another nickname for Varvara, or Barbara), and that she'd told fanciful tales about this doppelganger. Vaginov himself probably learned something of Lidia's life from the real Alexander Ivanov. The two men had a friend in common, Mikhail Kuzmin, one of the great poet-dandies of Petersburg's Silver Age, also a balletomane, who in the 1920s entertained a select group of former *intelligents*, Vaginov and Ivanov among them.[28] Vaginov knew intimate details about Ivanov and his family—not just Lidochka's storytelling habits, but also the shape of Ivanov's army career, the location of his regiment, the color of Lidochka's Norwegian child costume. He must have seen the real Lidochka's room that her father preserved unchanged, or at least a photograph: he's given that room to Varenka. In the novel, the ballerina's father retreats there often to sit alone.

The novel suggests that the father's cult of his daughter began even earlier than her birth, when she was still in the womb.[29] "I wanted to insure that Varenka would grow up in different surroundings," says Yermilov as he starts on the tale of her death, "that there wouldn't be that ubiquitous black divan with oilcloth nailed over it, that mirror with flies sitting on it, those awful glances from provincial officers. I spoke with my wife; I left the regiment; I had myself sent to Petersburg. I ordered furniture from Finland, cheap but anyway stylish; ordered a child's costume from Norway—so that everything would be simple, and full of light."[30] When Varenka is a little older, it's her father who decides she will become a violin prodigy, though in the end Varenka turns out to have no talent for the violin.

Did the real Lidochka fail at the violin? If so, such a setback might have sent father and daughter to the Theater School as an alternate path to fame. In the novel, Vaginov doesn't tell his readers how his Varenka progressed from the violin to ballet. He doesn't even connect Varenka's violin studies with the real Lidochka's best trait as a dancer, her musicality. If the novel is right, Lidochka had had music poured into her as a little girl. But Vaginov isn't interested in what that might mean to her dancing. He never describes her dancing. He doesn't even seem to like this father and daughter, who inhabit only a corner of his main plot about a young postrevolutionary adventurer. His Yermilov is a compulsive talker; his Varenka is obsessive about her body. The fictional Varenka seems almost to embody the female vices of the NEP (New Economic Policy), that period of limited capitalism decreed by Lenin in the early 1920s, whose bourgeois excesses were hated by "real" Bolsheviks. The father-daughter duo also harks back to older literary antecedents dear to the city, especially the work of the late eighteenth-century German author, E. T. A. Hoffmann. In the Silver Age and up through the Revolution, Hoffmann's tales with their air of magical doom were a cult item in Petersburg literary circles. It's as if Vaginov gave his unsavory father and daughter some of the incestuous traits of Hoffman's best-known literary pair, Dr. Coppelius the mad inventor and Coppelia, the doll he creates and falls in love with. Vaginov even "plants" a volume of Hoffman's tales on Varenka's bookshelf.[31]

Even if Vaginov wasn't interested in Lidochka's ballet career, the novel is proof that people in Lidochka's time had already connected her story with haunted Petersburg myths. And Vaginov goes a step further when he dwells on the father's possessiveness, as if he's implying that the young ballerina's death was linked to her unbalanced father. Could it be that the real Lidochka's father bore some responsibility here? His obsessive attention might have inspired an offstage recklessness in his daughter, even as it bolstered her onstage daring. Who can know such things? It's clear, though, that the real Ivanovs present a more complicated picture than the fictional Yermilovs. They weren't just a father-daughter duo: the mother, Alexandra Ivanova, was present if marginal in her daughter's childhood. She was certainly there on Lidochka's first day at the Theater School, when Mikhailov saw the family.[32] Was Lidochka self-obsessed like Vaginov's Varenka? Senior ballerina Elizaveta Gerdt thought she was, and also not respectful enough, but older ballerinas are not the best judges of younger. To her friends, Lidochka was a real artist, tormented perhaps, but warm, impulsive, and fascinating. Most people loved and even adored her, onstage and off, and were drawn to her vivid emotions, her mania for work, her big smile and loud laugh, even if some also saw melancholy and anxiety beneath the ebullience.[33] Lidochka was a much bigger personality than Varenka.

Questions remain, though, about Ivanov's role in his daughter's life. Even after Lidochka was grown, he went around with her, taking her to ballet classes, watching obsessively when she appeared onstage, chatting up the critics during intermission. Many contemporaries commented on his presence. No one mentioned her mother. Was Ivanov the Hoffmannesque figure Vaginov implied, who thought he'd created Lidochka himself? Was his attention to her obsessive? Was she struggling near the end of her life to escape his influence?

Answers can only be suggested. It's clear, though, that Lidochka was already a personage when she entered the ballet school, already strong-willed and self-contained. And if the Ivanov family in Mikhailov's description seems closed in on itself, it had good reason to be. In late August 1914, when Lidochka started ballet school, World War I had already begun. Russians were marching west to meet the Germans and Austrians. Ivanov's regiment had been called up. He would leave for the Ukrainian front in less than a week.[34]

Perhaps Alexander Ivanov put his daughter in the ballet school for safety, to ensure her the tsar's protection while he was away at war. Both father and daughter were entering—or in Ivanov's case, reentering—an extreme service to the monarchy, the father in the imperial army, the daughter in the Imperial Theater School. On August 26, Ivanov wrote the usual form letter to the school's inspector to request his daughter's enrollment. He signed it with his name and his new rank, lieutenant, 8th Automobile Regiment. But he added some things that other parents didn't put in such form letters. He wrote Lidochka's birth date (October 3, 1903) at the top, perhaps to underscore her suitability for admittance. Below that he added, from no other motive, it seems, than excessive affection, her exact age: "10 years, 10 months, 21 days."[35]

FIVE

Theater School: Girls

Lidochka, school age.

Courtesy Saint-Petersburg State Museum of Theater and Music.

Ten-year-old Lidochka passed into the sealed domain of the Imperial Theater School, like Georges before her. She exchanged her own clothes for the cornflower-blue uniform dress and the white or black apron, the regulation underwear kept in a washroom locker, the puff-sleeved gray dancing frock and antiquated "Penguin" overcoat. She joined forty-eight other girl boarders, ages nine to seventeen, sixteen more than the boys upstairs. Fifteen additional first-years came daily for dance and school lessons. Lidochka, with her father away at war, probably boarded from the start. How did she react to her new environment? A photo shows the ten-year-old in her own striped blouse, elbows crossed over the back of a chair, hair pulled back in the single braid required for Theater School girls under fifteen, looking out with a composure that's striking for her age. Perhaps she and her father had switched to ballet earlier. Maybe Ivanov studied up on ballet as he had the violin, and put her in a private dance school even before her Theater School audition. This would explain her rapid progress in her first two years.

The girls' quarters on the school's first floor, raised above street level, were a replica of the boys' above and the drama school's above that: a long tunnel of spacious rooms, separated into living quarters on the left side (as one faced the façade), including kitchen, dining room, dancing rooms, and dormitory. Schoolrooms were on the right. Three stone stairways led to the upper floors: the "kitchen stairs" at the far left, the "formal" stairs in the middle, the "theater" or "church stairs" on the far right.[1] The girls had their own versions of school routine: early morning wash around the big copper basin, regimented walks, morning ballet classes, meals at long tables, afternoon academics with the boys but on separate sides of the classroom, evening dance classes, nights in the high-ceilinged dormitory that looked to Karsavina like "a vast hospital ward."[2] But the girls' routines were subtly different from the boys'. The older girls were supposed to play a maternal role in the younger ones' upbringing, which implies a mentoring absent among the boys. Senior girls were assigned younger protégées for extra dance classes after supper. The younger changed again into dancing frocks; the older girls kept on day dresses and watched. Some worked conscientiously with their pupils; others simply asked them to hold a leg in the air or repeat *tendus* fifty times while they talked to their friends. Older girls were also expected to befriend young ones at night in the dormitory, to sit on their beds and tuck them in.

For Lidochka, this regulated life meant just as abrupt a change as for Georges. She hadn't been to school either. But she'd chosen to come here, and so expected, maybe even welcomed, the newness. In return for leaving a small, obsessive family, she got a female society of friends, rivals, and role models. Her air of quiet certainty impressed the others, even older ones who guarded their hard-earned places in this miniature society. Among the luminaries when Lidochka arrived were Ekaterina Geidenreich, eighteen; Valentina Ivanova, seventeen; Lidia Tiuntina, fifteen; and the mischievous twelve-year-old Alexandra (Choura) Danilova.[3] Danilova would soon become Lidochka's main rival and friend. Even though two years older, she was small for her age, with honey-blonde curls and mock-innocent blue eyes. She was a survivor, a quick study, a charmer if she chose, outspoken about injustice, and endearingly matter-of-fact.[4]

Choura Danilova would soon become important to Georges too. And since she's also more typical of Theater School girls than Lidochka, her story is worth telling. Alexandra Dionisievna Danilova was born November 7, 1902, in Peterhof, outside St. Petersburg, to parents who supposedly died while she was a baby. She said she knew nothing about them, but rumor has it that her mother was a peasant and her father a young unmarried army officer. When her mother and grandmother died abruptly, the officer's father, goes the rumor, took the infant to raise.[5] That grandfather-guardian might have been Dmitry Dimitrievich Gotovstov, State Councillor (5th rank), whose high-society wife, Lidia (born Nestroeva), had just lost a child of her own. But six years later, Nestroeva divorced Gotovstov and married a much older army general, Mikhail Ivanovich Batianov. Guardianship of the now eight-year-old Choura was handed over to Batianov.[6] The seventy-five-year-old general, though, didn't want a new child; he had eight by earlier wives, some of whom lived with him in his grand apartment at 28 Moika River

Embankment. He set about getting Choura into the institution that traditionally took in semi-high-born but unwanted children, the Imperial Theater School.[7]

Despite the application deadline having passed and the child being underage, Batianov's *protektsia* (patronage) got Choura as far as the school's audition. She herself was smart and quick enough to pass it. Unlike Georges and Lidochka, she'd already studied for a year at a girls' day school, something the Theater School favored, and danced a butterfly in that school's pageant. Like Georges, Choura wasn't told she was boarding when the Batianovs left her at the school in August 1911. She misbehaved so much in her first year that she didn't make the year-end cut. But Lidia Batianova begged the school directors in a May 29, 1912, letter to take the child back, and again *protektsia* won out, though Choura had to repeat the first year. Then Lidia Batianova herself died suddenly of meningitis, and Choura, grasping her shaky position in the general's family, started to work enough to stay at the school and fit in.[8] "I weep and weep when the door shut out my home," Danilova later said about her first dormitory night, "but afterwards I adore the school."[9]

It seems curious that young girls wrenched from whatever homes they'd known would thrive in the Theater School, especially when their caretakers were far from nurturing. Memoirists portray the school's inspectress and her lieutenants, the five or six *dames de classe*, as Russian variations on Dickens characters. By 1914, Inspectress Varvara Ivanovna Likhosherstova had been at the Theater School twenty years, and, according to Karsavina, had been the girls' enemy since the beginning.[10] She was a graduate of the prestigious Smolny Institute, founded by Catherine the Great in 1764 for girls of noble birth: she was gentry, fallen on hard times.[11] Mikhailov later recalled Likhosherstova as almost beautiful, with a cloud of white hair and severe black clothes. But he didn't know her at close range. To the girls, she was a malevolent giantess who looked like the statue of Catherine the Great they walked past every day. Despite her imposing size, Likhosherstova would glide around the school sneakily and soundlessly, dropping into the academic classes, staring down the pupils through her lorgnette, demanding perfect curtsies in the hall, criticizing hairdos with escaped strands—and more. "She stuck her nose into all the corners of our lives," wrote 1919 graduate Natalia Lisovskaya, "sitting in on our breakfasts, lunches, and dinners, our walks, our doctors' examinations in the infirmary, our dance lessons and rehearsals, our church services. Even at night she would walk the rows of beds, peering into the faces of sleepers and removing the beds' striped covers, which we liked to throw over our thin blankets because it was cold in the dormitory."[12]

Theater School: Girls

The *dames de classe* who served under Varvara Ivanovna, known in student jargon as *"klassiukhi,"* came from the same lesser nobility, though fallen probably on even harder times. Some had Germanic names—Baltic Germans were prominent in Russian court service.[13] One spoke fluent French but little Russian. Another had a habit of prefacing anything she said with "And please, and please . . ." Another wore her hair puffed up in front on an old-fashioned "roller," had shifty eyes, and liked to confiscate girls' diaries. "But they all held the students at arm's length," said Lisovskaya, "never spoke with us on family terms, never gave us questions about literature or art. They looked after our health, cleanliness, manners, etc., but were never tender with us. They seemed to feel some kind of iron directive, which they didn't dare contradict."[14] Like the school priest boasting about his exalted station in life, the *klassiukhi* by their very manners represented the social hierarchy outside the school on which most of the pupils would have occupied lower rungs. *Klassiukhi* weren't involved in the girls' dance training. Nor were they academic teachers, except for one French *klassiukha*; it was the boys' caretakers who doubled as schoolmasters. The *klassiukhi* were chaperones pure and simple, reminding the girls by their own "superior" behavior that they were charity cases, here to learn manners.

The assumption seemed to be that girls needed more vigilance than boys, to reverse the degradation of their impoverished or questionable origins. The boys were taken into the school as if into the military, into a regiment that served on the stage rather than at the front. They were rowdy and had their own games, almost like regular boys. "We played Robin Hood," Balanchine remembered. "And war! We invented a special game, without sabers. We weren't allowed to play with swords and other sharp objects. We could hurt ourselves. And if you were hurt, you couldn't perform."[15] It was more complicated for girls. Their future profession, theatrical service to a theater-loving monarchy, included possible intimacy with some of their patrons. If the theater could be thought of as part of a charged symbolic-religious "field" surrounding the monarchy, the Imperial Theater's female dancers were almost like Asian temple dancers. "Vowed to the theater," wrote Karsavina," we were kept from contact with the world as from a contamination."[16]

The nature of this arrangement is hard to pin down in written sources. It was certainly connected with the patronage that had long characterized tsarist society. A person got somewhere because of the favor-exchanging or sponsoring called *protektsia* that went on routinely—or else through a wild stroke of luck. If both *protektsia* and luck were lacking, one got nowhere.[17] Members of the many-branched Romanov family were the best source of *protektsia*. Female ballet students, having landed in the Theater School through *protektsia*, were being readied to receive it again as adults—and they were its ideal objects, at least of the intimate kind offered by high-placed men. They were young, alone, kept supposedly innocent by their schooling, made graceful by their dance training. The Romanov tribe included an unusual number of tall, rich males, who sat in Mariinsky boxes above the tsar's, connected by a special passage with backstage. As the imperial capital became Russia's industrial center in the early twentieth century, lesser nobles and even businessmen embraced Romanov customs. Many female Mariinsky dancers had discreet "protectors" who furthered their careers within the theater and supplemented their meager salaries.

But already by 1890, the discretion of such arrangements had been partially compromised: a Theater School graduate, Matilda Feliksovna Kshesinskaya, small, curvaceous, with black eyes and fatal charm, became the semi-official mistress to the Tsarevich Nikolai, oldest son of Alexander III, an arrangement condoned and perhaps initiated by the father. When Nikolai abandoned Kshesinskaya in 1894 on his father's sudden death to marry Princess Alix of Hesse-Darmstadt and become tsar himself, the young dancer was consoled by several of his grand duke cousins, one of whom fathered her only child, the frail and coddled Vladimir, Vova. Until the revolution, Kshesinskaya wielded astonishing power both inside and out of the Mariinsky.[18] She had a famous salon of her own, a place of barely respectable demimondaine goings on. She was a gifted entertainer. She was also a gifted and mesmerizing ballerina. But one gets a sense from later Theater School memoirs that Kshesinskaya's social triumphs may have tightened school life, or else Likhosherstova and her cohorts were hardening with age. As Kshesinskaya's star rose in the early 1910s, increased vigilance kept the school's female students supposedly even more unsullied and sheltered from the world.

And yet the results were the opposite from the intended. The more Likhosherstova and her minions bore down on students, the more the spirit of mischief and camaraderie bubbled up in them. Over the years, the girls devised rituals of defiance to counter the school's propriety, handed down through student "generations": illegal food trading (such as mashed potatoes exchanged for meat patties, as per weekly menus); forbidden hair curling; illegal putting on of "plays" in the "Ricci" living room (supposedly named for a music master suicide); illegal hide-and-seek; illegal reading of novels during academics, or asking for autographs from grown-up dancers, or writing in journals. An underground life ran merrily underneath the school's official surface, invented and reinvented among the girls themselves and devoted to besting the authorities. Girls covered for and shielded each other: Lisovskaya wrote her classmates' math homework along with her own. If a certain *klassiukha* seized someone's diary, others little and big surrounded and distracted her, so its owner could snatch it back.

The real-life class system outside the school sometimes impinged on this underground solidarity. When parents and relatives came on visiting days, Thursdays, from 5 to 7, they brought chocolates and other treats.[19] The more expensive the candy, the better its recipients were treated by the *klassiukhi*. There was also a hierarchy of age, which made it possible for some older girls to lord it over younger ones. But the camaraderie was real, to the extent that young orphans like Choura Danilova were cared for not by the adults in charge but by the alternate society of girls, which seemed able to satisfy most psychic needs. The littlest were buoyed by maternal attentions from the oldest, and by the shared defiance. Karsavina, who often veered into naughtiness with her best friend Lidia Kyaksht, later summed up the unlooked-for effect of this manners dichotomy on individuals. "As I look back now upon my school years," she wrote, "I see that . . . the rarified air of discipline was a proper school for temperament." Then she added the key phrase— "inasmuch as it concentrated its growth on one single purpose."[20]

That "single purpose" was learning ballet in the manner of the Mariinsky Theater. As pupils progressed, dance values came to count for even more than manners or anti-manners. In the end, dance trumped all. The school's administration, for all its prissiness, was attentive to signs of dance talent emerging among the pupils. It promoted the talented ones early to higher classes and put them on display in the graduation concerts. In the girls' case, the uniform-happy tsarist system devised a crude symbolic way of making its approval visible: it awarded a pink dancing frock to the few, usually senior, girls who showed the most promise. Pink frocks stood out in dance classes among the light gray ones. An even higher award was the white frock, given only to future prima ballerinas. Anna Pavlova, destined for world fame, received a white dress in her 1899 graduating year at the school. Karsavina got one in her second-to-last year, 1901. Olga Spessivtseva got the white dress in 1912, as did her classmate Maria Scherer.

Neither Lidochka nor Choura had the chance to earn a white dress before the tsarist monarchy disappeared. But both received the pink one strikingly early in their school careers, when they were twelve and fourteen respectively, still in the Middle Division. The times, though, were not normal. World War I, though waged far from the muffled halls of the school, added an air of urgency to normal school practices. And both girls were undeniably talented. But what's interesting about them as a pair is their different training "generations." Choura had one set of teachers, Lidochka another. The fact that Lidochka, after only two years of training, caught up with four-year veteran Choura points to the effectiveness of her teacher, who came to the Theater School in the same fall of 1914 as she.

Before then, the Junior Division of youngest girls was taught by Varvara Trofimovna Rykhliakova, an ex-Mariinsky soloist known for clear and sparkling technique. Rykhliakova had long, curly hair and a winsome, delicate air. She'd started her performing career in 1890 in a blaze of glory. But she was Kshesinskaya's classmate, and so was destined to remain in the shadows. Each time Rykhliakova rose up the hierarchy with pay raises and acclaim, she was pulled down again, removed again and again from ballerina roles by Kshesinskaya's decree. Even when away on tour, Kshesinskaya sent repertory and casting instructions to Imperial Theaters Director Vladimir Teliakovsky, who, though increasingly irritated, was powerless to countermand them. In 1906, heartbreak and frustration forced Rykhliakova to turn teacher to supplement her theater salary. Though "protected" by a prestigious married doctor, she was raising their son by herself. Rykhliakova, wrote Lisovskaya, was a "dry and strict" teacher, though she did "put our legs and bodies into places. In terms of the arms, however, in that time they almost didn't pay attention to the arms—well, except to make sure they didn't catch on our tutus. The elbows were held down, the wrists lay nonchalantly above."[21] But Rykhliakova's lifelong struggle for ballerina roles had left her in delicate health, and in November 1913 she took a two-month leave. A more prominent Mariinsky ballerina took over her classes. The next summer, that of 1914, Rykhliakova left the school altogether, and the same guest teacher returned in the fall to the Junior Division. And so Lidochka began her official course of training with the astonishing Olga Preobrazhenskaya.[22]

The year before, Preobrazhenskaya had retired definitively at forty-two from the Mariinsky stage after twenty-five years of dancing. Small, dark-haired, and highly intelligent, she was one of the most fascinating characters to come out of the tsarist ballet system. She was self-made, or as close as one could get in the Mariinsky system. She'd entered the school in 1880, a semi-orphan, mother dead and father neglectful, small, frail, with a crooked spine. But she'd had *protektsia* from a young but already imperious actress of the Imperial Alexandrinsky Theater, Maria

Preobrazhenskaya as Italian soldier, for her own dance number.
Courtesy Saint-Petersburg State Museum of Theater and Music.

Gavrilovna Savina (1854–1915), a friend of her maternal aunt, who was a music hall singer.[23] In young Preobrazhenskaya's schooling and afterwards, she'd had to fight not only physical weakness but Kshesinskaya, who graduated a year after her and was first friend, then bitter rival. And fight she did, but quietly. She bided her time. She didn't complain. She took on any role, no matter how small. She went abroad to study with renowned teachers.[24] She worked tirelessly at home with the transplanted Italian virtuoso Enrico Cecchetti to understand the mechanics of her technique. Even so, and even with the warm support of the Mariinsky's chief ballet master, Marius Petipa, she had to wait till she was thirty to become an official ballerina.

But Preobrazhenskaya's late rise meant that she'd had time to develop a particular aesthetic force field around herself, her own version of ballerina charm. It wasn't histrionic-virtuosic charm like Kshesinskaya's but its opposite. Preobrazhenskaya could do *Swan Lake*'s fast fouetté turns in place that Kshesinskaya was famous for, but she disdained such "tricks." In place of Kshesinskaya's evil Black Swan's thirty-two center-stage revolutions, Preobrazhenskaya performed instead a fast circle of *piqué* turns, which she thought truer to the drama.[25] Preobrazhenskaya's sequence didn't stop-time the action with incessant spinning, but enclosed the infatuated prince as if in a circle of deceit. Overall, Preobrazhenskaya's style featured clarity, harmony, and a seemingly effortless musicality. As a mature ballerina she was still very short, and her legs had "slightly pudgy calves," as critic Akim Volynsky wrote in "Golubok" (Little Dove), his October 18, 1912, *Birzhevye Vedomosti* (Stock Market News) article. And yet there shone in her "somewhat mocking eyes," he added, "a fervently intelligent gleam." And with the music she was transformed. "Something eternally radiating with joyful little lamps, flutters, and whirls across the stage," was Volynsky's description of the small ballerina in Petipa's *Les Millions d'Harlequin*. By precision and musicality, Preobrazhenskaya changed her stage from the usual whirlwind to a refuge of harmony and delight.[26]

In life, too, Preobrazhenskaya had developed the opposite character from the conniving Mathilda. Grand dukes fell in love with her, but she preferred to stay independent (even if one protector, a Count Z, lurked on the margins). She fell in love late in life with pianist-composer Alexander Labinsky, but continued to live alone in her own "smart" apartment, on Fontanka 68, in a building she owned. She eschewed airs and graces; she said what she thought; she was sympathetic to underdogs. She was the first ballerina to perform at a Narodny Dom (people's theater). For a command appearance at a gala honoring Kshesinskaya, she made a solo for herself as a *matelot* (sailor), a cabin-boy on a ship, dancing the hornpipe, swaggering, even "spitting" once over her shoulder in a pantomime gesture that brought down the house. She got along with everybody, from horse cab drivers to the tsar himself, whose private palace quarters she visited to play cards *en famille*, which further rankled

Kshesinskaya, since the palace was off-limits to a former mistress. Preobrazhenskaya had a quick, warm smile, not a gracious, hierarchical one. And having officially left the stage except for charity concerts, she was ready, in fall 1914, to pass on ballet's art and craft. In effect, she'd been devising her own teaching methodology for years. Colleagues knew this; even the great ballet master Petipa had sent her his younger children to train. In 1913, she'd opened a private ballet school in three rooms on Dmitrovsky Lane, where she taught afternoons and supervised an impressive range of guest teachers.[27] Admission was sought after for Petrograd's bourgeois daughters, but only the gifted were taken.

And now Preobrazhenskaya added the morning class of youngsters at the school that had trained her. One can imagine the gray-frocked ten- and eleven-year-olds on their first school day, holding the barres of the smallest girls' dance hall, faces turned toward the door.[28] In came their teacher, "graceful and fragile, in an elegant black ensemble that emphasized her slender figure, giving off a refined scent from her perfume (it was always Patchouli)," remembered Lidochka's classmate Nina Stukolkina.[29] She always wore black, another student remembered: black dress, stockings, and neat black street shoes that "had a bow on them, like ballet slippers." A third remembered her long necklace of Chinese wooden beads and her "strange, husky voice that seemed to break now and then."[30] The students were pleased that Olga Osipovna (Preobrazhenskaya's first name and patronymic, the usual form of respectful address in Russia) didn't look like a retired ballerina who'd gotten fat but was still trim and elegant. Her impromptu manner was the opposite of the *klassiukhis*'; yet she "personified Ballerina."[31]

Preobrazhenskaya began that first day as she would begin all future classes. The girls assumed the heel-to-heel first position at the barre and performed sixteen *battements tendus*—leg extensions along the floor, to the front, side, back and side, first standing upright, then again in a knees-bent *demi-plié*. Preobrazhenskaya believed that *tendus* were the crucial starting point for training their legs.[32] The next exercise, *grand pliés*, was meant for strengthening backs and aligning backs with legs, so the girls wouldn't throw off alignment by "sitting" on one leg. Four *grand pliés* were performed with torsos upright in each of the ballet's "positions:" first position, turned out with heels touching; second, feet apart; fourth, one foot in front of the other "like a little box"; fifth, feet slid in close together. After these nuts and bolts beginnings, Preobrazhenskaya led her pupils into ever more complicated and intricate exercises in the center of the room. The class was no light or entertaining affair, but a series of fiendishly hard tasks building from simple to complex. The girls worked willingly; their teacher came prepared, her combinations written down in a notebook.[33]

Preobrazhenskaya also worked throughout the class on the girls' arms. She would shake a girl's wrist at the barre to loosen her grip. She wanted "natural" arms, as in a spoken conversation. "The arms are the equivalent of words," she liked to say, and the hands should be "expressive, right out to the tips of the fingers."[34] But most of all she wanted her students to know what they were doing, to think as well as dance. Thinking was *her* specialty onstage. As students improved, she sometimes read an *enchaînement* of steps out loud instead of showing them: the girls translated the French terms into movement. At the end of the class, she had them improvise short études on the spot; she herself was known for such impromptu dances and improvised encores (though she formally choreographed many dances too). She placed them around the dance hall, each in a favorite pose, no two poses alike. The pianist played music Preobrazhenskaya had chosen, and students moved from their poses into a dance they made up as they went along, to which their teacher offered reactions and suggestions.

The little girls began to acquire the straight backs and proud heads of future dancers, and the articulate legs, pointed feet, and fierce physical and mental concentration they also needed for the stage. They began to balance on one leg, turn cleanly, fit their gestures to the music—and to experience something that's hard to put into words. As the bodies of those ten-year-olds found a new alternative "home" in the turned-out leg and hip position, a sensation of power resulted, almost of enlightenment. Ballet's retraining of muscles, if done wisely, seems to increase the charged interior space of a body, infusing the psyche with something like an urge to cover great distance, to show by means of ballet's ritual motions all the energy that's lodged inside. The effect of good ballet training then and now is that it bypasses thought—or *becomes* thought, not analytic thought but the kind that's bound up with emotion. Emotional energy flows into turned-out positions, and the child feels she can stretch farther, move bigger, matter more in the world. It's as though a young body is gradually opened up, not just to the flow of movement but to a more buoyant and effective being. Anything unresolved—frustration, anger, yearning—can be loosened and let go in a ballet combination, swept into the energy of motion and the exultation of self-mastery.[35]

Lidochka was the best student in the class; she would be the first to be nominated by Preobrazhenskaya two years later for the pink dress. But even if the Revolution precluded other pink dresses, other future star dancers still stood beside her at the barre. Three would go on to substantial careers in Soviet ballet: Nina Stukolkina, Olga Mungalova, and Nina Mlodzinskaya (though Mlodzinskaya's sharp tongue would get her exiled under Stalin to Belorussia). They would all graduate a year after Lidochka, not because they were younger but because revolutionary crises would soon derail orderly progress. Still, it was an exceptional group that began in that first wartime winter with Preobrazhenskaya, or maybe their teacher made them so. She knew them as individuals; she stuck up for them. For their first-year examinations in May 1915, she tailored a combination for each—and even interfered in results. Young Nina Stukolkina got so flustered in front of the Examining Commission of senior dancers at "the big table with the red table-cloth" that she messed up the order of steps. The Commission put her on the list to let go. Without a word, Preobrazhenskaya led the mortified little girl to the center of the floor and had her do advanced *entrechat six* jumps with beats, which changed the Commission's mind.[36]

And Lidochka? A pencil drawing shows her a little later, in a seated pose, wearing her puffed-sleeve dancing frock—it could be the pink one. Her hands lie beautifully crossed in her lap, her calm face is serious. She'd passed the year-end exams easily and would do that every year, progressing without a break up through the levels. This fact alone seems to suggest that she'd studied ballet earlier, maybe at Preobrazhenskaya's own school. As for the effect on *her* of Preobrazhenskaya's personality, we can only guess how a little girl with an overbearing father and a semi-effaced mother would respond to a woman like Preobrazhenskaya, whose authority came from herself, from her own experience and intelligence. The excitement of studying with Preobrazhenskaya would have reached into Lidochka's psyche and emboldened her, as it did with her classmates who've left memories. If Andrianov "made" Balanchine and his companions, Preobrazhenskaya "made" Lidochka and her peers—the last generation to be trained under the tsars, the first to emerge under the Soviets.

In an imaginary cross section of the school on a typical 1914–15 morning, one could have seen the boys and the girls in their identical studios on their different floors, practicing almost identical steps. Georges and Lidochka didn't yet know each other as fellow dancers, only as fellow students on opposite sides of academic classrooms. But their teachers knew them both. Balanchine later said that the only two adults in the school who encouraged him in his painful beginnings were his own teacher, Andrianov—and Preobrazhenskaya.[37]

Georges was now in his second year. His dance classes were again in the hands of the kind and handsome Andrianov. But even if he was still smallest, he was no longer lowliest. The previous year's older boys had passed to the Middle Division and now studied with young Mariinsky principal dancer Viktor Alexandrovich Semenov. Georges was a "senior" Junior, one of those who knew his way around a ballet class. Even so, he remained fiercely unhappy about having been put in what he still saw as the wrong school—until something happened. With his haughty looks, his attention to detail (learned perhaps at the piano), and the encouragement of his teacher, Georges began to receive coveted child roles on the Mariinsky stage. His smallness probably helped him here: rehearsal directors liked the littlest, especially if older and smarter. His first chance came in *The Sleeping Beauty*, a production thoroughly overhauled the season before. And with this stage debut, as Balanchine wrote later, "everything changed."[38]

The original 1890 *Sleeping Beauty* had been an affair of gaudy seventeenth-century colors, devised by the old courtier Ivan Vsevolozhsky, the Imperial Theaters director at the time. But after fourteen years, it was faded and frayed. The artist chosen to renew it was the fashionable Konstantin Korovin, from Sergei Diaghilev's circle, known already in theater circles for his red and gold treatment of Rimsky-Korsakov's old-Russian operas, *Sadko* and *The Golden Cockerel*. Korovin stylized *The Sleeping Beauty* too, replacing the seventeenth-century gaudiness with an eighteenth-century palette of opulent pastels. Some critics accused him of straying from the Louis XIV court setting and sacrificing the ballet's gossamer narrative to "all sorts of magnificence." But even with weighty new decor, the ballet was full of wonders. The mighty machinery of the Mariinsky pumped real water into onstage fountains and caused real fire to blaze up for magic effects. A profusion of Mariinsky dancers in rich pastels finery filled the stage, gesturing, bowing, parading as to the manner born.

One day in the winter season of 1914–15, Georges was called out of school with the other lucky children—leaving in mid-lesson was one of the joys of performing—and brought, in one of the six-seated, gold-trimmed coaches the students called "Noah's Arks," to the rococo sea-green Mariinsky Theater reposing in its vast Theater Square.[39] The children came afternoons to rehearse a ballet, returning the next evening to perform it. Georges was outfitted backstage in a pastel peasant suit and wig for the Garland Waltz in Princess Aurora's first-act garden party, then allowed to watch from the house with the other children as the princess was christened in the ballet's Prologue and the uninvited evil fairy Carabosse appeared at the party. A half-century later, Balanchine remembered with fresh excitement the "huge garden with cascading fountains" and "Carabosse's great coach . . . drawn by a dozen mice." After the Prologue, the children were brought backstage again, lined up in sixteen pairs, and sent out to join grown-up "peasants" waltzing with flower baskets. The Garland Waltz blended lilting rhythms and regimental intricacy. The miniature waltzers wove among the adults. After this, Georges was recostumed as a cupid for the ballet's final Act III, then sent out again to watch as Aurora pricked her finger on the fatal spindle and met the evil fairy, shrouded in a cloak. "There she was, a bent old lady, harmless," Balanchine remembered, "and the next moment her disguise had fallen through the floor and she was black and shiny, the wicked fairy. Fire came up all over the stage and everyone despaired." To the rescue came the Lilac Fairy onto a lilac-festooned stage (those fierce lilacs of the Russian spring), miming her countercharm—not death but sleep—waving her wand to summon trees and vines to cover the palace.[40]

What the ten-year-old had suddenly seen was the connection between his daily ballet class and the magnificent action on the ballet stage. He'd already made such a connection with music. He'd stopped hating the piano at seven when he'd realized that practicing could bring a Beethoven sonata to life. "And now I was learning the same thing about dancing: it took work, but when you saw what the work could produce, you wanted to work very badly."[41] Here was the deciding moment in his student life, when this revelation absorbed the confusions of Mother abandoning him to the ballet school, Father disappearing, the misspent family money, the loneliness of a family life he didn't belong in anymore. It was as if he'd been pushed through the thin waist of an hourglass where he'd been stuck, but now he'd swum out into the other hourglass globe. Music coursed freely through both globes—it was the constant in his life. But the *theater's* music now became his emotional food. No wonder Balanchine later constantly invoked Tchaikovsky, whose orchestrations tend to penetrate to the bones of lonely listeners. Dance wrapped in music was Georges's new religion, though he would be tested many times before it became his ultimate faith.

Georges wasn't alone in connecting lowly ballet exercises to glorious spectacle; an avid ballet culture was a feature of this hierarchical city. Ballet was a focal point, fusing the city's sensual love of beauty with its fetishization of social prestige. Most ballet-goers didn't focus on the dancers' training; they just enjoyed the effect of dance, music, and décor converging. But the city's numerous balletomanes, whether highborn or low, made a point of informing themselves about technicalities. In the Mariinsky's top gallery sat junkers, cadets, and petty civil servants who voiced their enthusiasm for this or that ballerina. In the first rows sat the more substantial balletomanes, often the ballerinas' protectors—*chinovniks*, officers, *commerçants*, men of letters. The solidity of their social niche helps explain why a former Horse Guards colonel, Vladimir Teliakovsky, would serve from 1901 to 1917 as the ballet-oriented director of the Imperial Theaters. Or why a distinguished army general, Nikolai Mikhailovich Bezobrazov, would be invited along to Paris and London with Diaghilev's Ballets Russes as an official éminence grise.

In the decade or so before Georges and Lidochka came on the scene, dancing had grown even more vital to the city's culture. Russian-born virtuosos, especially ballerinas, had begun to emerge around the time of *The Sleeping Beauty's* premiere, 1890. Earlier, practically the whole imperial lyric theater system had been stalled in Italomania. Italian stars were imported for ballet as well as opera. *Sleeping Beauty's* first Princess Aurora was the compact, and technically crystalline prima ballerina from Milan's La Scala, Carlotta Brianza. But even as Brianza's Aurora dazzled her court, went to sleep, and woke resplendent, ambitious young Russian dancers like Kshesinskaya, Preobrazhenskaya, and future superstar Anna Pavlova were waking up too, mastering the Italians' secrets and co-opting their roles. Another virtuosic Italian, Pierina Legnani, was Petipa's favorite muse up to his final years, but Kshesinskaya fought her way into prima roles too, and legitimately. She was the first Russian to master Legnani's famous thirty-two Italian-flavored fouetté rotations at the heart of *Swan Lake* (the ones Preobrazhenskaya later resisted).[42] Others followed suit.

The rise of Russian dancers signaled the maturing of the imperial capital's ballet culture, just as *The Sleeping Beauty* itself marked not a beginning but a culmination of the career of the diminutive, shrewd, neatly bearded, French-born ballet master Marius Petipa. He'd come to Russian as a dancer in 1847 and had been choreographing since the 1860s; this ballet was his fifty-fourth work. This, and his other works too, were majestic yet intricate ballet machines: panoramic, yet tightly constructed on the inside, with large-scale steps for the ballerina and her cavalier, smaller articulations for the soloists, and imperial-scaled architecture-in-motion for the corps de ballet. Petipa's settings came from the fanciful French *romantisme* he'd brought with him from Paris—India, Egypt, Spain, medieval Europe. But the ballet's content, perfected in *The Sleeping Beauty*, blended precision and high lyricism in a way that resembled the city's own magical mix of these antithetical qualities.

Historians have fixed *The Sleeping Beauty* as the start of the cultural flowering known as the Silver Age, that multi-genre embrace of *Jugendstil* and art nouveau ideas that would prove especially triumphant in Russia. The Silver Age was permeated by its artists' sense that their world was in its final bloom. A circle of highborn arts connoisseurs, artists, and dandies collected in the late 1890s around the young and boisterous Sergei Diaghilev, with his cousin Dmitri Filosofov and their friend Alexander Benois, calling itself Mir Iskusstva (World of Art). Two members had shared a youthful passion for *The Sleeping Beauty*. The circle's gorgeous magazine, begun in 1899 and also named *Mir Iskusstva*, emphasized at first the decorative arts in a European context, then turned to dance as the best local example of the wildly popular Wagnerian concept of *Gesamtkunstwerk*. Dance had become the art of the hour for other Silver Agers too: poets, novelists, philosophers, and painters like Blok, Bely, Akhmatova, Mandelstam, and Prince Serge Wolkonsky. To them, dance was the supreme art, in whose wordless flow a fearful and divided culture could be made whole, or else find oblivion. Some of Alexander Blok's most famous lines—like "The night, the street, the lamp, the drugstore"—came from a group of poems called "Dances of Death." At the heart of this cultural matrix was the embrace by educated Russia of Friedrich Nietzsche, and the Nietzschean Creator's ultimate advice: to learn to dance.

In 1904–5, as Georges and Lidochka turned one year old, another event had catapulted dance to the forefront of the zeitgeist. The young American solo dancer Isadora Duncan gave a series of performances in St. Petersburg which struck dancers and choreographers of the Imperial Ballet like a thunderbolt. Duncan practiced "free dance" in bare feet, wearing the puckered silk tunics of Grecian nymphs in Renaissance paintings, slit up the sides for freer motion. She fit her steps to the emotional dynamics of music not originally meant for dance—by Chopin, Schumann, Beethoven, Wagner. Her interpretations proved revelatory, not just to dancers but also to the rich, already experimental world of Russian avant-garde theater, and even to ordinary progressive Petersburgers who believed the arts could unite the tragically separate parts of the social body. Isadora's mock-ancient dancing got mixed up with the political currents of the time, especially the first revolutionary outburst in 1905. Still almost a girl, she seemed to embody the very spirit of revolution.

Duncan's free dance, reclothed in Silver Age ideals, even wedged itself into the sacred confines of the imperial ballet. In 1905, the dancers struck for more artistic freedom and also, ironically, for the return of the aging Petipa, who'd been fired by new Imperial Theaters director

Teliakovsky. The leader of their strike committee, dance star Mikhail Fokine, began to subject ballet to his Duncan-inspired vision of a contemporary art. He composed one-act tone poems rather than multi-act tales, in which he turned Petipa's geometry into art nouveau swirls and Petipa's mannerly court pageants into erotic dramas or stylized pictorial sketches—*Daphnis et Chloé, Chopiniana, Cléopatra*. But Fokine's greatest accomplishment was bringing the normally self-enclosed ballet out into the realm of Russian drama, which had itself begun a period of brilliant experimentation with the founding in 1898 of Stanislavsky's Moscow Art Theater. Fokine threw open the windows in ballet's stuffy world of court intrigues and pirouettes and let in the spirit of a new century. The *World of Art* circle, especially Diaghilev, with his lightning-quick sensitivity to aesthetic breakthroughs, grasped the new cultural meaning of dance and the new forces at work within it. In 1909, Diaghilev borrowed some of the Mariinsky's first Russian virtuosos (Kshesinskaya, Pavlova, Gerdt), and some of their juniors (Tamara Karsavina, Vaslav Nijinsky, Bronislava Nijinska, Ludmilla Schollar), put them into Fokine's colorful ballets, dressed them in Leon Bakst's hallucinogenic *Orientale* costumes, and unleashed them on Paris and London. *Cléopatre, Shéhérazade, The Firebird, Petrushka* sent multiple shock waves through these cities' Edwardian air, since in every new Ballets Russes season Diaghilev found new ways to harness ballet's expressive power to the latest avant-garde sensation.

Left at home in that first decade of the Diaghilev European triumphs (1909–17) was the still-mighty Mariinsky imperial ballet, now mostly drained of the excitement of the new. This was the ballet of Georges's and Lidochka's childhoods, which Soviet historians have called undistinguished and dull. It's true that the ultraconservative rehearsal master Nikolai Sergeev had risen to chief ballet master and that hardly any new works appeared, only some by Fokine, who'd returned home in 1912 after quarreling with Diaghilev, then left and returned again in late 1914. Fokine's new ballets, though (*Islamey, Francesca da Rimini, Stenka Razin, Eros*), seemed merely to echo his earlier. But it was wartime. The constrained imperial purse put limits on innovation. Karsavina had come home too, to add her magical performing to what she called the "sorrowful years"—years in which the Russian army met defeat after defeat, and wild patriotism alternated with outrage and gloom. But even if Fokine's new efforts were weak, a vast array of ballets survived through the war, his own older tone poems and Petipa's lavish, intricate spectacles as well.[43] "The stage," Karsavina explained, "was fulfilling its mission in the war by protecting the eternal treasures, the high cult of beauty

sheltered all through the world." Skilled artists danced on it: "old" soloists like Kshesinskaya and Karsavina herself, and just emerging ones
like Piotr Vladimirov, Elena Smirnova, Elena Lukom, Boris Romanov,
Viktor Ponomariov, Viktor Semenov, Elizaveta Gerdt . . .

Can an art be called lackluster and dying if audiences poured into the
theater and first-rate artists performed for them? The start of the war
even boosted attendance. The French, English, and even Belgian national anthems were played at the start of every performance, along
with the Russian. Then the curtain rose on fragrant India, mysterious
Egypt, the timeless peasant hamlet of *Giselle*, the medieval court of *Swan
Lake*, the turreted castle of *The Sleeping Beauty*—even the Spanish village of Fokine's *Jota Aragonesa*, his penultimate 1916 work for the Mariinsky, based on a study of Spanish dance he'd made while stuck in Spain at
the start of the war. The Theater School children in Spanish peasant
clothes, including Georges and Lidochka, joined the grownup Russian
Aragonese onstage. "It would be vain to ask them [the Russians] to go
without their theatres, music and ballets," wrote French ambassador
Maurice Paléologue in his diary after a 1914 evening at the ballet. "One
might as well ask the Spanish to give up their bull fights." And it wasn't
only the "upper and propertied classes" who flocked to their local art,
Paleologue noted. "The cheaper seats were crammed to the roof."[44]

The imperial theaters throbbed with life, like lit-up ocean liners plow-
ing through dark waters toward unknown destinations. Russians and foreigners avidly patronized the ballet throughout the hopeful war campaigns
of the 1914–15 winter, the great Russian retreat from the 1915 German offensive, the 1916 victory on the Austrian front, and the disastrous 1916–17
third war winter, when inflation and food shortages plagued the capital
and accusations of treason were hurled at the tsar and tsarina from the
floor of the Duma. As Georges and Lidochka grew from children to
young adolescents, they lived in this ballet repertory. He was a soldier, she
a doll in *Fairy Doll* (about a toy store coming alive at night); they were
Spanish street children in the Russian-Spanish *Don Quixote*; he was a
monkey in the Indian setting of *Le Talisman*; both were small Egyptians
in *Daughter of the Pharaoh*; they were angels, soldiers, mice, or dressed-up
children in *The Nutcracker*, miniature pages in *Pavillon d'Armide*, child
Hungarians in *Raymonda*; they were peasants, cupids, pages again in *The
Sleeping Beauty* (Georges was also a mouse in Carabosse's train, then a
boy in "Tom Thumb and His Brothers"), Spanish street children in *Jota
Aragonesa* . . . Besides dancing in ballets, Theater School boys and girls
were conscripted for child roles in the Mariinsky's operas and in the Alexandrinsky and Mikhailovsky drama theaters.[45]

But the essence of what they learned came from dance's own rich language, epitomized perhaps in the second-act *Mazurka des enfants* from *Paquita*, Petipa's first staged ballet on Russian soil (1847, though he added the *Mazurka* in 1881). Twelve child couples, boys in white tights and military tunics, girls in military-flavored white dresses, all with red capes and red pillbox hats, danced this upper-crust Polish ballroom maneuver from the time of Nicholas I. Even in 1916, the children's *Mazurka* remained a proud and careful procession that opened into side steps, running steps, circling formations, the boys heel-clicking and kneeling to the girls, the girls answering with haughty nods.[46] This would have been the first dance in which Georges and Lidochka were paired—he knelt to her; she gave him her hand. It was infused to the core with the dashing manners and military bravado that was about to be lost to the murderous technology of modern war.

Inside the Theater School, the children were mostly sheltered from news of the war and even from the unrest on the home front. One day each week they went without sugar, for the war effort. When the War Department tried to install wounded soldiers in the school's infirmaries, the Court Ministry refused, though it let the children sort bandages in their free time.[47] But gradually war's signs became ubiquitous. The city's name had already been changed by imperial decree, from the German-sounding St. Petersburg to the patriotically Russianized Petrograd. Army conscripts poured into it from all over Russia, to be gathered and sent on to the western fronts. Many regimental barracks were located in the city center itself. Recruits were drilled in open squares, especially the Mariinsky Theater's own. Ragged refugees displaced by fighting to the west thronged streets and sidewalks. Petrograd's society embraced their causes and held balls and performances to aid them and wounded soldiers. Mariinsky dancers took part. They rehearsed in the school's dancing rooms, observed through chinks in the door by the students. Karsavina was an especially active charity performer, loved for this by Petrograd citizens. Some Mariinsky female dancers trained as nurses and went to the front, soloist Ludmilla Schollar among them. Private hospitals were created by society ladies. The tsarina herself and her daughters made one in Tsarskoe Selo and worked in it nursing their beloved subjects. Not to be outdone, Kshesinskaya set up a hospital and graced it with ceremonial visits, after which Preobrazhenskaya made one too in her own building, though she took the nurses' training courses and tended the wounded men herself.[48]

In summers, Georges and Lidochka went home to talk of the war. Georges's mother, Maria, was volunteering in a hospital for wounded

officers. A surviving photograph shows her in the midst of many soldiers, posed on the steps of a palace somewhere: she's not in nurse's
clothes but in a frilly blouse, as if she managed rather than nursed. She'd
already sent first-born Tamara off to Mikhailov, a town in Ryazan province near Moscow where Meliton's brother Ivan now commanded the
prison. Ivan's wife Emilia would take charge of her education. The
summer of 1916 Meliton traveled to Mikhailov to see his daughter and
help his brother's household move to another nearby prison city where
Ivan had been transferred, Kasimov. The youngest Balanchivadze,
Andrei, had been enrolled at a Petrograd *Realschule*, a more task-
oriented high school than the classical gymnasia. He would begin in the
fall of 1916 and live in town with Aunt Nadia.[49]

Lidochka's family was even more directly affected by the war, since
Alexander Ivanov was serving throughout 1914 and most of 1915 with
Brusilov's Eighth Army on the Ukrainian front. He was by now an *avto-
mobil* master and chief of the regiment's garage, which was behind the
front lines. This meant he'd managed to evade the army's summer 1915
devastation on the northern front. He'd been sent back instead to Petrograd to serve on a commission on "lids, inner tubes, and hoses," and
prolonged his leave to stay with his family. He also got a new rank,
shtabs-kapitan, which put him on the Table of Ranks, at least for the one
and a half years left of it, though not as a hereditary noble but a "personal" one: he couldn't pass his rank to his children. Ivanov's war luck
held. In fall 1915, he was posted home for good to Petrograd's First
Reserve Armored Car Division and put to work converting Italian Fiats
to armored cars.[50]

In late August 1916, when the ballet students returned to school, the
war still raged. On the home front, inflation deepened. Food shortages
grew acute. But ceremonial occasions continued. On the tsar's name
day, December 6, Nicholas II, Alexandra, and their children attended
the Mariinsky—probably for the last time—to see the tsar's favorite
ballet, *The Little Humpbacked Horse*, with its German march finale performed by the ballet children. Georges and Lidochka both danced. As
always on this day, the theater was filled with schoolchildren: in the
boxes sat the girls in blue, red, pink uniform dresses with white fichu
collars; in the parterre were the cadets, boy pages, and grammar students in miniature uniform jackets. After the ballet, the child dancers
changed into their own immaculate school uniforms and processed to
the royal box to be presented to the tsar. It was "like a colossal apartment," remembered Balanchine, with "chandeliers, the walls covered in
light blue." Each student was called forward by a schoolmaster or

mistress: girls first, boys second, "hands at our sides." Each was greeted, each given "chocolate in silver boxes, wonderful ones!" and an "exquisite" porcelain mug, with light blue lyres and the imperial monogram." Balanchine remembered the Tsar as "not tall," with "protruding, light-colored eyes." The tsarina was a "very tall, beautiful woman . . . dressed sumptuously"; the four daughters were beauties, the Tsarevich Alexei, who was just his age, born in 1904, alert and handsome.[51]

Sheathed in antiquated ceremonies, the monarchy was nearing its final apotheosis. Nicholas II's name day was followed ten days later by the violent murder of the peasant priest, Rasputin. This self-styled holy man with strangely light, hypnotic eyes, born in 1869 in a Siberian village, had wandered the whole of Russia before finding his way into the royal couple's favor as a healer of their son's hemophiliac bleeding. But after the tsar left the capital in 1915 to command the army in its Belorussian headquarters, Rasputin appeared almost to rule along with the tsarina. In his memoir of the revolution, the revolutionary politician Sukhanov refers to the Petrograd government as the "Rasputin régime." The capital was scandalized by Rasputin's high-handedness and his private orgies in restaurants and gypsy cafés. Politicians and royal family members tried repeatedly to warn the tsar against him, but the Tsarina held such a fanatic trust in this curiously effective muzhik that Nicholas refrained from action.

Others took it. On Saturday, December 17, 1916, several young aristocrats, together with an aging Duma parliamentarian, invited Rasputin to a tryst, then poisoned and shot him and dumped him, still breathing, into the Neva River. This was their panicked way of trying to force the tsar and tsarina to abandon the so-called decadent behavior that was fueling the unrest. Even before Rasputin's corpse was found, speculation about the murder had already mingled in Petersburg drawing rooms with enthusiastic comments about Smirnova's arabesques in that evening's Sleeping Beauty. The monarchy was engulfed in rumors about Rasputin and the treacherous "German spy" tsarina, but the ballet system and its school seemed to be immortal, destined to go on forever, school graduates passing each spring into the theater, nine- and ten-year-olds entering the school each fall.

In that crucial winter of 1916–17, Georges and Lidochka turned thirteen. Her face, with its pointed chin and upturned nose, seemed thin after a spurt of growth. He was still small and thin too, but also strong, with dark eyes and the haughty air he'd had from the beginning—except with the youngest students. One of the newest girls, a nine-year-old boarder with a long face and watchful eyes who'd started at the school in

August of 1916, encountered each of them and never forgot it. Her name was Vera Kostrovitskaya. Like Balanchivadze, she lived too far away to go home every day, so she boarded from the beginning. Vera was the child of a very high *chinovnik*, identity unknown even today, and a bohemian mother whose own mother was a professional pianist. She was terribly homesick, missing her grandmother's piano playing most of all. Older girls played tricks on her, stole her food, made her cry. She stopped sleeping, lost weight, and could barely stand up after morning dance class. Only Lidochka was kind, reassuring the child and later making her a friend.

Another comfort came to Vera unexpectedly. One winter evening she thought she heard a Chopin étude coming from the floor above, played "seriously and exactly" like her grandmother played at home. She went to the dark hall by the stairwell and pressed against the door to listen. That night she finally slept. Every evening after that she would escape the older girls' predinner banter and slip away to that locked door to hear the phantom pianist play the things she knew from home. One day she learned from the school's music teacher that a gifted Middle Division boy was studying piano—Balanchivadze. A little later, in mid-February 1917, she met Georges in person at a Lent service in the school chapel. He was serving the communion wine for Batiushka Pigulevsky. "Very thin, pale—almost transparent," remembered Kostrovitskaya, "with black smooth hair, wide-apart dark eyes and a generous mouth." "You can drink it, it tastes good," he whispered to the little girl. "Don't worry, I'll pour some more." Kostrovitskaya remembered those gentle words all her life.[52]

Outside in the streets, emotions were building that would soon erupt in violence. The third winter of war was ending, a winter of bitter cold. On the home front, food shortages grew drastic and inflated money bought nothing. Nearly two million soldiers had already died in what Russians angrily called the "European" war. Rumors abounded about the debased monarchy. Off in Tsarskoe Selo, the royal court was frozen in its own kind of sleep. The "German" tsarina, her face set in a mask of grief, was nursing her children through an attack of measles. All four of her pretty daughters had it, as did the Tsarevich Alexei, whose body also contained the constant threat of hemophiliac bleeding, a condition the populace knew nothing about.

On Wednesday, February 22, the weather abruptly got warmer and the sun came out. The next day, February 23, was International Women's Day, the eight-year-old socialist holiday inaugurated in America. Masses of working-class women turned out in the streets to riot for bread.

Over the next few days, crowds of workers joined them. On Saturday night, February 25, the tsar in his faraway headquarters finally ordered the capital's army units to restore order. On Sunday, soldiers opened fire on crowds on the Nevsky Prospekt; a hundred or so demonstrators were killed. But it was too late. On Monday, February 27, other Petrograd soldiers who'd been called out refused to fire on civilians. They'd sat idle, disgruntled and overcrowded in the city's many barracks, waiting to be sent to the front. Now, in a burst of action, they held meetings. They spoke about their frustrations and came to the tricky decision to side with the people. "The enormous coercion machine manufactured by the government was spinning its wheels," wrote Viktor Shklovsky, then an officer like Lidochka's father in the First Reserve Armored Car regiment.[53] Regiments mutinied, one by one. Some arrested or killed their commanding officers. Many marched in ragged order to the Tauride Palace to proclaim their loyalty to whatever new government was being formed by a hastily assembled Duma committee.

On that fatal Monday, even the Theater School students heard the commotion in the street. The girls in their dancing rooms ran to the windows to see what was happening. Their teachers implored them to come away. Choura Danilova disobeyed, climbed onto the window casement, and saw a soldier in the street raise his gun and take aim. She fell, as if shot, crying, "I am wounded, I am wounded!"[54]

She wasn't wounded; fright had made her fall. But high in the window was a bullet hole. The walls of that sacred sanctuary of the Romanov monarchy had been breached. The revolution had begun.

SIX

1917

Armored car in February Revolution.

Despite the bullet through a Theater School window on February 27, nothing changed for another day inside its hushed interior, in the center of a city surging with crowds of workers and soldiers. Many of these were armed, from raids on the many arsenals also in the city center. New regiments hourly joined the mutiny: Pavlovsky, Volynsky, Litovsky, Izmailovsky. Bands of soldiers and workers searched out pockets of tsarist resistance. Rumors put police machine guns on roofs. Rebels fired at roofs; other guns were shot into the air. Trucks and cars raced around the streets with soldiers hanging from their sides. On Tuesday, February 28, the second day of the "great mutiny" that would become the February Revolution, a new hail of bullets flew into the school's windows—a spillover from an assault on another nearby incubator of the tsarist system, the elite military Corps des Pages.[1]

Now at last caretakers snatched the children out of windowed classrooms, handed them their school overcoats, and deposited them on benches in the inner corridors, boys on their upper floor, girls on their lower. Then they retreated, terrified for themselves as the regime they'd served melted away. Late in the night, the half-asleep girls huddled on the benches saw, far down the corridor, the usually stately Varvara Likhosherstova approaching at a run at the head of a crowd of men in military uniform. The lead soldier held a revolver to her back. "Search!" he said. All headed to the dormitory, where soldiers looked under the beds for monarchists. The littler girls giggled. The soldiers left in disarray. The next morning, March 1, the families of the students came for them.[2]

The city had cast its lot with the insurgents. It had no choice: on the streets were masses of factory workers, students, and assorted citizens, along with 180,000 or so armed and unorganized soldiers who couldn't return to their regiments without risking reprisals. Already the clock could not be turned back. Ragged groups of rebellious soldiers were streaming to the city's northeast, to the Duma's seat in the Tauride Palace, conferring the status of impromptu political center on the stately old edifice. Inside, Duma members were trying to keep pace with street events. Should they assume leadership? The tsar was still tsar; he was heading back on a train from General Staff headquarters to his family near the capital. If they acted, punishment might await them—or glory. Duma chairman Mikhail Rodzianko retired to an empty chamber to think. He emerged to sanction a Provisional (temporary) Committee of the State Duma that would try to restore order in the capital. A revolutionary act, to save the status quo.

At the same time, radical intellectuals from an array of leftist parties, as well as worker-leaders just freed from the city's prisons by rampaging soldiers, gathered at the Tauride Palace too, finding empty rooms at the other end. Some were veterans of the 1905 revolution and speedily reconstituted earlier revolutionary workers' councils, or (using the Russian word for "council") soviets. From these emerged a Provisional Executive Committee of the Soviet of Workers' and Soldiers' Deputies, abbreviated Ispolkom in Russian, which set about responding to the chaos in the streets and organizing supplies for the now homeless and hungry soldiers. The soviets noisily and raggedly occupied one end of the imposing neoclassical palace. The left-bourgeois members of the Duma Committee wandered about the other end, drinking tea and debating.

On the defining night of Wednesday, March 1, more citizens crowded into the Palace, as the two ends—Soviet Executive Committee and Provisional Duma Committee—reached a tentative agreement to improvise a government. Key to the agreement was the lone figure who belonged to both soviets and Duma (its only socialist member), the flamboyant lawyer Alexander Kerensky. He went running back and forth between the two factions. Soon he would accept a minister's portfolio in the impromptu new government. But on that same night, in the Palace's left-wing end, a mass of soldiers took over a meeting of the soviets and pushed through, with the help of an impromptu military committee of intellectuals, the notorious Order No. 1, banning the officer-soldier abuse that had been part of army procedure for so long. It mandated soldiers' or sailors' committees in each unit to challenge officers' orders; it gave legal sanction, in other words, to the masses of rebelling soldiers.

On the next day, March 2, the tsar in his railway car hours away near Pskov met with a Duma delegation and gave up the throne to his brother Michael, who refused it. The mood on the streets was joyous. A decadent monarchy had collapsed. Utopia had arrived. The soldiers were suddenly human beings. They couldn't be slapped in the face anymore by officers, or shot for deserting, or addressed by the pronoun *ty* used for children and other inferiors. The workers glimpsed dignity in the form of an eight-hour workday and a say in management decisions. Even the intelli- gentsia felt a shaky jubilation: they'd longed for this fashionable liberation from embarrassingly antique gentlemen rulers for half a century. "Revolution . . . a dream of generations and of long laborious decades," Nikolai Sukhanov called it, in his penetrating eyewitness account.[3] Red flags appeared in windows. Street crowds waved them too. Everyone embraced. Impromptu speeches were heard on street corners. Impromptu bands of people tore down tsarist statues and other imperial symbols or hunted down the hated police, who'd been exempt from military service. Everyone sang a Russian version of the anthem of that earlier revolution that had torn France apart, the *Marseillaise*. "It was like Easter—a joyous, naïve, disorderly carnival paradise," wrote Viktor Shklovsky, another brilliant revolutionary memoirist.[4]

How bewildering it must have been for the ballet students, stumbling out of their school into a huge outdoor celebration with random gunfire. They'd rarely been allowed into the streets in normal times. Vera Kostrovitskaya and her grandmother went on foot the long route home down the Fontanka, passing bonfires on street corners, where throngs of people with "joyful excited eyes" warmed themselves and burned police papers. The grandmother explained to the little girl that revolution had come and there was no more tsar. What Vera understood was that she'd been freed from older girls' bullying.[5]

In some ways, these child ballet students resembled the soldiers and workers. They'd put up with ancient humiliations from haughty caretakers and senior students, because that was the order of things. They'd been passive pawns, not just of their education but of school rituals designed to remind them of their "place." Now this arbitrary arrangement had ended, and something more human was on the horizon. These children might not have seen it that way at first; for now, all they could feel was bewilderment. What would become of their school, with its patrons deposed? They'd stared daily at imperial portraits on their classroom walls, celebrated imperial name days, performed in the presence of grand dukes, met them in their school's halls . . . Just two months earlier they'd danced the tsar's favorite German march and received his thanks in person.

Each family offered its child a different explanation of events, depending on its earlier politics. Lidochka Ivanova heard about the soldiers' grievances: her father's armored car division was in the thick of the action. Many armored cars had been garaged in Petrograd waiting for repair or retooling. The rioting soldiers had raided garages as they'd raided artillery storehouses, taken cars out and excitedly driven them around, even men who'd never sat behind a wheel. "And throughout the city rushed the muses and furies of the February revolution," wrote Viktor Shklovsky, "trucks and automobiles piled high and spilling over with soldiers, not knowing where they were going or where they would get gasoline, giving the impression of sounding the tocsin throughout the whole city."[6] The vehicles' armor made them look like constructivist sculptures on wheels—a square mass topped by a circular mass, with a gun barrel pointing out. If one image encapsulates the chaos of the February Revolution—its working-class origins, its lurch toward modernity—it's those armored cars careering through snowy winter streets with crowds of fur-hatted soldiers clinging to them.

Ivanov had risen in the army by caring for them: he was a repairman, a master tinkerer. At the front, he'd wrangled gas for his beloved cars; in the rear, he'd worked to improve them. But he was an officer too, a *shtabs-kapitan*, and that meant danger as soldiers turned on their officers, arrested them, marched them to the Tauride Palace, even killed them in the heat of the moment. Ivanov, though, belonged to the First Reserve Division, which had gone "red" even before February.[7] Once again, he'd managed a switch to the winning side. In fact, in most armored car divisions officers did not resist when their men joined the rebellion. Many had been workingmen themselves, like Ivanov. Shklovsky's captain received a soldier escort to protect him from other soldiers' violence.[8] Ivanov would soon make a formal transition from the tsarist army to the Red. It seems he didn't shrink from the revolution but helped manage it.

Did Kapitan Ivanov take his daughter home from the ballet school in an armored car? Nobody remembered such a scene, though Ivanov's connection with technological modernity may have been a factor in the modern aura that later surrounded his daughter. But however he fetched her from the ballet school, he would have voiced his revolutionary excitement—one could suddenly speak one's mind—despite his pride at the pink dress she'd won in the now-hated tsarist regime.

In the Balanchivadze family, Meliton, though mostly apolitical, supported the revolution. Maria, still serving in a tsarist army hospital, was unsure. During the violent February days, Georges was taken from the school to the aunts' apartment in Bolshaya Moskovskaya Street. Twelve-year-old Andrei joined him from his *Realschule*. The brothers remained in Petrograd: trains to Finland were running, but the Russian infrastructure

Balanchivadze family and friends, Georgi in front.
Postcard, George Balanchine and group of Georgian men. BALANCHINE Is a Trademark
of The George Balanchine Trust. Courtesy of New York City Ballet Archives, Ballet
Society Collection.

there had collapsed. Their father, recently returned from his long trip to
visit brother and daughter, was probably stuck in Finland. Meliton was
facing not just revolution but the final collapse of his once-prodigious
fortune. Detailed records haven't survived, but even if he'd once rescued
family finances, he couldn't do it again. "Lacking a practical vein, and up
till now generous, kind-hearted, and trusting, he'd been drawn (even further) into obviously unprofitable industrial undertakings," wrote his
biographer, Khuchua. "After the February Revolution, M. Balanchivadze
did not linger long in Petrograd."[9] In fact, Meliton left for Georgia in
March 1917, expecting his family to follow when they could go as a group.
For now, however, his Russian sons were in Petrograd but his daughter
was still far away beyond Moscow. The children hadn't seen each other
for more than a year. But things were changing for Tamara in Kasimov, as
she herself wrote in a letter to her mother on April 2, 1917. Her uncle Ivan
Balanchivadze been recalled from his prison command to army duty.
He'd just left on the long train ride to the Fifth Army's Dvinsk front (now
Daugavpils in Latvia).

Tamara's April letter is interesting from many angles. She congratu-
lates Maria on the Easter holiday, the day before. She begs her mother to
join her in Kasimov. She doesn't ask about her brothers (she'd done that
in earlier letters) but focuses on her own needs, like any self-absorbed
fifteen-year-old. Did Maria get an earlier request to send a certain hat,

even if it wasn't finished? Some dresses would be sewn for her in Kasimov when her aunt got back from escorting her uncle to the train. They'd made an Easter dinner before he left, with Russian, Georgian, and Polish dishes (Ivan's wife Emilia Karlovna was Polish). Tamara, describing this to her hungry family, doesn't seem to grasp the capital's food crisis. She sends congratulations to her father about the revolution, but warns him too: "There's nothing to be glad about. On the contrary, everything is sad." In Kasimov, she writes, soldiers are stopping boats on the Oka River and turning them back, "and what the workers are allowing themselves, I won't write!" In the same defeatist mood she asks Maria why it's not worth sending her, Tamara, the German books she'd asked for, to continue earlier lessons. "On the contrary: they would be exactly right for now, even necessary." The Kasimov household like many others expected a German invasion. She signs the letter "your daughter, Tamara," adorning the "T" and the "r" of her name with little inked flags, and adding, in a forecast of her future profession, a bold curlicue under it.

The Balanchivadzes were spread all over the empire: Tamara in Kasimov, Ivan heading for Dvinsk, Maria outside Petrograd in a war hospital (Tamara had asked in an August 1916 letter if she'd already gone "into service"), Georges and Andrei in Petrograd, Meliton on the way to Georgia . . . Apollon Balanchivadze was farthest away of all: he'd been transferred from the Finnish border to a command on the Turkish front.

The Balanchivadzes weren't the only ones rerouted by February's mass rebellion. Russian revolutionaries who'd languished for years in Siberian exile, or lived hand to mouth as far afield as New York, were packing bags and coming home. On Easter Monday, as Tamara mailed her Kasimov letter, the most determined of them all stepped off the train a little after 11 PM at Petrograd's Finland Station—Vladimir Lenin. He was met with spotlights, delegations, and a cheering crowd of 10,000 workers. Hemmed in by the human mass, he climbed onto . . . an armored car! to give an impromptu speech, the germ of his "April Theses" announcing the Bolsheviks' refusal to cooperate with the Provisional Government. This position astonished the Ispolkom's motley welcome delegation of Bolsheviks, Left Mensheviks, Left Socialist Revolutionaries, and "Mezhraiontsy" (Inter-District Organization), all supporting the Provisional Government in the first flush of revolution. For the ride to Bolshevik headquarters, Lenin climbed into another armored car, one of the many available, since the First Reserve Armored Car Regiment had also met the train, (probably with *shtabs-kapitan* Alexander Ivanov along). On the way, the car stopped every few blocks so Lenin could mount it again to speak, as car and crowd slowly crossed the Vyborg Side to the Petrograd Side. Their destination: the art nouveau mansion of prima ballerina Kshesinskaya, which the Bolsheviks had commandeered.

No photo survives of their arrival. But as Lenin emerged from the car to enter the mansion, two aesthetic systems long bent on annihilating each other met and clashed. The car with its crude metal armor stood for the force of the proletariat. The white brick mansion, ostentatiously placed on the Neva's northern bank at the mouth of the busy Troitsky Bridge, stood for a once almost mystical social power that had suddenly evaporated. The Armored Car Division had taken possession of Kshesinskaya's palace even before the Bolsheviks arrived, for its spacious garage. The ballerina herself had gone into hiding with son and jewels on Monday night, February 27, and so hadn't witnessed the takeover. Twice she came back in disguise to view the state of her beloved home. Her closets were ransacked, her giant bathtub full of cigarette butts, her piano wedged in a corner between crumbling columns, and her bedroom crowded with the desks of the *Pravda* newspaper staff busily hammering out the revolutionary news.[10]

But what better act could revolutionaries devise than occupying the symbolic center of tsarist corruption? Other rebels took over other mansions in that February and March vortex, but none was as desecrated as Kshesinskaya's (nor were those others thought to contain "German gold," which she'd supposedly received from traitorous business deals). In the person of this deposed celebrity, all of ballet seemed to take on the old regime's aura: corruption mingled with eroticism. Hastily made movies—*The Secrets of the Romanovs, The Shame of the House of Romanovs, The Secret Story of the Ballerina Kshesinskaya*—would soon appear, in which Kshesinskaya looked as much a dissolute sinner as Rasputin and the empress. From her hiding place, the ballerina telephoned Kerensky in person to get her house back. He sent her across the palace to the Executive Committee of the soviets, where she was shocked at not being recognized. But the soviets were adamant: nothing could be done about the house without risking mob reprisals.[11]

The street celebration in full swing masked a fatal split between the middle classes, who assumed the new life would include the old pleasant routines, and the lower classes, who wanted life utterly transformed. In sentiment, the two factions corresponded roughly to the positions of the two governments frenziedly debating at different ends of the Tauride Palace. The ongoing war was the sticking point. How could Russia continue to honor its commitments to "the gallant Allies" (France, England, now suddenly America) with four million of its soldiers dead, its workers exhausted from war demands, its ordinary citizens made hungry by war's inflation? As the days wore on, the war problem shifted the whole political spectrum to the left. The moderate socialists, Mensheviks and Socialist Revolutionaries who wanted to win more battles to make an "honorable" peace, joined with centrist Duma members in an uneasy coalition, which slid increasingly to the right. The Bolsheviks, who demanded immediate peace, roped in the more radical Mensheviks and Left Socialist Revolutionaries, and that faction slipped centerwards as the war flailed on.

Despite political cataclysms, order gradually returned, at least to the capital's surface life, and so to its theaters. The Provisional Government showed surprising concern for the whole imperial theater apparatus, though the school's fate was not yet addressed. As early as the tsar's March 2 abdication, Duma chairman Rodzianko had appointed another landowning member (and theater enthusiast), Nikolai Lvov, to look after the former imperials. Petrograd's Mariinsky, Alexandrinsky, and Mikhailovsky Theaters had closed down, but guards were posted, and signs put up exhorting the population to "defend this building as national property!" The Imperial Theaters' tsarist director, Colonel Vladimir Teliakovsky, was asked to stay on to ensure a smooth transition. On March 3, Teliakovsky and Lvov addressed a *miting* (the English word was borrowed for mass political meetings) of theater artists at the Alexandrinsky Theater, in which the colonel thanked them for his years of service and Lvov implored them to side with free Russia. On March 6, the theaters were de-imperialized and renamed state theaters. On March 7, repaired city trams returned to the streets flying red flags. On March 12, the theaters reopened too, but with imperial portraits gone, gilt double eagles covered in red cloth, ushers' tailcoats discarded for "jackets of a dirty gray," tsarist coats of arms on programs replaced by a lyre, and the heavy, eagle-embossed dark-blue stage curtain retired in favor of the light, white, "Greek" (so revolutionary) curtain from Meyerhold and Fokine's famous 1911 *Orpheus and Eurydice*. A Requiem for the Fallen Heroes of the Revolution was given twice on reopening day, the *Marseillaise* played and sung with its Russian lyrics, and box-office proceeds donated to the families of the fallen.[12] The theatrical season resumed, but with a different audience. In the Tsar's box, rows of pale, ragged figures had replaced the resplendent uniforms and bejeweled ladies: the old revolutionaries, returned from Siberian prisons.

This audience shift was triumphant or disastrous, depending on who was judging. An aristocrat from England's military mission attended the first ballet performance of the new order, *The Sleeping Beauty* with

Smirnova on March 15, because he'd seen the last one under the tsars: the same ballet, with the same ballerina. He was displeased. The curtain now rose at 7 instead of 8, he noted in his casually snobbish (and anonymous) *Russian Diary of an Englishman*. As for the audience . . ."On the ground floor Imperial stage box to the left of the stage, where the Grand Dukes usually sat, were several lady dancers and one man." This was the box newly assigned to members of the profession by the Actors' Soviet. "And over their head, in the box where the Grand Dukes' children had congregated, now sat a Jew and a Jewess."[13]

Regardless of audience, the Theater School students were needed again for bit parts in the old ballets, so the school was willy-nilly reopened and its teachers regathered. The older students trickled back to their dormitories despite family panic and transport challenges, though the youngest lived at home for the rest of that spring and came only for day classes—to the delight of Vera Kostrovitskaya. On April 9, the theater artists, who'd held their own *mitingi* and elected their own soviet, held galas in the Provisional Government's honor at both the Alexandrinsky and the Mariinsky. The Mariinsky's featured speeches interspersed with opera and ballet excerpts, including Fokine's *Polovetsian Dances* from the opera *Prince Igor*, with Theater School boys in the corps. On April 14, fifteen older ballet students were requested for the May Day celebration, to be held on April 18, the equivalent in Russia's calendar of Europe's May 1. The Mariinsky's facade was draped with red flags, and orators spoke from a wooden platform to the masses in Theater Square.[14]

Even with students onstage, the school's future was far from assured. Its bookkeeper had to petition for items once automatically supplied, like carriages to take students to the theaters and paper to keep the books. On all requests he typed a small b. (for *byvshee*, meaning "former") on the letterhead in front of "Imperial Theater School." This was the solution for all the city's bureaucracies. As the government resumed its daily rounds, that little "b" for "former" was affixed to a vast range of office letterheads. Petrograd was a maze of "former" governing bodies. The Ministry of the Court still ruled over the imperial-turned-state theaters, but it too was a "former," a facsimile of itself. Everything had changed. Nothing had changed. Inside the school, the same routines started up, the lessons, the manners, the meals, though food supplies dwindled. The famine conditions pertaining in most of the city had finally reached this once-favored court appendage. Butter was scarce. Bread was cut into ever-smaller portions. Milk was diluted. And big questions loomed: how could the Provisional Government support an elite training institution with a starving population on its hands?

A 1917 graduation performance on April 30, with excerpts from *Harlem Tulip* and *Coppélia*, was held at the ex-Mariinsky itself. This marked the season's end and the students' release to their families, for a summer of escalating turmoil. A June offensive by the Russian army on the whole western front was followed by humiliating retreats, then violent street demonstrations—the so-called July Days—when a new revolutionary mob, including 10,000 sailors from the Kronstadt naval base, again brought Petrograd to a standstill. In response, the Provisional Government enacted a crackdown on free speech and planted allegations in newspapers of Bolshevik treason: it was a *German* train, readers were reminded, that had brought Lenin and company across Europe to Russia. Lenin fled again to Finland, disguised as a workingman. A new Coalition Government (the third) made Kerensky its premier on July 8, though without ending the war. On the front, the Russian army disintegrated as the Germans advanced. In late August, the Germans took the strategic Baltic port of Riga. General Lavr Kornilov, the half-Cossack, half-Kalmyk monarchist whom Kerensky had just appointed army chief, sent troops to Petrograd in a grand attempt to reverse the revolution. But the population rose up once more to save it, and Kornilov's troops went over to the other side. The double-dealing Kerensky exhausted himself with melodramatic speeches, but couldn't stop the Provisional Government's power from fading away in the face of chronic factory strikes, lengthening food lines, and universal expectation of cataclysm.

It's impossible to tell where any ballet students were during that volatile 1917 summer. Even if racy plays like *Gypsy Lover* ran at the summer theaters, even if conductor Malko played Tchaikovsky, Scriabin, and Stravinsky at the Pavlovsk Concert Hall and rumors of an August concert by a returning Pavlova caused a near-riot at ticket offices, severe shortages still plagued the capital.[15] Ration tickets were needed for bread, milk, and shoes. People stood in line for hours. Little coal or wood could be found: the coming winter looked scary. Inflation had cut the ruble's value by half.[16] Petrograders waited for invasion from without or a socialist coup from within. Balanchivadze family members in Petrograd—Maria, Georgi, Andrei, and the aunts—couldn't get to their garden in Finland to harvest vegetables. Lidochka was assured of safety and food by her father's army connections, no matter how shifting and mercurial that army in a summer of mass desertions. Alexander Ivanov even got his family to the country, as shown by a photo of him with wife and daughter on a wooded country road. Lidochka holds one of his arms; her now dowdy-looking mother in cardigan and shapeless skirt holds the other. The adored daughter is dressed up as if for a country estate—white frock, white broad-brimmed hat, white socks and shoes on her feet (turned out in ballet's third position).

The winter theater season bravely opened on the heels of Kornilov's failed invasion—opera on September 1, ballet on September 2 (Karsavina in *Giselle*). But no one could pretend things were the same. The great Pavel Gerdt, *danseur noble* for fifty years, had died on August 2, a clear sign of an era ending. And the school was again in limbo. At the start of the summer, reform had seemed imminent. A July Pedagogical Conference had proposed that the school's curriculum finally be aligned with other Russian high schools' seven-year programs. More acting, mime, aesthetics, and academics were recommended as well.[17] This was actually a revolutionary program. In the old days, explained a *Birzhevye Vedomosti* (Stock Market News) columnist on June 11, Theater School students were trained as automatons and automatically put into the ballet troupe, where they sat for years, even if talentless. With the new utopian program, these students would get "a free choice of their life's path!"

But these visionary plans were dropped as the city's situation worsened and the ruble's value sank to the equivalent of 10 cents. The decision was made to close the school's dormitories and reduce its staff. Students were welcomed back in the fall, but only for day classes. On September 13, the school's acting head, Leonid Leontiev, requested 1,000 free student tram tickets from the Petrograd Tramway Commission. He learned only on October 9, in new worker-manager-officialese, that "to satisfy the ordered commutes is not represented a possibility." On September 17, the school asked permission to use the militia guard to deliver letters, since regular mails weren't working. On October 21, an urgent request went out for wood for the school's big tile stoves, along with more notebooks for bookkeeping and forms for taking attendance. Teachers were deserting. "In my last years, 1917–18 and 1918–19, things were very bad with teachers," wrote 1919 graduate Lisovskaya. "Many abandoned us. But even those who stayed behind had their salaries held back."[18] Students had left, too, including Choura Danilova, who fled the revolutionary city in September with her new guardian, the general's daughter Maria Batianova (the general had died in 1916).

Lidochka, whose father could ensure protected commutes, returned to the school for its day classes. According to Mikhailov, this is the moment when she surprised her classmates with her early maturity. "Yesterday's girl suddenly, as in a fairy tale, stood before us a young lady. In those three months out of our sight [Lidochka] had grown, and gotten more serious and better looking. In the theater they stopped putting her in children's roles. In concerts already beyond the school stage they began to cast her in more complex roles."[19] Her boy classmates were bewildered. Georges, back in school as well, was still small for his age. "I had known her since we were children," said Balanchine later. "I had always liked her. I was short then. I was so short that I jokingly signed my letters *Maloross* (the old term for Ukrainians from "Little Russia," Malorossiya in Russian; also a pun literally meaning 'grew little'), even though I was Georgian."[20] It was now that he was kept back a year, to start the fall 1917 term with boys his own age. Georges's new friends Mikhailov and Leonid Lavrovsky would provide crucial company in times to come. The comradeship helped too with the new Middle Division teacher, Viktor Semenov. At twenty-five a leading State Theater *danseur noble* with a body like Hermes, a handsome face (though with satyr-like pointed ears), wonderful elevation in jumps, and famously soft landings, offstage Semenov was a strange character. He spoke in a soft falsetto, except when he switched to basso to mock and abuse an offending student. Perhaps he liked teaching because of the power it gave him. He was, however, a "good teacher," says the eternally polite Mikhailov, which meant he showed the steps clearly.[21]

The boys' earlier teacher, Andrianov, wasn't around when school resumed, not even to offer a friendly word in the halls. He'd died in late summer of consumption at a faraway sanatorium on the Black Sea. Compounding the effects of this loss was Georges's anxiety about where his family planned to go. On September 2, Meliton wrote to Maria from Georgia about the Petrograd situation. He assumes in this letter that the children have already been sent to Ivan's wife Emilia in central Russia. He urges Maria to go to Kasimov herself, and to emigrate from there to Georgia with the children. An apartment and food provisions await them in Tbilisi. But Meliton can't help jumping from familial concern to delight at his own warm reception in Georgia and his excitement about designing its musical education. This is the tone of a man who's re-embraced the life he'd put aside for twenty-eight years and rejoined the extended family he'd always belonged in. He's been to the double wedding of his nephew Irakli and niece Katiusha, he reports (brother Vaso's children—she was a young singer whose Petersburg Conservatory studies he'd earlier sponsored), in the resort town Borjomi. He's visited his married sister in Banoja. How far away Meliton must have seemed to Maria as she read his news![22]

On October 23, Georges and Andrei answered their father in a joint letter, written not from Finland but Petrograd—they convey the Petrograd aunts' greetings at the end. Georges, the actual writer, says nothing about his own ballet studies, beyond informing his father of Andrianov's death. But he does this strangely. "We communicate this piece of news: the artist Andrianov is dead. He was in the hospital in Alupka. They buried him there." True, he's only twelve. But he expresses no ostensible grief for the jaunty *danseur noble* who'd been his only teacher for three years, who'd showed him special kindness and served as a lifelong model in both dance and deportment.[23] This bald announcement made to an absent father, about the death of another "father," implies a loneliness too deep to write about. More news follows, but not about ballet. Brother Andrei is taking piano lessons from a new teacher named Alina Karlovna (last name unknown). He's learned a Beethoven sonata. The two boys have been to the ex-Mariinsky once to see Rubenstein's opera *Demon*. The letter ends with a list of prices and shortages typical of the whole of Petrograd. Andre's piano teacher, they report, still takes the same price for lessons as before inflation and shortages—1 ruble 50 kopecks (that was a kind piano teacher). Milk costs the same, 1 ruble 50 kopecks a bottle, but they don't have any. Bread is 28 kopecks a pound; butter, 2 rubles, 60 kopecks, but there isn't any. They end with the news that their mother plans the move to the Caucasus for after Christmas.[24]

Georges at this moment believed he would soon leave Petrograd, which would mean abandoning his ballet education. But on October 24, a day after he and Andrei wrote this letter, the Bolsheviks, who'd been biding their time, winning soldier and worker converts and gaining the majority over the other squabbling parties in the soviets, moved to take over the revolution. From today's perspective, it's hard to imagine how anyone in that tangled political scene had the strength to act. For eight months, they'd slept on drafty floors on the edges of meetings, talked all night, and dispersed at dawn. They'd run out of food or forgotten to eat. They'd been in constant exhilaration or despair. But Lenin, ensconced in a hiding place in Finland since July, kept a clear head. As Kerensky on October 24 ordered Bolshevik newspapers shut down, Lenin wrote to his party that now was the time.

During the night of October 24–25, Trotsky's fledgling Red Guard occupied the city's key institutions: the railroad stations, telephone exchange, telegraph building, Peter and Paul Fortress, banks, printing presses, and finally the Winter Palace itself, where Provisional Government ministers were meeting. The Bolsheviks were now commanding from the former Smolny School for Noble Girls (Varvara Likhosherstova's alma mater), another white-columned tsarist building near the Duma, which had served since midsummer as headquarters for the city soviets. Lenin himself appeared in Smolny sometime after midnight—he'd made the secret journey back from Finland. As dawn broke with the news of success, Lenin, gray with fatigue, confided his astonishment to an equally gray-faced Trotsky. "From persecution and a life under-ground, to come so suddenly into power . . ." Lenin paused for words, and found them in German. "*Es schwindelt*—it's dizzying."[25] Violence was miraculously avoided in the next few days, even if violent rumors abounded. A Council of People's Commissars (Bolshevik-speak for cab-inet of ministers) was hastily set up, with Lenin as reluctant chief: he'd wanted to be just head of the party. The new officials fanned out to take up their posts, but chaos ensued instead, as bank, telegraph, and govern-ment employees vanished from their offices, taking files, money, and keys with them. The city's food deliveries came to a stop. "Famine is approaching," said the American military attaché in a communiqué home. On November 3, the Bolsheviks celebrated anyway, with brass bands. By mid-November, they'd abolished all titles and ranks, outlawed private property, nationalized banks and factories, shut down the stock market, canceled government debts, seized tsarist gold reserves, closed national borders, and made overtures to Germany for a general—not yet a separate—peace. The revolutionary transformation awaited so long was about to overturn the lives of everyone, not just in Petrograd but the whole vast former empire.

But first—more chaos. Workers' groups discovered the wine cellars of various palaces and mansions and imbibed their contents; so did the regiments sent to discipline them. Meliton wrote again on November 12. "Wife and Children my Dears," he begins, "how are you living in this terrible time?" The people of Petrograd have turned into savages, he's read. "How good it would have been if you'd gotten out of this accursed city when I wrote you that you should! Now it will be very difficult." He himself is all right because "our regiments are guarding Tiflis and Kutaisi." Commanding one of them was brother Ivan. Ivan, it seemed, had slipped out of the tsarist army amid the mass desertions of the Dvinsk front and returned to his own revolutionary country. Georgia was different from Russia. Moderate Mensheviks held the power instead of radical Bolsheviks, and had declared their own independence. They had their own Red Guard too, and they needed the military skills of the seasoned Ivan. With practically all the Balanchivadzes home again, Meliton finally summons his Russian family too. "Leave all the things in Petrograd," Meliton tells Maria. "We can worry about them later." He himself, he cheerfully reports, has tons of work to do, not only founding music schools but mounting his opera in Tbilisi. By the way, could Maria and the two boys please help persuade the Petrograd-based Georgian tenor, Alexander Dogonadze, to come home to sing in it?

On November 27, Georgi and Andrei wrote an answering letter. They repeated the family's intention to emigrate to Georgia. All that's holding them up, they write, is Andrei's gymnasium fee of 20 rubles that Maria has paid in advance for two school quarters (the Russian school system was parsed in four quarters). Maria wants her money's worth. But the second quarter is nearly over, so they'll come soon. They offer more news about their studies, but again, nothing is said about Georgi's ballet schooling. Nothing is ever said about Georgi's ballet schooling in any surviving family letters. What's said instead is that Georgi himself has learned a piece on the piano, a Rubinstein polka. Andrei is still playing his Beethoven sonata and will soon start on a Schubert piece, the one Meliton played himself. And by the way, they've located the tenor Dogonadze and given him the message that he should emigrate to sing in Meliton's opera.

It's as if the brothers' news has been specially censored for Meliton's benefit, and in the process Georges the ballet student has been all but obliterated. Or else the boy believes that, given their imminent move, a ballet career seems so unlikely he doesn't bother mentioning it in a letter. Or his father's longtime opposition to his becoming a dancer and not a musician has rendered him silent on his future profession. Later, Meliton would write his son again to try to get him to switch from ballet to music. The Georgi-Andrei team now moves on to the familiar privation theme. They've learned to repair their own galoshes, they write proudly, using rubber soles "bought by Mama." But it's the letter's tone that's disquieting. It's written in a younger, more dutiful style than one would expect from the writer, who's been singled out, after all, at the Imperial Theater School. It's as if Georges, "performing" on paper for an absent father, has become the littler boy Meliton had once known, and regressed back to one in a pair of brothers, a unit created by an uneasy family for its own convenience.

Only at the end of this November 27 letter does the old Georgi-Georges flash out. "Papenka," he writes, "who in the Caucasus has spread the rumor that Georgi is a composer, who's made up many songs? That he's a wonderful musician? This is not true. Because when we are in the Caucasus," he continues, "everyone will ask us to play, and we're not going to be able to play anything. So—you should tell everyone that we are playing only for ourselves." Here at last is that stubborn nine-year-old, now older and beginning to claim his identity. A reader can almost hear across 100 years the sudden fear for that identity, threatened less by the forces of history than by an old dynamic within the family. He was supposed to go to his father's unknown country and there be put on display. But by doing that he would lose the world *he* belonged in, the world they'd put him in against his will but which he'd gradually reshaped to his specifications. Georges had been praised in the Theater School not just for dancing but piano playing as well. But his little brother outstrips him even here. Andrei was already a music student outright, studying too at a respectable academic school. The threat of identity submersion must have been severe.

Sometime in November 1917, Tamara and Aunt Mila Balanchivadze set off from faraway Kasimov on the long road "home," to Georgia, a country neither of them had ever seen. In January 1918, at the end of his school term, twelve-year-old Andrei left for Georgia too, alone, by train, truck, and horse cart. It took him a month of narrow escapes and near starvation to find his father and resume his musical studies under Meliton's supervision.[26] But Maria and Georgi/Georges didn't leave their devastated city. Something had happened "offstage," beyond the arena of family letters, to keep them there. Could it have been the news of the Theater School's coming revival? Or was it Maria's own stubborn pride? She'd held the family together so long by sheer force of will that she must have hesitated to go to a country where her husband was the prodigal son and she knew no one. Or was Georges the force behind their staying, as he finally acknowledged his desire to belong to the art that had chosen him?

Neither mother nor son, it seems, could abandon the only city they knew, and the selves they were in it. In early 1918, Georgi was living with Maria and the aunts, waiting to see what would happen with his school. He had his subliminal wish: he was alone on the scene with his mother. But he was already moving beyond her sphere.

SEVEN

Theater School: The Hungry Years

Lenin and Lunacharsky.

Who were the Bolsheviks who had taken over the Russian Empire and the fate of its 164,000,000 inhabitants? Technically they were the smaller half of the Social Democratic Labor Party, which had split in 1903 into radical Bolsheviks and moderate Mensheviks. Actually, the new rulers were a porous group that included long-time Bolsheviks and members of the other splinter groups on the radical Marxist front. They'd come from all parts of the vast empire, but shared a belief in the need for a working-class revolution to right ancient wrongs. This Marxist creed had allowed them as individuals to live poor, outside the law. Most had converted to the cause in adolescence. Virtually all had been caught by tsarist authorities and put in prison or exiled to the empire's remote north. Between incarcerations, they'd fled abroad to obscure corners of Munich, London, Geneva, Paris, Stockholm, or Vienna, where they'd studied alone, worked as journalists, spoken at meetings, set up illegal newspapers, created schools for workers, met up at international party conferences, lost each other, made political alliances, broken them, even married each other's brothers and sisters. Almost nowhere in the history of Western politics has there been such an oddly stable social category of people on the run, plotting and hiding, as these Russian revolutionaries.[1]

Now *they* were in charge. And they had an empire-sized laboratory to experiment in, but one with broken equipment, crumbling premises, and devastated personnel. World War I and the revolution piled on it were still depleting resources and energy. The Council of People's Commissars had to fix everything even as they changed everything, a dual task which all too often stalled in its tracks. And the hinterlands hadn't even gone Bolshevik yet. Could this small group of revolutionaries construct a government? The Petrograd-based

French diplomat Louis de Robien thought so in the beginning: "They are perhaps dreamers, but I prefer their dreams to the gross realism of the 'get-out-and-let-me-in' people of the first revolution."[2] Later he changed his tune.

However this group is judged in the end, they loomed up so suddenly on the screen of history (and vanished as suddenly later, by Stalin's hand) that they never registered as ordinary politicos. They've come down more as folk heroes—or villains: Lenin, their leader, somehow rascally, with slanted eyes, full lips, and workingman's cap; Trotsky, the Mephistophelian dandy with burning eyes and goatee; Stalin, the black-haired, mustachioed Georgian in the background, spinning his future web of power; Sverdlov, young, high forehead, pince-nez, black leather from head to toe (he started that look); Kamenev and Zinoviev, Lenin's shadows, the one red-goateed and anxious to please, the other flowing-haired and posturing; Alexandra Kollontai, stately and elegant, upswept curly hair, gentle blue eyes, courageous head of the Zhenotdel (Women's Department) . . .

And then there's the "cultural" Bolshevik, the rumpled, bear-like figure with the receding hairline, pointed goatee, and merry eyes behind his pince-nez, Anatoly Lunacharsky. On the night of October 26, when the Bolsheviks handed out portfolios, Lunacharsky got what had been two, the ministries of education and the court, now joined in the People's Commissariat of Education, or Enlightenment (the Russian word *prosveshchenie* means both things), called Narkompros. Born in Ukraine in 1875, he was one of the most idealistic of the group. He'd converted young to socialism, studied in Switzerland, lived in tsarist exile settlements, and married the nineteen-year-old sister of Alexander Bogdanov, the "God-builder" Bolshevik. Bogdanov's grandiose idea about a religious dimension to Marxism suited Lunacharsky's optimistic nature. But Lunacharsky had other faiths too. Even as he looked to the glowing Marxist future, he found un-Marxist solace in the bourgeois past, in mankind's glorious achievements in culture and art, especially after he left Russia for Europe in 1906 and became an astute arts critic for radical newspapers. Fortunately, he landed in 1912 in Paris, domain of that vibrant émigré enterprise, Diaghilev's Ballets Russes. He preferred its revolutionary aspects, its restoration of the antique roots of dance, or in his words, the "original dramatic ballet," along with the "purity, flexibility, and human grace of the whole dancing body." This, and the future commissar's perception that ballet could handle philosophical questions, moved it in his mind from effete to serious, and changed the fate of the Imperial Theater School.[3]

On becoming commissar, Lunacharsky shouldered his multiple tasks with his usual energy. But he had to tread lightly in the arts. He had to help the people love the arts, get the Bolshevik leaders to pay for them, and persuade the artists themselves to join the revolution.[4] He was rebuffed on all sides. He didn't know the scene—he'd been in Petrograd just since spring. In December of 1917, only a few *intelligenty*—Mayakovsky, Blok, Meyerhold—accepted his invitation to rally for the Bolsheviks, and the bureaucrats resisted. Before Lunacharsky could even enter the Ministry of Education, its coffers were emptied. The teachers' union fought him. The literati looked down on him. His former revolutionary colleagues on Maxim Gorky's paper, *Novaia Zhizn* (New Life), scorned him in print. All wanted autonomy. Lunacharsky wanted cooperation. "The laboring people who are now in charge cannot subsidize a state theater," he admonished them, "if they can't believe that this theater exists not for the entertainment of lords, but for the satisfaction of the cultural needs of the working population, because . . . Democracy should converse with Artists!"[5]

But why should Artists converse with Democracy (code word for Bolsheviks) when these artists had managed their own institutions very well over eight revolutionary months? Petrograd State Theaters chief Batiushkov refused even to meet the new commissar, then gave away his leftover budget money to performers. Lunacharsky merely fired Batiushkov, but he arrested Mariinsky opera chief Alexander Siloti, who wouldn't hand over the keys to the imperial box. Well into 1918, the theaters ignored state directives and tried to weather the postrevolutionary storm alone.[6]

Stealing was the Petrograd norm in that lawless winter of 1917–18. Soldiers stole food from their barracks and sold it. Famished citizens ransacked food shops. Individuals were robbed in the streets; the Fontanka embankment near the Theater School was especially dangerous.[7] The still-raging war added to the mess. Negotiations in the Polish town of Brest-Litovsk to end it had broken down in December. The new Foreign Affairs Commissar, Trotsky, couldn't bear to sign the punitive peace treaty. Not just Trotsky but all the Bolsheviks were waiting for the rest of Europe's proletariat to rise up. There were signs that that might be imminent: riots, strikes, and desertions in the French and German armies and Europe's industrial cities. In January, Trotsky tried a stalling tactic, proposing a joint declaration of "no war, no peace." Nonsense, said the German generals and invaded Russia again, seizing Ukraine, Belarus, the Baltics, and even Pskov, 150 miles from Petrograd.[8]

As the weary city geared up once more to defend the revolution, the Theater School closed again, not for ideological reasons but for general emergency. Civil guards needed it for barracks. The former Mariinsky grimly carried on with operas and ballets. But life was askew. At the start of 1918, Lenin jumped the old church-based calendar forward two weeks to catch up with the West. Russian citizens went to sleep in January and woke up in mid-February. The first order of business, though, was eating. To young Balanchivadze, back with his mother and aunt in Bolshaya Moskovskaya Street, the search for food "was fun, to a child . . . at first." (Did he mean fun if you were the only child?) "But finally, your mother sends you for bread, and there's no bread at stores—and that's sort of a novel game too, trying to find a store with bread—until you get really hungry yourself."[9] He often ran across the Fontanka to the school, the reverse of the route he'd once run away on, to see if a notice announced reopening. He met other new classmates. A band of them went out at night to steal fish from the barges on the Fontanka banks. One boy stole a live fish and beat it to death as they ran from a watchman.[10]

But stealing was risky. And Georges's mother and the maternal aunts, who did neither "physical labor" nor "intellectual labor" got only minuscule rations, though Maria would shortly find a job in a Soviet office.[11] So Georges, almost fourteen, sewed saddles, ran messages for banks, played piano in a little movie theater. Did such random labor seem unjust to him? The whole city, once so prosperous and rosy, was plunged into desperate poverty. Those who survived the postrevolutionary famine, disease, and bitter cold tended not to remember dates. Sudden influxes of food or heat were noted sensually, not chronologically. Life revolved around primitive bartering. You were paid for piecework with some matches or a piece of soap, tradable for scraps of food. But getting home from far-flung jobs meant walking hours alone in the cold and dark.

The girls let go from the school couldn't roam as the boys did, but they too learned to do things a ballet education had spared them: stand in a food line, light a stove with chair legs, boil potato peels in water to make soup, mash coffee grounds for "cutlets." Choura Danilova, back in Petrograd with the general's daughter, practiced her new skills in one bedroom of the general's once-grand apartment, cooking on a makeshift wood stove with family huddled around.[12] Lidochka must have learned these tasks too, though the Ivanovs were privy to extra rations and space. During the spring 1918 Brest-Litovsk crisis, Trotsky had begun to conjure the Red Army out of ragtag groups of Red Guards.

He'd persuaded a skeptical Lenin that a modern army couldn't depend on volunteers alone, but needed officers with military tactics and weapons training. Where to find these "specialists" but among the remnants of the old army? By the middle of 1920, 48,000 former tsarist army personnel were serving in the Red Army.[13] Alexander Ivanov, *shtabskapitan* of a "red" armored car division, was one of them.[14]

The Bolsheviks were finally forced by the threat of German occupation to sign the Treaty of Brest-Litovsk in March of 1918, ceding the new Baltic states, Belarus, Poland, and parts of Ukraine to the Germans, together with large chunks of the empire's population, industry, coal mines, and food crops. Many couldn't stand the shame. Even Lenin felt it. Russians "must measure to the very bottom that abyss of defeat, dismemberment, enslavement, and humiliation," he said.[15] And the Germans were still so near! On March 12, the Council of People's Commissars packed up and fled Petrograd for safer ground in Moscow. Moscow became the new capital, and the old imperial city was left to languish.

But all was not lost for Petrograd's culture, since Lunacharsky chose to reside there instead of Moscow, at least for a time. It's been said he was a hopeless administrator, but not when it came to his love affair with Petrograd. He delegated some Moscow tasks, which freed him to face, among myriad other problems, the future of Petrograd's trio of former imperial theaters, the Mariinsky, Mikhailovsky, and Alexandrinsky (later to become the Kirov, Maly, and Pushkin). They were already "nationalized." They'd been founded and administered by the court. Now Lunacharsky cut them loose from the other ex-imperials and made them a subdepartment with one budget (*khozraschet*) and one director, his longtime friend Ivan Vasilievich Ekskuzovich. Ekskuzovich had been an Izmailovsky Guards officer, then an architectural engineer, always a connoisseur of music and theater. His wife was a singer.[16] He turned out to be a wonderful administrator as well, bent on preserving as well as revolutionizing. In that famine-ridden spring of 1918, "Beloved Eksku," as ballet students called him, began the rescue of the Theater School from its regimental occupiers. Lunacharsky helped from above; the school stood at the intersection of his two passions—education and the arts.

The departing soldiers had left a mess, Balanchine remembered.[17] Dust was everywhere; the parquet floors were chopped up; wood for the big stoves was gone. But some kind of ballet training started again, even if students had to put on their old school dress uniforms for class, and over those their tsarist-issue bathrobes plus scarves and gloves. But they could work only in short increments before clustering around one of the makeshift cast-iron wood stoves nicknamed *burzhuiki* (literally "bourgeois ladies"). Lunacharsky even showed up in person among the anxious students. "Don't worry," he said with a tired smile. "Now is a very hard time, but we will keep your school, whatever it takes. Study! Master the art of ballet, so you can use it to serve our people!"[18]

He meant it. It's true that Lunacharsky was an early supporter of Proletkult, the intellectuals' and workers' movement that wanted to throw away the old arts and help the proletariat make the new. Lunacharsky welcomed such experiments. But he wanted even more for the people to enjoy those old arts as much as he did, including the ex-imperial ballet. For this to happen, the old spectacles had to be shown with full casts and scenery. Flooding into theaters were all kinds who'd never dared before to enter—the "dark people" in worn overcoats, leather jackets, peasant kerchiefs: workers, soldiers, sailors, house servants, students, peasants. They got free tickets through army units, factories, and trade unions. Many came from outlying districts on union-sponsored "culture excursions." They came not casually or indifferently, but "with a sort of trembling expectation," as Stanislavsky remembered. Before, the Mariinsky's prerevolutionary audience had exchanged noisy greetings and gossip before the curtain rose. The new audience was deadly silent, as if in a temple, then intensely involved once the performance started. They were a "passionate, exacting, impressionable" audience, Kostrovitskaya wrote.[19] And a puzzled one. They knew nothing of theatrical dance. They asked each other in whispers when the performers would start to speak or sing. Help came in the form of leaflets, guidebooks, annotations on programs, and live "introductions" from the stage. Dancers came from behind the curtain and talked to them. This was crucial, if their once lavishly supported art was not to lose its state subsidy and die.[20]

And the students got a chance to perform alone for the new public. Prominent ballet soloists organized a benefit for the Theater School on April 26, 1918, at the ex-Mikhailovsky Theater.[21] Earlier, the Mikhailovsky had been for French and German plays. But Ekskuzovich was finding new uses for it, such as hosting the ballet children who'd been in effect the private entertainers of tsars and grand dukes. Now even the proletariat could see them in cobbled-together evenings like this. First came a socialist-flavored propaganda skit, "It Was a Dream," written and danced by the older boys, about a sculptor and his capitalist exploiters;[22] then a suite of dances by Mariinsky soloist Leonid Leontiev called *The Seasons*, followed by divertissements, waltzes, pas de deux.

Georges, now fourteen, danced in two of the divertissements, a tarantella for five couples and the pas de trois from *The Fairy Doll*, as one of two sad Pierrots courting a ballerina doll. Or at least he was listed—in a surviving program, both numbers are crossed out. Were they canceled? Still, this is the first time in recorded history that Balanchivadze was given a role with his name attached. It shows how his teachers viewed him: not as a miniature prince, but as a *caractère* dancer and clown. In this time of theater cults and love of masquerade, clowns could be found in many parts of the old and the new tsarist repertory. Fokine's clowns were key modernist figures, cousins of Alexander Blok's and Meyerhold's Silver Age Pierrots, and ultimately of Picasso's Harlequins. Still, it is telling that the first time Georges danced, or would have danced, a featured role, he was meant to embody this archetypal woebegone commentator on life, a figure that would find its way, even if camouflaged, into many of his later ballets and even perhaps his offstage self-image.[23]

Lidochka, by contrast, received a grown-up ballerina part in this school benefit. She appeared in a romantic duet called *Adagio and Waltz*, which the boys' new teacher Viktor Semenov had choreographed to Tchaikovsky's *Nocturne* and Kreisler's *Schön Rosmarin*. Her partner was Semenov's gifted student Mikhail Dudko, two years older. If only someone had photographed them! Dudko the future Soviet male lead, with his blond looks and straight young body; Lidochka the child-woman, black hair and big "Mongolian" eyes (as her contemporaries said), her face with a look of pure expectation.[24] That Semenov would choose a thirteen-year-old to express romantic love offers proof of Lidochka's early maturity. She'd also acquired enough ballet technique to receive into her young body the singing cello phrases of Tchaikovsky's *Nocturne* and the animated pizzicati of the Kreisler waltz. One reviewer noted her "vital, full-blooded poetry."[25]

These strenuous efforts to show dance to the new public didn't stop when the theater season ended in June of 1918. Summer theaters opened again all over the city, despite privations and uncertainty. Scaled-down ballet favorites were offered in summer gardens, city parks, workers' neighborhoods, and army barracks, danced by the youngest and oldest dancers. Soloists joined in—they were paid in chunks of bread. Students were thrilled to dance with their idols.[26]

Even as Petrograders flocked to theaters, the fledgling Bolshevik state was in mortal danger.[27] In the south, old officers and Cossacks had formed the formidable Volunteer Army. In Samara on the Volga, disaffected socialists had created Komuch (Committee of Constituent

Assembly Members), a mini-state also with an army. The Germans were still poised on the western front: they controlled the Ukraine, the Crimea, and parts of the Caucasus. The English and the Japanese had landed forces in the north and far east. Caught in the vast middle were the approximately 50,000 soldiers of the Czechoslovak Legion, Czech nationalists who'd joined the Russian army to fight their Austro-Hungarian rulers, augmented by captured Czech prisoners of war. They were heading home on 259 trains, along the only route open to them: not west toward the still-raging war but east on the Trans-Siberian railroad to the Pacific Ocean. Along the way, they liberated newly Bolshevik towns, a fact which indirectly caused the death of the tsar with his wife and five children. When the trains got too close to the Ural town of Ekaterinburg where the royal family was held, the secret order came from Moscow to kill them.

But the Bolsheviks weren't even secure in the cities. In Petrograd, plotters, from monarchists to anarchists, held clandestine meetings. The peasant-linked Left Socialist Revolutionaries (Left SRs) were especially fractious. They still shared the government with Bolsheviks, but secretly hated their peace treaty and forced grain requisitions from the peasants. In summer 1918, some Left SRs returned to their prerevolutionary terror tactics, assassinating the German ambassador and then some high-profile Bolsheviks in a bid to get Germany to attack again. In late August, a rogue Left SR, Fanny Kaplan, shot Lenin through the neck and almost killed him—or that's the official explanation. A power struggle on high could have been the cause.[28]

The Red Terror was the response. The one-year-old VCheKa secret police (All-Russia Extraordinary Commission for Combating Counter-Revolution and Sabotage), known as the Cheka, stepped up its arrests and shootings of real and imagined enemies, though Petrograd was spared its excesses by the pragmatism of local chief Moisei Uritsky—until his own murder by an SR in August 1918. But even in turmoil, Bolsheviks continued their social engineering. Youth had to be shaped for the glorious future. But how? Debates inside Narkompros delayed the start of the 1918–19 school year.[29] The Theater School was caught in the crossfire: many Bolsheviks wanted to cut loose such an elite imperial training institution. The school, with Lunacharsky as advocate, finally reopened, later than other schools and with its stoves frozen and its rations nonexistent. Theoretically, it had been brought into the system, outfitted at last with the regulation seven-year high school curriculum. Practically, its future was shaky indeed.

But Lunacharsky and Ekskuzovich were a strong team, in mid-fall 1918 managing to reopen not just the Theater School but its dormitories and kitchens too, an event that saved the careers of Lidochka, Georges, and their whole generation. Lunacharsky had done some horse-trading behind the scenes. He'd taken over the unused space on the school's third floor, former site of a tsarist drama school, and installed there the new Narkompros School of Drama, where students boarded. That allowed him to put the ballet students back into *their* dormitories and divert enough rations to feed them three scant meals a day instead of breakfast alone, as in other high schools.[30] Placing the people's Drama School inside the old Theater School also put the idea of theater back into ballet, thus neutralizing the school's imperial associations and yoking it to the postrevolutionary theater mania. In Petrograd especially, the newly empowered lower classes were crazy about theater, not just seeing it but doing it. This was predictable. The amateur theater movement dated back to the early twentieth century, when gentry pioneers had devoted their lives to helping the people know the joys of putting on a show.[31] Then too, theater could "speak" more directly to the semiliterate masses than books or newspapers. After 1917, every factory, trade union, workers' club, and Red Army cell, it seemed, had formed a theater group and built, borrowed, or improvised a stage to perform on. "All Russia is acting," wrote Viktor Shklovsky. "Some kind of elemental process is taking place where the living fabric of life is being transformed into the theatrical."[32] But where were the worker-actors to people those stages? Applications both semiliterate and erudite flooded in for the new Drama School.[33]

Lunacharsky himself attended its opening on October 12, 1918.[34] One can picture him in his worker's cap and little glasses, standing on the school steps in front of the red banners, flanked by three of the city's beloved actors and surrounded by newly admitted students. "There are epochs when not just statesmen but whole peoples move human history forward!" he shouted to his teenaged audience. "And for Youth, endowed by nature with the love of risk and novelty, this is *your* time, the happiest time, the time to realize your dreams!" The ballet students too had come out from their dormitories to hear this Bolshevik paean to youth. Both Mikhailov and Kostrovitskaya pegged the moment as the start of ballet's resurrection via theater.[35] Balanchivadze was there too, pale, black-haired, now almost fifteen, stubbornly wearing his frayed imperial uniform with the silver lyre on its velvet collar.[36] To sixteen-year-old aspiring actor Yuri Slonimsky, Balanchivadze and the other young dancers seemed like elegant hosts welcoming rude guests. And so they were, in a way. If the acting school was taking in social classes and "nationalities" barred from imperial drama training (Slonimsky, for instance, was a Jew), the ballet school was taking back its old elite population (few Jews among them). Lunacharsky's vision had plucked these ballet orphans out of an already receding past and placed them squarely in a utopian future.

Maybe the glimmer of this thought came to Georges then. But it was the near future that worried him. Four days earlier, on October 8, 1918, he and his mother had received the precious Exit Passport No. 4385 from the Commissariat of Internal Affairs. Permission to travel out of the country—effectively, to emigrate—had been impossible to get for a year. This document authorized "Citizen Maria Nikolaevna Balanchivadze, office-worker in a department of the Petrograd 'Sovdep,' residing at 1–3 Bolshaya Moskovskaya [Aunt Nadia's address], to travel with her fourteen-year-old son, Georgi, to husband and children." It assigned her a border crossing at either Orsha or Kursk, forbade her to take more than 1,000 rubles out of the country, and demanded her and her son's return to Petrograd within a year.[37]

By now almost all the ex-Petrograd Balanchivadzes had reached Georgia: Meliton himself, Tamara, Aunt Mila, Uncle Ivan, and Andrei. Only Apollon was still in Russia; he'd joined one of the pro-monarchy White armies.[38] And the little country had been independent since May 1918. Its government was socialist, but of the milder Menshevik strain, which did not sit well with Moscow. The Bolsheviks also hated the support Georgia received from the enemy Germans.[39] In this precarious situation, Georgia needed cultural heroes, and Meliton Balanchivadze, folkloric specialist, musical educator, and composer of the first (still unfinished) Georgian opera, was an obvious choice. Naturally, he wanted his wife and missing son there too, in a city where cafes and restaurants were thriving. Georgia was a breadbasket compared to Petrograd.

Maria and Georgi came very close this time to leaving, thus altering the history of twentieth-century ballet. They chose again to stay. Which of them took the lead this time is hard to say, but the passport itself is revealing. Maria Balanchivadze didn't fill it out, fourteen-year-old Georges did. He signed for her by proxy, in a small, even hand. That doesn't mean he wanted emigration more, only that he could already handle a complicated bureaucratic transaction, whether at his initiative or her request. Maybe the reawakening of his once-hated profession in the unlikely hands of the Bolsheviks prompted their decision. Maybe it was Lunacharsky's stirring words about youth and dreams. Maria didn't go alone, either; she would stay in Petrograd for three more years.[40] Despite what Balanchine later implied about his mother's indifference, she stayed mostly for him, though other factors may have influenced her too: her mother (if that's who the mysterious "Babulia" was), her cousins, the city itself. Ironically, mother and son might have ended up in a closer bond if they'd left together for Georgia. Balanchine doesn't mention her again, nor do his peers. From this moment on, Maria, though only blocks away, ceased to play a decisive role in Georges's life. Whether she disappeared from his psyche is another story.

But their last-minute decision caused a problem: Georges wasn't registered for the school dormitory. He's not on the official boarders list drawn up on November 1, 1918, when the school's name was changed to the Petrograd State Theater (Ballet) School of the Department of Property of the Republic of the Council of People's Commissars of the Russian Republic.[41] Thirty-three students are listed, twenty girls and thirteen boys, including Lidochka, her fellow Preobrazhenskaya protégées, and the boys Georges had run wild with in the streets of Petrograd.[42] How did Georges manage, when Bolshevik regulations required an official domicile? To his rescue came Grigory Isaenko, the eccentric schoolmaster who'd looked after him since his first traumatic day at the school, the one reported to be in love with him. Despite being of respectable tsarist rank before the revolution, Isaenko had been promoted after it to school inspector, second in command. He'd received a coveted apartment in the building, earlier inhabited by the infirmary doctor but reassigned in early 1918 when the infirmary closed. Isaenko became Georges's official sponsor, though it's unlikely the boy actually slept in Isaenko's rooms on the boys' floor. Those rooms were in perpetual disorder. Isaenko kept piles of old newspapers and magazines. He would appear in his doorway in a large threadbare bathrobe. Still, students loved him: his gruff manner masked an excess of affection. Georges probably lived in the dormitory with his classmates while accepting part of Isaenko's rations. In their memories he's there with them, as their new stripped-down life began on the premises of the old.

On all the home fronts, the population was exhorted to sacrifice for victory. The Red Army laid first claim on the scant resources of a land where crops were hoarded, trains were broken, and factories were collapsing. Despite these daunting conditions, some minuscule but key improvements reached the Theater School at the end of the 1918–19 school year. The figure responsible was its new director Andrei Alexandrovich Oblakov, who took over in March of 1919. Oblakov was tall and gaunt, with stooped shoulders and a drooping mustache. He'd been a dancer in the Mariinsky, as had his father before him.[43] Oblakov himself, though, had been dismissed from the theater early because he was close to the radical group who'd struck in the 1905 revolution. He'd gone abroad and danced for Diaghilev's Ballets Russes. Now back in revolutionary Russia, he moved with his pianist sister, Ekaterina, into the apartment below Isaenko's, which opened onto the girls' floor.[44]

With his "burzhui" appearance, Oblakov seemed an unlikely type to wrest material sustenance from the Bolshevik bureaucracy. But his flair became apparent as he settled in. His first acquisition: more wood to heat the big dance rooms. "We carry logs; the stoves work in the dancing rooms; we begin again to learn to dance," is how Kostrovitskaya summed up the start of the 1919–20 school year.[45] A former dancer himself, Oblakov knew what dangers awaited young dancers who exerted themselves in the cold. Tendons can snap, muscles go brittle. Without warmth, no dancer can bring a body to the physical state needed to learn. Once the dance classrooms warmed up, Oblakov tackled what seemed the opposite problem. He walked through the halls and sniffed the musty air. Could the enormous windows be opened? "Impossible! It's already freezing! The children will be sick!" exclaimed Varvara Likhosherstova on the girls' floor (even the Bolsheviks hadn't dislodged her). "Fresh air is always good," replied Oblakov, and the windows were opened. The metaphoric implications didn't escape the students. "The revolution flung open the windows and doors of the aging school," wrote Mikhailov later with Soviet-style ardor, "and the wave of fresh air rushed into the dance halls, the long corridors, the dark corners."[46]

For Georges, Lidochka, and their classmates, picking up where they'd left off was the first order of business. This was more straightforward for the boys than the girls. They'd already studied with Viktor Semenov, albeit with interruptions, since the fall of 1917, when they'd passed from the Junior Division to the Middle. Nobody liked Semenov in the classroom, even if they admired him onstage. Still, they settled back in their routine, carrying their logs to their dance room, starting in at the barre in first position. These fourteen-year-olds, warming themselves back into life, already knew what they needed from a ballet teacher.

For Lidochka and her classmates, things were complicated. Sometime in the spring of 1918, their inspirational teacher, Olga Preobrazhenskaya, had left them.[47] She'd had to keep the students in her private school alive; she'd also returned to the stage. Even before the Bolshevik takeover, Preobrazhenskaya had put herself in the front ranks of dancers

Lidochka in school uniform.

Courtesy Carl Taggersell.

trying to win over the new audiences. In the summer of 1917, she'd gone on a two-month tour of the Russian south with her beloved pianist friend, Alexander Labinsky. She gave solo performances on all kinds of makeshift stages. After the October Revolution she redoubled her efforts, performing in workers' clubs, trade union halls, and amateur theaters, even if her misgivings grew about the new regime.[48] While she was gone, the ubiquitous Viktor Semenov took over the Middle Division girls' class too, teaching not just Lidochka but the other promising Middle Division girls. In the spring 1919 graduating concert, he displayed them in *Fantaisie Chorégraphique* set to the music of Glinka.[49]

Lidochka was his favorite. Even if she now wore the gray dancing dress instead of the imperial pink—the Bolsheviks did not favor social distinctions—her talent stood out. Semenov's romantic duet for her the previous spring was proof. But she didn't like studying with him. She asked and was allowed to transfer to the class of an older teacher, Zinaida Frolova, sweetly encouraging but undynamic.[50] But all was not lost, since in early 1919 Oblakov coaxed Preobrazhenskaya back. The small ex-ballerina was now forty-seven, but still in dancing shape. She took up her mentoring again to the girls she'd formed since their first days. She demanded again technical precision and expressive arms, and short original dances at the end of class.

Since Preobrazhenskaya herself was a choreographer—she had often composed her "Petipa" variations, and other dancers' too—it's worth noting how she worked.[51] Georges's classmate Mikhailov saw one of her concerts at the Liteiny Theater, a longtime amateur stage still run by the old theater enthusiast Pavel Gaideburov. Watching, he forgot that she was "the same small, not young, not beautiful woman" he'd passed daily in the school corridors. On a bare stage with only the piano, backed by dark blue curtains and wearing a simple gray chiffon tunic, Preobrazhenskaya danced her own Grieg, Chopin, and Scriabin dances in the manner of Isadora Duncan, free-flowing, not classical. To the Grieg piece, she offered a dance sketch in which she evoked, by means of gestures and rhythms, each member of a peasant family—heavy, doubting father; impatient, headstrong son; mother kicking up her heels in a folk dance. It contained "all the joy in the world," wrote Mikhailov. The Chopin Prelude "contained all the sorrow," as she danced a grieving woman who'd lost her lover to the war and was bringing flowers to his grave. Mikhailov thought her emotional depth unequaled, except later by the younger ballerina Elena Lukom, and even later by her own student, Lida Ivanova.[52]

Preobrazhenskaya is known today in the West primarily as a Petipa favorite and later a brilliant ballet teacher in Paris, but she must also be counted among revolutionary-era dance experimenters. She'd seen Isadora Duncan perform in 1904–5. She'd been on the spot as Fokine searched for his art nouveau innovations—she'd originated the Prelude in his 1907 *Chopiniana*, called *Les Sylphides* in the West. Now in the early years of the revolution, before Duncan herself returned to Russia in 1921 to found a school, this small ex-ballerina-crony of the tsar was exploring the Duncan spirit. Inscribed in Preobrazhenskaya's body was ballet's old, court-flavored language. But she'd adapted that body to a different task: communicating something simple and true to a mass of non-connoisseurs. Her vision contained a modernism that Balanchine himself would later adopt: no décor or fancy costumes, just a body. She asked the same of her students, inviting them to rethink the meaning of classroom steps and gestures. Not only Georges and Lidochka owed a debt to her but all the others who stayed in Russia to create Leningrad's Kirov Ballet.

In the fall of 1919, Georges, Lidochka, and their classmates settled back, with the help of the big stoves, into the routine of ballet class. Much had been lost, but something had been gained: a sense that their training regimen was worth saving; that they were responsible for the future of the art. And not in the classroom alone. They danced more than ever at the ex-Mariinsky State Theater, where operas and ballets were offered in the hardest times. Ballet performances were even increased. In the imperial schedule, forty or so ballets were usual for a season. In the early Bolshevik years, more ballet performances were added, till by 1919–20 sixty or seventy graced a season.[53] That's not counting the shows dancers gave in the workers' clubs, factories, and army barracks.

And the repertory was varied. Eighteen different ballets were shown in the 1918–19 season alone: old favorites like *Giselle, Swan Lake, The Sleeping Beauty*, and ballets nowadays mostly forgotten—*Esmeralda, Bluebeard, Le Halte de Cavalerie, Le Talisman*, and Fokine's parable *Eros*. In the 1919–20 season, six more ballets were retooled and put back on the stage, several of them imbued with the *commedia dell'arte* atmosphere so crucial to those times and also to Balanchine's later career: Petipa's *Harlequinade*, Ivanov's *The Nutcracker* (with its *commedia*-flavored toys), Fokine's *Carnaval*.[54]

Georges, Lidochka, and their school friends danced all the ex-Mariinsky performances, often replacing corps de ballet members who'd fled Russia. They had to learn fast and keep a large number of steps in their memories. Or else they watched from the wings. They saw the magnetism of the only officially ranked ballerina of those difficult years, Elena Smirnova, a brunette beauty, especially sultry when she danced *Esmeralda*'s gypsy. Smirnova was partnered by Georges's teacher, the catlike Semenov, or by the younger princely Piotr Vladimirov. They admired the younger ballerinas coming up: Elizaveta Gerdt, with her icy elegance—"wonderful, like crystal," Balanchine said later; the winsome Elena Lukom; the effervescent Elsa Vill; the melancholy Olga Spessivtseva. They saw the great *caractère* and *grotesque* dancers of the day transforming their bodies into hunchbacks, wizards, evil fairies, helpless clowns—Leonid Leontiev, the comic Ivan-Durak in *The Little Humpbacked Horse*; Alexander Chekrygin, *The Sleeping Beauty*'s evil Carabosse.

It wasn't easy for the theater to mount these performances. Ekskuzovich scrounged for the simplest materials: paint and glue for the scenery, makeup for faces, the pointe shoes that had been imported from Europe before the revolution. The female dancers wore out their remaining pointe shoes, falling over their feet. The dancers were as hungry, cold, and sick as the audience. In 1919 Ekskuzovich addressed the situation through an inventive agreement with the Red Army: dancers and singers performed for the soldiers; soldiers shared rations with the theaters.[55] Performances started at 6 or 6:30, so the audience could get home to their makeshift iron *burzhuika* stoves. Meanwhile these soldiers, peasants, and workers sat like lumps, bundled in multiple coats, blankets, fur hats, and felt boots, but grateful to be taken out of their daily struggle. Dancers in the wings threw off coats and blankets just before they ran onstage. Dancing, they could see the steam of their breaths. Smirnova once danced all of *The Fairy Doll* with big leggings over her tights, a sweater over her bodice, and a shawl wrapped on top.[56]

For the ballet children, the biggest challenge was getting home at night from the theater. Their court coaches were long gone. The city's trams had no petrol. At first they went on foot with a teacher, for safety. But it's not a short walk between the two points: to cross the canals one must loop around back streets to bridges. Once when Balanchivadze and Mikhailov missed the group's departure, they walked home alone, saw someone shot, and ran opposite ways, each thinking the other wounded. A little later Ekskuzovich located some ancient wooden carts in a theatrical storehouse. These *lineiki*, or "Babylonian contraptions," as Kostrovitskaya called them, waited at the stage door when the shows finished late. They were black and long, with a lengthwise black wall down the center. The children climbed up wide side steps to sit back to back against this wall, twelve on each side, facing into the street. On a front pedestal sat a coachman in a big coat and top hat. A "pitiful old half-starved nag" (*kliachka*) pulled them.[57]

Kostrovitskaya's description of the *lineikas* highlights not just their quaintness but also their riders' high spirits. On the shorter route through the seedy Sennaia Ploshchad (Haymarket Square—Dostoevsky territory), homeless street kids would shout at the coachman to "take those kids to the dumping ground!" The children liked this, but the coachman didn't, so he mostly took them the long way, up the once splendid Bolshaya Morskaya Street with its deserted palaces to the 25th of October (formerly Nevsky) Prospekt. The spectacle of their city's frozen grandeur caused delight. "We all fell into the lyrical mode," wrote Kostrovitskaya, "and started to call out, in unison, lines from a poem we all knew by Alexander Blok that paid tribute to their beautiful city, 'Petersburg, snowy twilight, a glance at the street, roses in the house . . .'"[58]

The city had lost more than half its former two million inhabitants to disease, to flight, to the villages where there was a chance of finding food. The Belgian-born son of revolutionary Russian exiles, Victor Serge, arriving in January 1919, was shocked at the desolation. "The broad, straight thoroughfares, the bridges astride the Neva, now a river of snowy ice, seemed to belong to an abandoned city," he wrote; "first a gaunt soldier in a gray greatcoat, then after a long time a woman freezing under her shawls, went past like phantoms in an oblivious silence." He called it "the metropolis of Cold, of Hunger, of Hatred, and of Endurance."[59] But to the ballet children heading home on their *lineika*, this same city was a theatrical backdrop of unearthly beauty, and they were onstage in the surprisingly joyous play called their lives. After years in strict gender seclusion, they were shouting poetry in unison.

"It wasn't always grim!" Balanchine himself later said, meaning life inside the school.[60] Even with the numbing cold everywhere but the dancing rooms, the dubious bread and blackened potatoes, the scarce wood, the typhus-bearing lice that had to be picked off bodies, the boils on skin from malnutrition (Danilova had four, Georges thirty), the students shared sensations at a depth rarely experienced.[61] Living in close proximity, they formed a primitive tribe. Boys and girls were still relegated to separate floors, but both groups moved their beds out of the dormitory halls to the former infirmaries, to sleep close for warmth. Sooty iron *burzhuiki* were set up there by the old priest Pugulevsky who'd turned handyman. Their pipes fed out through open windows. These hazardous little stoves were all over Petrograd in those years, puffing out smoke through the broken windows of palaces. The children grew closer in their gender-segregated groups, but in the dining room boys and girls ate together. Separate squads of girls and boys prepared the meals, but the boys of the Students' Committee (the Uchenicheskyi

Komitet, or UchKom) supervised. They'd devised a technique for cutting the bread into equal pieces—*osmushki* of 1/8 pound each—so the crumbs weren't lost. The old imperial training institution had become, almost by accident, a paragon of Bolshevik education. Everything in Lunacharsky's ideal was there: coeducation (in rehearsals), active participation in school life (the UchKom election), "exploration of labor through simple physical tasks" (ballet class!).[62]

The UchKom student committee had been chosen in a full student body meeting on October 8, at the beginning of the 1919–20 school year. This was the bleakest time of all for the Bolshevik state. Former imperial White commanders were advancing on its shrunken territory: toward Moscow came General Denikin from the south and Admiral Kolchak from the east. General Yudenich, based in now-independent Finland and Estonia, was marching toward Petrograd. Trotsky, who'd augmented and stiffened his newborn Red Army, deployed it against all these enemies. He himself raced, in a special armored train containing weapons, pamphlets, strategy room, and movie theater, among far-flung trouble spots. In mid-October 1919, Yudenich's forces made it to Gatchina, twelve miles from Petrograd. Lenin turned fatalistic about the city's fate, but Trotsky sped there to inspire another last-ditch effort, and the Reds beat Yudenich back. The second anniversary of the Bolshevik Revolution, November 7, 1919, became a victory celebration.

Even hounded from outside, the new Soviet order spawned committees, delegations, commissions, departments, and subsections of departments in an attempt to instantly democratize daily life. The Theater School's UchKom was part of this, staffed by the boys, voted on at least by the girls. Balanchivadze, liked by everyone, was a member. Once formed, the UchKom promptly ordered another general meeting, where even the youngest girls spoke out for the first time about the petty humiliations of the old school life. The license to put such things in words was exhilarating. As time went on, the UchKom expanded its duties. It thought up special projects, such as mixing with the drama students. If something was left over from ballet rations, the UchKom boys put it into jars and took it upstairs. The drama students came downstairs to take *caractère* dance with the teacher inventing the curriculum, Alexander Shiriaev. The ballet students received parts in the drama students' productions. Georges, who loved to transform himself with stage makeup and gestures, played an old servant in Chekhov's *The Bear* to Choura Danilova's landlady, and another old servant, Karp, in Ostrovsky's *The Forest*. That production was so successful it got a showing in the former Alexandrinsky. Lidochka played lead roles; she loved the stage. The once-empty school theater on the third floor was busy with rehearsals and performances.

On free evenings, the UchKom gathered the ballet students alone for ballroom dancing, games, songs, poetry. That's where the boys and girls deepened their friendships. Lidochka and Georges "performed" at these. She sang the passionate Russian romances, earlier forbidden. "I'm in Columbine dress/a red fan in my hand/You're in Harlequin clothes/with a pointed fool's cap . . ." went one of the favorites.[63] She had a small, true soprano and would soon study opera. Georges played the piano. Even without the UchKom's initiative, the students put on plays. They even acted out D.W. Griffith's silent film *Intolerance* in the washrooms. Sometime in the winter of 1919–20, Lunacharsky had given them a rare treat: he'd opened the city's vast unheated Splendide Palace movie theater on Karavannaia St. especially for them, and screened D.W. Griffith's multiple-story-track epic. They forgot the theater's icy air as "the Assyrian forces, with the tsar, Belshazzar, in the lead, with torches . . . came on the screen," in flickering black and silver, "and the Mountain Girl . . . exultant in victory . . . And suddenly, the luxury of Paris restaurants and suspicious haunts—the fight for survival on the lowest edges of Paris. And again, the Babylonian war—amazing, riveting us for three and more hours!" Fifty years later, Kostrovitskaya still remembered the thrill. In washroom recreations of Assyrian Babylon, Lidochka took the part of the Mountain Girl. The Mountain Girl's longed-for prince was Balanchivadze.[64]

Against all odds, it was probably the happiest time in both their lives. They were fifteen in the fall, sixteen in the spring. If not in love with Lidochka, Georges was in awe of her. She was restless, inquisitive, marked for future stardom. But she looked up to him too. He was favored by his teachers, even if too thin, pale, and dreamily absent-minded to think of courting her. But nobody was courting anybody yet. Or rather, more important than pairs was the life of the group, which had caught fire. These ballet students drew closer to each other in proportion to the severity of that struggle. They coped together. That was their job: to become individually creative and collectively selfless, as befitted the new Soviet man and woman. And in the former Imperial School, where girls and boys had been prudishly kept apart, there was special joy in discovering real comrades of the opposite sex.[65]

Just how comradely they'd grown emerged one miraculous night in this coldest-yet winter of 1919–20. Batiushka Pigulevsky, even if he wasn't a priest any more—the school chapel lasted till early 1922, but no one could officiate—had already atoned for his former haughtiness by putting the stoves in the infirmaries. Now he roamed outdoors while students were in school, searching the city's outskirts for work projects he could "contract out" to the UchKom's brigade of boys, which included Balanchivadze, Mikhailov, Lavrovsky, and others. Evenings, he brought the boys back to these sites, to saw logs off old fences or clean up garbage from basements. They earned loaves of bread, herring heads, frozen potatoes. When such work dwindled, Batiushka looked for anything "carelessly secured," even the checkerboard wooden *shashki* street pavings, which the brigades could remove under cover of darkness. On the freezing night in question, the boys discovered, in a ruined basement, two half-buried cases of Georges Borman chocolate, a local luxury brand. Instead of eating it on the spot, they brought it home—and played Santa Claus. They carefully cracked the glass in the door to the girls' infirmary, took off their boots so as not to wake the sleepers, climbed through the hole, and left chocolate slabs on the girls' beds, marked as to each person's portion. In the morning the girls woke up to this. "The taste of chocolate had been forgotten for a long time," is how Kostrovitskaya put it.[66] Punishment was threatened. The boys had broken the only rule still sacrosanct: gender segregation at night. But cooler adult heads prevailed.

A few vestiges of the old school remained, notably the punitive Varvara Likhosherstova. She was still the girls' head inspectress; she still got the youngest to curtsy to her in the halls and ask permission to go to the toilet in French (*puis-je aller là-bas?*). But her power was waning, like the evil fairy Carabosse of *The Sleeping Beauty*. She could be overruled by Oblakov or Isaenko, both now above her in the chain of command. If those gentlemen went to her apartment to confer, students heard shouting. If she was abroad in the halls when an UchKom evening began, she would slip away like a ghost. But by now she was almost alone. Starting in spring,1919, the school was directed by a small group of odd and singular adults who didn't meddle in the Uchkom's self-governing activities, but merely offered tactful guidance. Each had arrived by a different route. The former school porter, Pyotr Kuzmich Shatilov, who'd stood for years in tsarist livery at the school's door, had been a secret Bolshevik. He was now Deputy Director of Administration. But instead of punishing students for his years of servitude, he wrangled what extra rations he could. "We owed the welfare of our daily lives in this difficult time to Shatilov," wrote Mikhailov.[67] The new porter who replaced him, Stepan Khristophorovich (surname unknown— the boys called him Khristofor Kolumbych), jumped into school life too, raising and lowering the curtain for student plays. He was mad about the theater.[68]

Varvara Likhosherstova and Theater School Girls.
Courtesy Saint-Petersburg State Museum of Theater and Music.

Another colorful soul, Alexander Viktorovich Shiriaev, taught *caractère* dance, which meant any nonclassical style, including balletic folk dance, and also the exaggerated rendering of clowns, Harlequins, witches, or sorcerers known as the *grotesque* genre. But Shiriaev by implication taught much more. He was fifty-one in 1918 when he'd returned from Europe. He had what Slonimsky remembered as a patrician

Roman profile and a bandy-legged, thickset, and expressive body, and his heritage was one of pure theater. He was the grandson of the Italian-born ballet composer Cesare Pugni, who'd created the music for canonical ballets like *Esmeralda*, *The Little Humpbacked Horse*, and *Carnival in Venice*. He himself had been a brilliant *caractère* dancer in the old Mariinsky, the original Buffoon of the 1892 *Nutcracker*, and Petipa's trusted assistant. He knew the old repertory, not just from rehearsing it but from filming it too. In 1904–5, Shiriaev had spent "an amazing amount of money," in Fedor Lopukhov's words, for a movie camera, and proposed to record the great dancers of his time (Kshesinskaya, Pavlova, Preobrazhenskaya).[69] The Imperial Theaters declined: the new *kino* was lower-class entertainment.[70] But Shiryaev persisted, replacing dancers with puppets he made himself, manipulating their joints frame by camera frame—wearing out a groove in the parquet floor between puppets and camera—then projecting them into motion. He recorded the repertory on a miniature stage he made.[71] Saddened at ballet's small-mindedness after Petipa, he'd left Russia with wife and children in 1909 and danced in Europe. When he returned in 1918, with only his son (his daughter had tragically drowned), he was given a room in the school and put to work by Oblakov creating the school's first *caractère* curriculum.

Shiriaev was important to all the students, but especially Balanchivadze, who learned from him to assume the characters of servants and the other colorful characters he loved to portray. Students thought Shiriaev a reincarnation of one of the ballet's Hoffmanesque characters, a Drosselmeyer or Coppelius. They were drawn to his mysterious room full of stage masks from forgotten ballets, musical instruments, antique landscapes, ballet engravings, old theater posters, objects from Asia and Africa, and an aquarium with brightly colored fish.[72] Isaenko in *his* apartment was just as eccentric. "If a door opened slightly and disclosed—a stomach, we knew Isaenko would appear," wrote Kostrovitskaya. This short fat man with "flabby swollen features and watery eyes" also knew about the theater and theater life; he'd once booked tours for the Imperial Alexandrinsky. "My dear," he told the girls, "you must learn to glitter without spangles; *with* them even a fool can shine."[73] For the older boys, he thought up puns and quips and a nonsense game. Meeting one in the hall he would point his finger and say, "Dear boy . . . go there! Die!" The boy was supposed to throw himself to the floor, then get up as bidden or be left lying while Isaenko went about his business. They were afraid of "Grishka," yet knew he was their friend. He'd been there, after all, from the beginning. At one

point, Georges got too old for the "Die" game and told the older n
that he would rather die for real than lie down. Isaenko slunk away.

Oblakov, their chief, was as otherworldly as they and even more ge
erous. He offered his own apartment as a salon where students coul
ask the questions suppressed in earlier times. In the evenings, his ta
stooped form would appear in his doorway on the girls' floor and "with
a shy smile" he would invite them in, to sit among the antique furniture,
rare books, and old Indian and Russian fabrics. The younger girls and
boys came separately and voiced opinions on school life. The older students came later, boys and girls together. "In the apartment it was cold,
half-dark, the electricity in the whole city was only working at half-
capacity," remembered Kostrovitskaya. "But it wasn't about that! We sat
at a round table, beautifully set with ancient porcelain, to drink tea
made of dried carrots, little patties [*lepioshki*] made of potato skins, and
listened to theater tales about the works of Fokine or the dancing of
'Annochka' Pavlova, as Oblakov called her." The Oblakovs lent their
books to students. Ekaterina Oblakova played the grand piano—
Stravinsky, Debussy, Ravel—the modernist music of Europe rarely
heard in Russia.[75]

Quixotic and surprisingly steely Oblakov, "the quietest person in the
school," said Kostrovitskaya, was interested as much in intellect as
dancing. He hired new teachers to make classes interesting. He invited
young painters, actors, and musicians in to talk with his dancers. Isaenko
felt the same; it was he who'd first noticed sixteen-year-old Yuri Slonimsky at the drama school and brought him into the closed world of ballet,
telling the youth that learning ballet was a "prerequisite" for acting. Balanchivadze gave Slonimsky dance lessons and smuggled him backstage.
The young actor fell in love with the art and brought along his Bohemian painter-buddies, Vladimir Dmitriev and Boris Erbshtein. He'd
bonded with the pair in 1918 on a train home from a ballet performance
in Pavlovsk, when he'd noticed their odd mix of peasant shirts and old
jackets. Dmitriev was blond, with high cheekbones and steely gray eyes;
Erbshtein was swarthy, long-faced, kindly. Both were delighted to
observe especially the girl students firsthand. Dmitriev put on dance
britches and joined the lesson. Oblakov made sure all three were welcome, despite icy looks from Likhosherstova.[76]

It was Oblakov who'd given the students the Blok poem they
shouted out from the *lineika*. He promoted all the Silver Age poets,
but especially Mayakovsky, icon of the revolution, the tall boisterous
man with the shaved head and plebian suit. Balanchivadze in particular took to Mayakovsky and became a walking encyclopedia of his

verses, absorbing their peculiar duality: their revolutionary machismo coexisting with the Pierrot-like moans of unrequited love. Balanchine described himself all his life with the Mayakovskian phrase, a "cloud in pants." Oblakov met privately with the most talented of his charges, especially Georges, Lidochka, and Nina Mlodzinskaya, a beautiful dark-haired ballerina-to-be. He was listener, advisor, and counselor, probing to find out what interested them, what they dreamed of. He steered them to certain music. He looked the other way when the boys snuck out at night to dance in movie houses for half-loaves of bread. He wanted his students to see themselves as artists. He hoped for choreographers.[77]

With his encouragement, both Lida and Georges began to find their adult identities. Lida read books on art history and ballet history; she wanted to see how dance stars had fared in other times and places. Her father, who'd kept up his contacts in the art world, took her to experimental plays, arts exhibitions, poetry readings, even to the famous House of the Arts, the half-ruined palace on the Moika Canal that Maxim Gorky had wrangled as living quarters for writers and artists. Viktor Shklovsky lived there, and Mandelstam. Young Lidochka asked them questions. She sought out the dance critic-philosopher Akim Volynsky, who knew about her from her teacher Preobrazhenskaya. One day, in front of his seat at the ex-Mariinsky, "a very young girl with her braid undone and slightly Mongolian features in her lovely face . . . curtsied, and introduced herself," he remembered after Lidochka's death.[78] He invited her to the private ballet school he'd just started himself. Her father brought her. She did a few steps at the barre for Volynsky's head teacher, ex-soloist Nikolai Legat, then astonished them both with two airborne *saut de basque* leaps across the floor of the practice room. Men jumped like this, not ballerinas. But Lidochka wanted to be a ballerina of the future.[79]

Georges's case was more complicated. Inside the school, he'd cultivated a persona that was detached and a little mysterious. He'd won his elders' special support and protection. He'd found at the school, in fact, the close family that eluded him in life, with admiring classmate siblings and quite a few fathers. But the longing for his real parents never went away. Music was synonymous in Georges's mind with his real father, who'd been lost to him in 1909 when the boy was lodged in the Theater School. Now Meliton wrote to his son from the Caucasus, urging him to become a musician. Georges was split in his own mind between dance and music. In January 1920, he enrolled in his father's old school, the Petrograd Conservatory, in the piano class of revered old Sofia Frantsevna

Tsurmiulen (Zur Mühlen), a student of the Polish-born pianist Theodor Leschetizky, himself a student of Carl Czerny, of piano exercises fame.[80] Georges saw his teacher once a week: the Conservatory was across the street from the ex-Mariinsky. He did his piano practicing at his own school, warming his hands with gloves he'd cut the fingers out of. Isaenko made sure the other music students stayed away when he was playing.[81] The pieces he prepared were virtuosic: Weber's *Rondo Brillante*, a Beethoven sonata in E flat major, Bach's E major Prelude and Fugue, Arensky's "Bakhchisarai Fountain," a Chopin A flat minor waltz and C minor étude ("Revolutionary"), a piano "novelette" by Schumann, and Tchaikovsky's "Chanson Triste." Georges was also known as a prodigious improviser, and even composed some songs.[82]

But he started to choreograph too in that spring of 1920, in an unexpected style. He had already been given his *emploi* (as the Russians say) as a dancer, his future style. He wasn't destined to be a prince. His legs were too thin and his style histrionic. He was better as a buffoon or wild virtuoso, or so his teachers thought, and he agreed. "I wanted to be dashing—leaping and turning," he told Taper later. "I wanted to have more character, like what I now hate. I used to love primitive kind of thing—kind of Turkish, Persian prince, harem dances, national dances. Dagger dances. Saber dances."[83] (Georgian dances! In the 1921 graduation concert, Shiriaev would make a Georgian *lezginka* for him.[84]) Such *caractère* flair no doubt earned him praise in ballet class. In the fall of 1919, when his class moved to the Senior Division, Leonid Leontiev, the soon-to-be Petrushka, taught them until he got too busy running the theater. Then another great *caractère* dancer, Alexander Chekrygin, took over and brought the boys to graduation in 1921. Both men could have reinforced Georges's love of this wild virtuosity.

But Georges didn't make a *caractère* solo for himself, even if ballet training usually prompts young choreographers to work first on their own bodies. He made instead a dance for two bodies not his own, a woman's and a man's.[85] Nor did he choose a dashing piece of music like the ones he liked to dance to; he used the most sentimental number imaginable: the violin and piano sonata in B flat by his father's old mentor, Anton Rubinstein, all yearning arpeggios and swooning chromatics. It's known as *Noch* (*Night*), after the Pushkin poem fitted to its melody, which is what Georges called the piece. To dance it, he invited another Preobrazhenskaya student a year below him, Olga Mungalova, and his close friend from the same younger class, Piotr Gusev (though he himself would dance its first performance). They worked behind closed doors, with only Oblakov and Isaenko allowed in. But the whole school knew what was happening. Kostrovitskaya claims that *Night* debuted in 1920 in the school's theater, and Oblakov hired a young violinist to play for it. Mikhailov sets *Night*'s premiere in summer 1920, at a vacation village students were sent to. Whenever it first appeared, *Night* surprised its viewers with a passionate undercurrent not often seen on the ballet stage, and an impressionistic palette. No foursquare preparations, no cavalier supporting a ballerina's turns, but "half-poses, half-arabesques . . . tender transitions to adagio," as Kostrovitskaya wrote. It didn't look like Fokine's art nouveau either; its dancers weren't Fokinesque dramatis personae, but Man and Woman in the abstract. Both wore the most neutral of costumes, a tunic or chiton, like Preobrazhenskaya's—rare for a woman, rarer for a man. The chiton signaled that the dance was revolutionary, pure, "Greek." As for Mungalova, she wore no diadem on her head, just a neoclassical ribbon encircling her curly blonde hair.[86]

His friends had long known that strong passions lurked under Georges's dreamy exterior, erupting rarely. That summer, Georges, pushed by other schoolchildren into a pond, climbed out and emitted what classmate Mikhailov called "a pure animalistic wail." It was one of those rare times when "his southern blood boiled inside him."[87] Probably Georges's friends assumed that his cool Russian blood usually held his "hot Georgian blood" in check, except when he danced his favorite wild numbers. But they hadn't pegged him as a romantic. *Night* was about a longing for women, maybe in the manner of Mayakovsky. And something else: Georges seemed to know how women moved. In those "tender transitions," a man's body was linked with a woman's in a newfound parity. It was as if some part of Georges harbored a double-gendered insight into a man's dancing body and a woman's too—as if he were choreographing for two halves of himself.[88] Did the partners' eerie synchronicity stem from the way Georges had entered dance: taking his sister's place in the profession? Might the missing sister-dancer have lived on inside him, doubling his own body, or might Maria's maternal vision of a dancing daughter become his own, as he chose his ballerinas?

Even if Georges had thought about using the talented, brunette Lidochka in *Night*, and not the untried blond Mungalova, Lidochka wasn't available. She was making her own choreography, the first version of her later famous solo *Valse Triste*, to the haunted modern waltz by the Finnish Sibelius. Georges helped her as consultant; they also worked in secret. The dance was about being trapped and fighting with death. Later versions were vivid almost beyond the bearable. Earlier versions, unveiled at the time of Georges's *Night*, weren't yet as strong.

Still, it's worth noting that a young dancer known above all for conveying delight chose to make for herself a dance about death and entrapment. A part of Lidochka was hidden deep inside; one only saw it onstage.

On May 5, 1920, Georges and Lidochka made their performance breakthroughs together in *The Magic Flute*, she playing the sassy peasant girl, he her flute-playing peasant love. Besides showcasing the talents of these two, the *Magic Flute* encapsulated the school's collective spirit. Everyone collaborated. Shiriaev reconstructed the steps choreographed first by Lev Ivanov in 1893, last performed in 1898 when graduate Fokine had played the lead. Shiriaev and Preobrazhenskaya cast Lidochka and Georges. Even if the old master didn't think Georges was a *danseur noble*, he liked him in a comic ballet. The two teachers coached the leads, though Lida already had the habit of "fantasizing" her character into existence by herself. Students under Shiriaev painted the *Magic Flute* scenery, worked the lights, altered costumes from the school's storerooms. Dmitriev and Erbshtein pitched in with the decor. Their friends and classmates danced too, or else appeared again in the assorted numbers that followed (Choura Danilova joined Lidochka and Georges in Paquita's *Pas de Trois*). Isaenko and Oblakov stood in opposite wings to prompt and encourage, as they did at every student performance.[89] *The Magic Flute* marked the pinnacle of Georges's and Lidochka's success as student dancers.[90]

These two were the school's dominant personalities, but not the only ones. Other vivid characters were growing up around them: Choura Danilova, a class above, with her imperious manner and light, clear style onstage; Piotr Gusev, a class below, whom Preobrazhenskaya had brought in from her own school for his partnering skills; lithe blonde Olga Mungalova; dark, serious Nina Stukolkina; preternaturally wise Vera Kostrovitskaya; earnest Mikhail Mikhailov; cheerful Vasily Vainonen . . . few were mousy or bland. That's what this school had produced in this utopian interlude: a close society of strong individuals, united in purpose, watched over by caring adults. No one was jealous that Georges and Lidochka headlined in *The Magic Flute*; everyone was proud, like family members.

After the concert, the whole school traveled for the summer to the former Tsarskoe Selo, Tsar's Village, where Nicholas II and his family had lived in the old days (a mere three years before), next to rich *chinovniki*. In 1918, the Bolshevik state had handed over the grandly idyllic town to its future perfect citizens, the children, and renamed it Detskoe Selo, Children's Village. Petrograd's schools and children's homes received vacation quarters in abandoned mansions and palaces. In 1920, the Theater School was assigned two structures next to a big park: the big, domed Yusupov Palace, with its two columned wings, back veranda and lush garden, and the smaller mansion of a Colonel Kuris across the street. The girls lived in the palace; dance classes occupied its mirrored circular ballroom. The boys lived in the Kuris mansion. Choura Danilova's class of 1920 had graduated already, so Georges and Lidochka's class was on top in Detskoe Selo. The senior males—Balanchivadze, Mikhailov, Kirsanov, Efimov—got their own "adult" room separate from the younger boys.

The ballet students performed some evenings in the village's town hall for the rest of Detskoe Selo's summer population, the half-starved schoolchildren of Petrograd. But on free evenings the boys came across the street to the girls at Yusupov. Boys and girls sat together on the back veranda, in the ghostly translucence of the northern summer nights. The lilacs poured their scent into the air. The littler girls picked bouquets and put them in glasses on the veranda table. The students pooled their rations, and the boys caught fish in the ornamental lake of the adjacent park for the housekeeper to cook. Balanchine was half in love with Mungalova, his ballerina in *Night*. Was she the first elusive blonde in his life? (She later married their mutual friend Gusev.) The first one who wasn't already a star like Lidochka, so would let him help mold her? Classmates remember Balanchivadze on that porch practicing his new trade, asking Mungalova and others to try some lifts.

On another part of the porch, sixteen-year-old Lidochka withdrew with the younger Vera Kostrovitskaya for long talks. Sometimes they went into the garden and sat on the roof of a baroque chicken coop. Lida had made the precocious Vera a friend in whom she confided, whom she told about the roles in the repertory she dreamed of dancing. She already knew which beats of music she would inflect, how she would stand and gesture and move across the stage. Sometimes the two girls would go alone to the palace's ballroom and conduct a dance class together. "See, Vera," Lida told her, "you can do each step in a beautiful way, and a not-beautiful way."[91] Vera already suffered from the tuberculosis that would curtail her dancing career. She'd missed key parts of her training. Lida worked with her to improve her steps and help her understand what they could *mean* on the stage (the way she had been encouraged by her teacher, Preobrazhenskaya).

In that long, hot, idyllic 1920 summer, Georges and Lida crossed from childhood into maturity. Both had started on the road to stardom on the stage, or so they thought. They'd exposed their most intimate selves in *The Magic Flute*. They'd imagined new kinds of dancing too,

Boy Theater School Graduates, 1921.
From left: Mikhailov, Balanchivadze, Efimov, Kirsanov. Courtesy Saint-Petersburg State
Museum of Theater and Music.

Lidochka in her eerie solo and her talks with Kostrovitskaya, Georges in his first pas de deux. In their art, they could almost be counted as adults. In other ways, they were still children. As the summer ended, the four senior boys were left behind in Detskoe Selo waiting for transport home. They wandered through the empty Yusupov Palace to the basement, where a box of empty wine bottles was left over, as Mikhailov later wrote with revolutionary disdain, "from a lush count's life." They brought the box upstairs and started throwing bottles off the veranda. One boy threw a bottle; another would try to hit it with a second. If the bottles crashed in midair the four felt "indescribable delight." Bottles flew. At the climax of the game, portly Isaenko appeared in the doorway. "Stop that immediately! You huge morons! You were so happy to stay behind without adults!"

The boys stood with eyes lowered. They had another year under his watchful eye before they tried their luck in the world outside.[92]

EIGHT

The NEP Economy

Javotte rehearsal, spring 1921.
At center, Georges holds Lidia. Courtesy Saint-Petersburg State Museum
of Theater and Music.

Georges and Lidochka's final 1920–21 year at the Theater School was also the last year of the Civil War, and in terms of food and fuel, it was even worse than the ones before. During the ballet students' idyllic Detskoe Selo summer, the Red Army had fought what were supposed to be its final battles. On the Western front they'd pushed back the Polish forces of nationalist general Pilsudski, grandiosely seeking to recreate the medieval Polish-Lithuanian empire. In the south, they were beating back the only remaining White Russian army, under Baron Wrangel, which was advancing up from its Crimean stronghold. A peace treaty with the Polish Army was signed in mid-October 1920, and in early November Wrangel's army was forced back to the subtropical Crimea, soon sailing for Constantinople in 126 scrounged boats along with the civilian horde it had protected.[1] As the Red Army demobilized and sent home almost a million soldiers, resources should have been freed up for civilians, and life in Petrograd should have improved.

But by a cruel twist of fate, the summer had been hot and dry, lethal for farmers. The weather, plus rusting farm machinery and the Bolsheviks' grain requisitions, meant that the 1920 fall harvest was meager. Yet another cut was ordered in Petrograd food rations. "In the towns everything was slowing down to a death sleep," wrote Petrograd professor Pitirim Sorokin about the fall and winter of 1920–21. "Railways were broken down. Buildings were falling in ruins."[2] By winter, blizzards and the decaying railways had further reduced the flow of food and fuel. In February 1921, sixty of the city's biggest factories, including the mighty Putilov Iron Works, were forced to close and dismiss their already starving workers.[3]

Food grew scarcer in the relatively protected Theater School as well (and we'll never know to what lengths Oblakov went during the whole

Civil War to obtain it). And the older girls' teacher Preobrazhenskaya left Russia in the winter of 1920–1. She didn't want to emigrate, but her beloved pianist Alexander Labinsky insisted. Helped by friends, carrying her little dog Kleva, she made the dangerous crossing in February 1921 on foot over the frozen sea to Finland.[4] It was devastating for the girls she'd trained from the beginning. She'd already started work on their graduation concert, choosing another bucolic ballet, *Javotte*, about the peasant lass Javotte who defies her parents to marry another peasant, Jean. She'd commissioned it for herself nineteen years before from the Mariinsky's longtime *danseur noble* Pavel Gerdt (also a sometime choreographer).[5] Preobrazhenskaya cast Lidochka in her own title role; Jean, of course, would be danced by the girl's "peasant" partner from *The Magic Flute*, Balanchivadze. This was a step up for the pair. *Javotte's* music was not the usual oompah-pah fare but an impressionistic musical idyll written in 1896 by the French composer Camille Saint-Saëns. Conservatory chief Alexander Glazunov had even composed an extra number for Gerdt's *Javotte*.[6] Rehearsals had begun in December 1920.

And then Preobrazhenskaya left. Where could Oblakov find another expert teacher quickly, for his oldest girls?

As it happened, the city's dire conditions had already created a training ground for ballet teachers. After Lunacharsky had saved the Theater School in 1918, smaller dance studio schools had sprung up to join it, some private, some government-subsidized. They resembled the acting studios that had popped up earlier, except that dance demanded more space and more-specialized teachers. Preobrazhenskaya's own school was one of the few to survive the revolution. Now, former dancers Moskaliova, Lilina, Kusev, and Alexander Chekrygin and ex-Mariinsky head Boris Romanov started schools too.[7] Romanov proposed to train orphans. Free-form dance was available as well, in a Petrograd Institute of the Rhythm of Perfect Movements, and a Duncanesque "Geptakhor." A movement school/studio wasn't a bad idea; if the government approved it, one could get a requisitioned palace and rations for students (and oneself). But some students could actually pay. The city, in fact, was full of aspiring dancers: "bourgeois" youth declassed by social upheaval, working-class youth empowered by it.[8] Even Bolshevik wives wanted to don tutus. Shady personages got into the ballet school game, including a Hungarian-born Baron Miklos,[9] who obtained for his school a gem-like yellow palace on the Neva that had belonged to Princess Yurieva, Tsar Alexander II's mistress—though later he had to relinquish it when he was caught selling its priceless furnishings.[10] (Many Petrograders now lived in such grand abandoned premises, haunted by "ghosts" of recent vintage.)

It was at this Baron Miklos's school that Preobrazhenskaya's replacement began her teaching career—Agrippina Vaganova. Eight years younger than Preobrazhenskaya, she'd been a Mariinsky star, too, and would go on to codify the Soviet Union's official ballet methodology that now bears her name. She'd also come from humble roots: her father had been a soldier turned Mariinsky Theater usher. And she'd inherited, like Preobrazhenskaya, a less than ideal body for ballet; hers was long-waisted, with a large head, pointed chin, and stiff arms. But she'd worked hard, earned the title "queen of variations" for her brilliant renditions of the difficult solos in Petipa's story ballets, and finally made ballerina status in 1916 at the end of her career. Even if suited to teaching, Vaganova hadn't begun it until a family tragedy forced her to. Her common-law husband, a tsarist official, shot himself from political grief on Christmas Day, 1917, leaving her penniless, with their son and a niece and nephew to bring up.

For a while, Vaganova presided over the Miklos School faculty. She taught, and managed the other teachers, coaxing several former colleagues out of freezing apartments. Two former tsarist high officials played piano for the classes.[11] Then Vaganova moved on to another of the semiprivate dance studios, the Second State School of Ballet, begun in 1920 by critic Akim Volynsky, who'd snagged a palace off Nevsky Prospekt. It was also known as the "BaltFlot School," since Volynsky got his financial support from the Navy's Baltic Fleet funds earmarked for experimental theater.[12] Volynsky, who saw ballet as a reincarnation of ancient Greek dance, wanted to turn out dancers who were also little philosophers. He lectured them on philosophy while Vaganova and former Mariinsky soloist Nikolai Legat, gave them technique. Volynsky's dream of seeing his own school dictate a new ballet training methodology eventually curdled his objectivity as a critic. But by then, Vaganova had been summoned to her alma mater, the ex-Imperial, now State Theater School.

And what a different temperament she brought to its senior girls! In place of their impulsive and affectionate former teacher, this cool, unflappable younger ex-ballerina of forty-two didn't show emotion even if the students danced well. She only said, calmly, "*vot, vot . . . tak*" (yes, yes . . . like that) and quietly adjusted their bodies.[13] The younger girls had vowed to act out their grief at losing Preobrazhenskaya by doing everything backwards, but came around to respecting her.[14]

Lidochka probably did too. No link has been made in dance history between Lidochka and Vaganova. The later Soviet cult of Vaganova meant that her first graduating class, which was really Preobrazhenskaya's, has been glossed over. But Vaganova did "finish" Lidochka's and her classmates' training. It might have been good for the impulsive girl to be subjected to Vaganova's penetrating gaze and steely standards. Yet Preobrazhenskaya too had taught precision in her own way, connecting it with expressive meaning, and Lidochka already had strong ideas of her own. She could have quietly resisted Vaganova and continued creating herself.

Georges's teacher Chekrygin took over staging the unfinished graduation ballet *Javotte*, and the divertissement dances to follow. Shiriaev helped. He also made his extra number for Georges, a *lezginka* fast-paced Georgian warrior solo with knives, keyed to the boy's special wild virtuosity.[15] Did this solo represent a symbolic repatriation to Georges's unknown homeland? By now the boy was secure enough in the school community to flaunt his exotic side. In spring 1921, he and Piotr Gusev had created an "orchestra" together, using the primitive materials loved by the avant-garde: pots, pans, basins, tin cans, combs . . . and a piano, played by Georges. Georges also handled the arrangements, repertory, and rehearsals. The orchestra's opera potpourri was so successful it took up half an evening—just like Georgi's and Andrei's earlier musical "menus" for family guests. Some songs were staged with dance, such as "What are you dancing, Katenka? Polka, polka, Mamenka!"[16] The orchestra's pièce de résistance was the overture from *Carmen*, in which half the "musicians" fell down as if dead on the first chord of the theme of "fate," the other half on the second. Oblakov and Isaenko attended every performance.

The students also continued dancing in the ex-Mariinsky, itself struggling to stay alive as the city was dying. Even with its new name, the State Academic Theater of Opera and Ballet, or GATOB (usually just called the Ak Theater, or even the Mariinsky), it had managed only one semi-new production since the revolution, *Petrushka*, on December 12, 1920. Diaghilev had presented *Petrushka* in 1911 in Paris, with choreography by Fokine and music by Stravinsky, but never in Russia. Now Leonid Leontiev pieced back together the ballet's panoramic old Petersburg street fair and its life-sized puppet theater. He'd danced the Moor puppet in Paris; now he took over Nijinsky's part, the sad Russian Pierrot in love with the ballerina doll. In Karsavina's part as the doll, he put Elena Lukom. *Petrushka*'s scenery was repainted by its original designer, the indefatigable Alexander Benois, now head of Mariinsky stage décor and one of an elected triumvirate advising Ekskuzovich (with music scholar Boris Asafiev and conductor Emil Cooper). The spring before, Benois had brought back his own first Diaghilev collaboration, *Le Pavillon d'Armide*. Now he and Leontiev made an all-Fokine program with *Petrushka*, *Chopiniana*, and *Islamei*, which ran constantly that spring and used the advanced students. Georges and Lidochka would have heard a lot of Stravinsky's lyrical-percussive sounds.

But even as the class of 1921 prepared for graduation, their city's fragile daily life was threatened again, as was life across the whole vast country that had been so depleted in the Civil War. The Bolsheviks' forced grain requisitions had especially infuriated the peasants, who took up arms in the summer of 1920 in Tambov province, southeast of Moscow. The former Socialist Revolutionary Alexander Antonov mounted an anti-government operation, well-organized, with peasants and deserters both Red and White. These "Greens" stole Bolshevik weapons and murdered Red commissars and tax collectors. The Red Army set out to destroy them, but more revolts sprang up elsewhere—118 of them by the winter of 1920–1.

In February, the worst possible group, from Lenin's viewpoint, joined the fray: the Kronstadt sailors on the naval island west of Petrograd (where Lidochka's father had begun his military service). They'd been in the revolution's vanguard. Now they created a defiant populist collective to correct the revolution's broken promises. In early March, Red Army divisions tried to cross the still-frozen sea to crush them, but these stood out against the snow, and Kronstadt cannons picked them off. The big guns could be heard even in Petrograd. At the height of the impasse, Lenin made a surprising move. Delegates from all over Russia had converged on Moscow for the 10th Party Congress. To them, on March 15, Lenin decreed that food requisitions would cease. Instead of compelling the peasants to surrender their crops, the government would collect a tax in kind, one-quarter of their harvest, less than amounts seized earlier. The rest they could sell on a not-yet-existent "open market."[17]

And so began the astonishing New Economic Policy of the 1920s, the NEP, which was to last for another eight years before Stalin shut it down. What Lenin imagined was a simple exchange: peasants would sell their grain in the towns and receive the manufactured goods they so desperately needed. But there weren't any such goods. What transpired instead was a massive shift in priorities. Earlier visions of universal social welfare gave way 1921 to a new slogan: productivity at all costs.

That meant increased factory output and decreased state spending. Failing state enterprises were leased out to private owners, successful ones held to account, workers dismissed from the swollen state bureaucracy, and rations no longer handed out at workplaces. A massive famine struck the Volga River region that summer, but in the cities conditions slowly improved. The once furtive black market merged with the new grain exchange. Bakeries cropped up, then grocery stores, commission stores selling hoarded valuables, repair shops, factories, even restaurants, and with them the old villains of capitalism, "profiteers, currency traffickers, speculators, pawn shops, swindlers, shady intermediaries and other types of sharks . . ." as one Bolshevik-minded observer put it.[18] The Bolsheviks had to hustle up new laws to keep pace. The NEP was an admission of defeat, but Lenin used his best mental acrobatics to argue the opposite: that regenerating the bourgeoisie would save socialism.[19] He'd effectively halted the revolution to insert the middle-class takeover that Marx had mandated before proletarian rule. The Party's idealistic wing reacted with shock and disbelief, and the arts with fear. Now instead of searching for ways to reach workers, artists would have to search for profits.

For Georges, Lidochka, and their classmates, the NEP's coming was miraculous and daunting. Looking out from their cave in their ex-imperial school, where they'd been freezing, hungry, and dirty but fused together in a primitive tribal warmth, they saw lights coming on, window glass returning to windows. They saw, as Schwezoff put it, "almost a resurrection," as if their city was rousing itself to welcome them into it.[20] And yet, revived urban life posed problems not only financial—dancers wouldn't be the ones making money—but psychological. Alone without each other, how would they fare? Their May 1921 graduation concert may have reflected the confusion. Lidochka got sick with a high fever. Instead of calling the concert off, Oblakov made the last-minute decision to replace her in *Javotte* with her classmate, Nina Vdovina. Vdovina had been on the Estrada music-hall stage before coming to the school; she could learn fast. Balanchivadze taught her the role and partnered her— his first experience of quick staging. Nor was Lidochka's illness the evening's only mishap: Mikhailov's partner for a *Coppélia* pas de deux, Lyubov Platonova, fainted in the wings. He didn't get to dance at all.

Javotte was a hit, even with substitutions. But everyone was sorry for Lidochka. The next day a "small delegation of her large circle of friends," as Mikhailov put it, went to her family's new apartment nearby at the corner of Sotsialisticheskaya and Pravda Streets—the Ivanovs had moved—to tell her about it. Mikhailov had been there before. Lida had often brought two or three classmates home to feed them, including Mikhailov and Balanchivadze. Her father, whom Mikhailov describes as an *intelligent* drawn mistakenly into army service (Ivanov didn't let on he'd been a volunteer), had treated them warmly. During that post-concert visit, Lidochka lay among the snow-white sheets, her tearful dark eyes "like wet cherries" as she followed their account. She didn't burden them with her grief at not dancing; she seemed genuinely happy for them. "Lida," wrote Mikhailov, "was joyful by temperament (*zhizneradostna*). In any case, that's how she lives in my memory."[21]

Despite performance mishaps, all fourteen members of the class of 1921 were passed by the official commission, consisting of the several dancer-teachers and the students' ballerina idol Elizaveta Gerdt. A few days later, on June 1, all joined the ex-Mariinsky as "Artists of the Ballet." Thirteen began in the corps de ballet; Lidochka alone received the soloist rank.

There they were, professionals, heading into summer. But they couldn't stray far from their school even if they'd wanted to, since the theater used the school's rehearsal halls, and rehearsals multiplied as the NEP settled in. A better economy meant more summer theaters. Old favorite ballet epics and various divertissements rotated among these; Petrograd's Bolshoi Opera Theater hosted a full-cast production on Sunday, the outdoor Letnii (summer) Bouffe took the same one pared down on Wednesday, the Tauride theater on Thursday—and so on through the summer.[22] Lidochka left the school dormitory to live in her family's apartment, where she had her own room, but she came daily to the school to rehearse. Later that summer, she went out on tour as Viktor Semenov's ballerina. Semenov often employed the youngest so he could pay them less, and she'd apparently reconciled herself to working with him.

Balanchivadze barely left the school at all. No family apartment awaited him after graduation, except perhaps a corner of Aunt Nadia's where his mother lived too. Isaenko helped him get a room on the school's top floor, unheated but private. He'd remained close to his schoolmaster-patron. They were often seen conversing in the halls. And Georges haunted the school rehearsal studios with his three eager male classmates. They could be found in studio corners, endlessly turning and jumping. They were just seventeen, not fully grown, not as strong as they would have been without Civil War interruptions and privations. But they knew they were needed. Among the ex-Mariinsky's dancers who'd decamped to the West was a critical mass of promising young males—Piotr Vladimirov in 1918, Anatoly Obukhov in 1920, Anatoly

Vilzak that summer of 1921 . . . In the Civil War years, the ex-imperial ballet troupe must have seemed to audiences like the orchestra of Haydn's *Unfinished Symphony*: slipping out one by one, before the end of the show. Those remaining often fiercely resented those who'd left. The ballerinas at home—Elizaveta Gerdt, Elsa Vill, and Elena Lukom— were overworked and missing partners. They eyed the newest male recruits.

Georges was the first to be singled out. On June 19, 1921, a month after graduation, his *Lezginka* was put on the program at Pavlovsk Concert Hall, the most prestigious of the summer venues. He danced fourth among ten *Choreographic Divertissements* that followed a Petipa one-act, *The Awakening of Flora*. A few weeks later, in the rehearsal studio, Gerdt, whom Georges especially admired, called him out of a corner. "Stand next to me and try to hold me for two turns," Mikhailov remembers her saying.[23] She was slated to dance *Swan Lake* with Vladimir Ponomariov at Pavlovsk on July 17, a version with three acts instead of four (Act I, the prince's birthday party, was gone). But Ponamariov, also staging the production, chose not to take on the strenuous ballroom scene with the evil Swan Queen Odile. Another prince was needed for that act. Gerdt's regular younger partner Mikhail Dudko fell ill, so Georges got the part.[24]

Partnering Gerdt as Siegfried, even for one act, was a very big deal: pulling it off would have put Georges on a fast track to the top. Dudko and Boris Shavrov, two and four years older respectively than he, were already top-billed dancers who partnered reigning ballerinas. Georges's natural competitiveness pushed him to rival them, even if he preferred the exotic solo roles. But fate got in the way. Rushing between school and theater to find a Siegfried costume that fit him, he arrived at the Vitebsk Station to see his Pavlovsk train vanishing in the distance. He borrowed a bicycle from friends and pedaled the twenty-five miles at top speed, clutching the packet with his costume. He made it at the end of *Swan Lake's* lakeside scene (where he was supposed to have danced a hunter) just in time to don his prince costume and assist Gerdt in her evil seduction of him. Did the swan theme swelling to brass seem to sound his doom? Did the frenzied horns of the next ballroom scene call him back to life? *Swan Lake* is the only tragic ballet classic Balanchine restaged himself thirty years later, in a compressed and splendidly agitated version (the other classic he redid was *The Nutcracker*, not a tragedy). But at that moment, limp from pedaling all that way, Georges made a lackluster impression. Mikhailov believes this *Swan Lake* trauma destroyed Georges's performing ambitions, that afterwards he practiced less and thought about making dances more. But other factors would soon arise as well to discourage him from a dancing career.[25]

In late August, Georges joined the other Mariinsky dancers, including Lidochka back from her tour, to prepare for the new season. The ballet's October 2 opening would feature the only really new work the company had attempted since the Revolution, a *Firebird*, based on the Russian tale about a magic bird caught by a tsarevich. Georges and Lidochka were in it. Diaghilev had commissioned the original 1910 *Firebird*'s music from Stravinsky, its choreography from Fokine. Now, in 1921, Alexander Benois wanted to bring as much of Stravinsky's lyrical-dissonant modernist music as he could to a revolutionary Russia that hadn't heard it. But what about *Firebird*'s choreography? Fokine had left Russia three years before in a huff when Mariinsky directors wouldn't make his wife a ballerina. Ekskuzovich's advisory triumvirate, especially Benois, who'd worked with Diaghilev, wanted a renewed *Firebird*. Was there a choreographer somewhere in the Mariinsky trained in the old ways but thirsting for the new?

A marginal Mariinsky ballet master named Fedor Lopukhov seemed a likely candidate. He was thirty-eight years old in 1922, tall and thin with long, blond hair and strangely light blue eyes, "not handsome, but *vivace*, with a long-nosed profile, like Gogol's,"[26] wrote Danilova. His mother was a culture-loving Scots-Estonian, his father a Russian ex-serf who'd wanted to sing opera but ended up a Mariinsky usher. Fedor had come up through the Imperial Theater School, as had practically his whole family. His older sister Evgenia and younger brother Andrei were Mariinsky soloists. Another sister, Lidia, was a ballerina-soubrette in Diaghilev's company: she would soon marry the British economist John Maynard Keynes and become a London Bloomsbury legend as Lydia Lopokova.[27] Young Fedor had joined the dancers' strike in the 1905 revolution, a "mistake" that forced him out of the Mariinsky and into Moscow's Bolshoi Ballet, then pushed him farther afield on a series of tours, including a long one in America with his sister Lidia. In San Francisco, he was so homesick that Pavlova, on tour nearby, made a special trip to comfort the young Russian she didn't know. The two sat in a park and wept as they remembered St. Petersburg.[28]

Back in Russia (he'd kissed the customs official upon reentering), Lopukhov had rejoined the Mariinsky as a *caractère* dancer, and staged dances for smaller amateur theaters. When the Bolsheviks arrived, he was ready, along with the other ex-1905 "agitators" reinstalled by Lunacharsky in the Ak Theaters, to play a bigger role. To prepare for his

Firebird challenge, he consulted constantly with theater experts Benois and Asafiev. He learned to read orchestral scores from conductor Emil Cooper. Lopukhov wanted his *Firebird* to evoke the old fairy tale's cruelty: his magic bird would be fiercer than Fokine's (even if he had to cast ingénue Elena Lukom), his monsters scarier.

The finished product was received with puzzlement. Denis Leshkov, balletomane turned Narkompros bureaucrat, gallantly wrote in the weekly *Zhizn Iskusstva* (*Life of Art*), that audiences would understand this *Firebird* in a few years.[29] But confusion about the new work only underscored the dire conditions in the ex-Mariinsky's ballet. It hadn't known real hands-on artistic leadership since Fokine had left. Boris Romanov, its provisional head from 1918 to 1920, had been too daring and eccentric a choreographer to make new sense of the old repertory. Leonid Leontiev, who'd taken over in 1920, was well liked but couldn't make good new ballets. The caretaking triumvirate of Benois, Cooper, and Asafiev weren't dancers themselves; they couldn't coach or rehearse. Three ballerinas—Gerdt, Lukom, and Vill, with help from the soubrette Borshakova—carried the repertory on their shoulders, but for everyone else, discipline was lax. "The dancers didn't have to go [to the theater] every day," Balanchine told Taper later.[30] They'd spent the Civil War starving and freezing; new hardships loomed in the NEP. The barter economy was fading; paper money and credit were reemerging; factories, even "artistic" ones like the ex-Mariinsky, could no longer double as social welfare agencies. The extra rations from Ekskuzovich's Red Army arrangement disappeared as the army drastically downsized. Dancers had to buy their food on salaries that could barely support them. Ideological confusion reigned too. Without free tickets, would the workers still want the ballet, as Lunacharsky claimed? Or would all of theater be overrun by the new "Nepmen" and "Nepwomen" in their flashy clothes, and slide backwards into decadence? *Zhizn Iskusstva* erupted in mid-August in think pieces—"The Paying-ness of the Theater Audience," "The Market and Art." By late November 1921, ads for clothes stores and restaurants, not seen since tsarist times, were back in the papers. As Eric Naiman has shown in his provocative book *Sex in Public*, NEP society was haunted by the specter of the just-repressed bourgeoisie rising as if from the dead.

The youngest company members felt this aesthetic crisis, and they certainly noticed the salary gap. They would meet in corners of rehearsal studios and vow to save their art. But their lives weren't easy. A morning class at the school, usually taught by Vaganova, was followed by all-day rehearsals. A wide range of ballets was on the roster in 1921–22: Petipa tales, newer Fokine ballets, and Lopukhov's newest *Firebird*. These offered excellent training for a future ballet master, or so thought Lopukhov. "Installed in the corps de ballet, I had to be onstage for most of the performance, learn a wide range of parts, remember them all," he wrote about his own first dancing years. "I acquired, straight from the hands of the classical choreographers of the last century, dance 'words,' dance 'phrases,' whole dance 'eras.'"[31] One can imagine Georges too, absorbing his future choreographic "material" in endless onstage evenings. But unlike in tsarist times, he and his friends had to work on the side. Their salary fed them till halfway through the month, but that was all.[32] Housing was needed too. And their three-month summer holidays were unpaid.

Starting in 1921 and for the next two years, Georges played the piano three hours a day for school ballet classes. Choura Danilova saved money by walking between home and theater, forty minutes each way. Lidochka wasn't quite as needy, since her father still had army perks. But overall, they were hungrier than before. They performed in out-of-the-way, freezing movie houses, dancing "numbers" between the films, compensating for such debased work with increased devotion to the ballet ideal. They'd received the best of the tsarist tradition from extraordinary figures like Preobrazhenskaya, Andrianov, Shiriaev. They'd absorbed the purest revolutionary idealism from Oblakov and colleagues. Nobody had engineered these conditions, but Georges's and Lidochka's class, together with Choura Danilova and a couple of her 1920s classmates and the next two classes of 1922 and '23, constitute a magical mini-generation unto itself. Their bodies contained the means to synthesize the old and the new, and they meant to do this.

But for now, they had other pressing things on their minds. As the new economy took shape, they faced not only money problems but personal challenges that graduates before them, even recent ones, couldn't have imagined. Earlier classes had entered a world unified by wartime deprivation. This 1921 class faced a reborn consumer society, for which nothing in their school lives had prepared them.

They needed clothes, for instance. This sounds like a small thing, but in Civil War years no clothes were manufactured or imported. People made do with what they could find. Dresses were sewn from umbrellas, shoes from chair leather, outerwear from anything. "Often the seats of first-class railway carriages were cut completely away," wrote Igor Schwezoff about those times; "people made velvet and plush coats out of them."[33] Or they borrowed things. For a special event, a person went running among friends and neighbors to put an outfit together. The ballet students had an advantage: the school's costume storehouse, which they freely pillaged. For official school occasions, they'd worn their old uniforms, boys' military-style suits, girls' blue wool dresses topped with white aprons. But these uniforms had frayed and shrunk as the wearers grew.[34] They were presented to the students anyway as graduation gifts, together with one set of underwear. But what could ex-students do with uniforms in the NEP fashion frenzy? Twenty years before, in 1902, the just-graduated Karsavina had gone with her thrifty mother to a secondhand Jewish clothes dealer to be readied for the world beyond school. But such shops didn't exist now. Where could the 1921 graduates find the street wear to proclaim their special artistic status? In the competitive NEP, each needed a style, not just for clothes but hairdos, music, movies, manners. The Civil War had wiped the slate clean. You could be anybody—if you had the money. But you had to be somebody.

Each of the classmates reacted differently. Mikhailov decided to support his mother, who'd long supported him by sewing tutus. He took a new apartment for them—rashly, since salaries were so paltry.[35] Georges did no such thing, even if his mother was right there in Petrograd. But a family letter suggests a closer relationship than has been supposed. Younger brother Andrei wrote to Maria Balanchivadze from Tiflis on September 21, 1921, just as Georges started his first season in the company. He enclosed a separate letter to be given *only to Georges*, as he instructed Maria (it hasn't survived).

To Maria, Andrei enlarges on family news, some of which she seems to know already. Tamara, now nineteen, is living with a new Georgian husband in the country outside Tiflis. Andrei sees them often, but he himself, he writes proudly, has been accepted into the Tiflis Conservatory for piano and composing. Aunt Mila, who'd come to Georgia with Tamara, is grieving over her husband Ivan's death in a battle with the Red Army. The Bolsheviks had finally conquered proud little independent Georgia in February 1921, ousting the Mensheviks. But Maria shouldn't worry about Aunt Mila or him, writes Andrei: the family was taking care of both. "Better worry about yourself and Zhorzhik," Andrei says, then adds with younger-brother wistfulness, "I can't believe I haven't seen him for five years! And during that time . . . I've become an artist." Was Maria herself really taking care of Georges, as Andrei implies, doing his laundry, bringing him food? Had she seen his school graduation performance? Had she traveled to Pavlovsk for his *lezginka* or his semi-failure in *Swan Lake*? If not, why not? A postscript at the end of the letter only deepens the mystery surrounding this inscrutable family. "I'm very sorry about Babusia," Andrei writes, "maybe she's happy now." This seems to mean that Babusia, who we assume was Maria's mother and so his and Georges's grandmother, has died in Petrograd. Maybe Maria has been preoccupied with nursing her. But how odd for Andrei to write like this about a grandmother's death—as if he wasn't personally involved. Balanchine, the brother on the spot, never even mentioned a grandmother.[36]

Whoever and wherever Georges's family was, the adult image the boy was cultivating emphatically did not include it. To peers and caretakers, he was already a solo figure, courteous, detached, and eerily self-confident. This was an extension of his school self, the proud little boy supposedly unfazed by anything. Even in his earliest school years, he'd made a mystical acrostic about his fate, in which the last sound of each line rhymed with a syllable of his family name. "Upon me smiles fate (*sudba—Ba*)/ My lot in life is already given (*dan—Lan*)/ To success I see the keys (*kliuchi—Chi*)/ I will not now turn back—(*nazad—Vad*)/ In spite of tempest and thunder (*groze—Ze.*") Somebody in his circle remembered the acrostic, and it became, as Yuri Slonimsky remembered, the "verbal calling card of the beautiful, merry and quick youth who was 'our guy.'"[37]

And now Georges had grown his hair long; a lock of it fell over his eye. He'd found in the school's storage a pair of white summer pants that were the envy of his peers—dandy clothing. He used eyeliner to make his eyes soulful. And who can blame him for recreating himself as a creature of the theater? His family had left him little to go on. His mother's origins were so carefully obscured that even her children probably didn't know them, beyond an impression that Germany or Austria might be relevant. The explanation Andrei later furnished, about a German father named Almedingen or Von Almedingen[38] who'd supposedly left wife and daughter to return to Germany, makes no sense. If Maria's parents had parted amicably, why would she hide her mother and reject her father's name? How were the "aunts" related to her? By contrast, the origins of Georges's father were knowable, but inaccessible. Meliton had passed on his music in some form to his two Russian sons along with his compulsively ironic Georgian humor. The grown Balanchine and Andrei both loved jokes. But the rest of the paternal heritage—the language, the web of cousins, the legendary landscape of Georgia—all this was out of Georges's reach without a father to embody it.

In terms of a sexual identity, Georges had already firmly declared his in his first choreography, though he was still close to the gay schoolmaster Isaenko. And he'd made another male-female duet too while still in school, to another lyrical tone-poem (*Poème*, by the Czech composer Zdeněk Fibich), purer and dreamier than the first one. *Night* was about longing, *Poème* about detached beauty. *Night's* ballerina was the younger Olga Mungalova, *Poème*'s the slightly older Choura Danilova, though both girls were blondes beyond his reach. Olga Mungalova was already his friend Gusev's girlfriend. Choura, a year older, was marked already as a Mariinsky soloist and known for her "cold chiseled features" and stage style to match. Nevertheless, Balanchivadze danced the piece with Choura, and held her at the end in arabesque above his head, so that "she herself, without the support of a partner, appeared to be floating away to some far distant place," as Kostrovitskaya remembered. This "air lift" was an original move, Kostrovitskaya wrote, not yet seen in a pas de deux, though afterwards many claimed the invention as their own.[39]

That fall of 1921, Georges grew interested in yet another young blonde, Tamara Zheverzheeva, or Tamara Geva as she was later known in the West. She was a student in the Theater School's new evening dance classes, created for older students under NEP commercial pressure. It was a competitive program with rigorous auditions, organized by the ever-present Viktor Semenov. Geva was a year younger than Georges (though she later changed it to three), a veteran of the city's private ballet schools and tall and limber like his first two Galateas.[40] The way Geva remembered it, Georges, slim and long-haired, entered her evening ballroom classroom together with Isaenko and took over the lesson from the regular teacher, arranging the students in interesting patterns and joining them himself. He was already thinking bigger than duets. He came back a few days later to ask Geva to be his partner for some concert appearances. Then he paid a Sunday call to her father's home on Grafsky Lane, not far from Aunt Nadia's apartment, bringing Mikhailov with him. Mikhailov, Geva writes (but perhaps with her signature fanciful approach), became a lover on the spot of her ex-courtesan mother, one more in a string of them. And Georges was auditioning the daughter. "So I became the Galatea to his Pygmalion," wrote Geva later, though the dance she describes him first creating seems to be *Night*, the one he'd already made for Mungalova.[41] After a public performance, the two became a couple, though Georges didn't tell his friends. He kept Geva a secret, as was his habit. The different parts of his life didn't know about each other.

It seems odd that Georges would choose someone outside his circle for his first girlfriend, when there were so many younger girls in it.

Maybe he didn't want to spoil the circle's intimacy, though most of his male friends would find girlfriends here, many of which would become wives.[42] Maybe he wanted to protect the other girls from Isaenko's ire, which did fall on Tamara. Or he was shy about sex and wanted to experiment outside his circle. Or he liked Geva's bohemian glamour. But Geva brought something more than looks: an artistic "dowry" from her father, Levkii Zheverzheev. Before the revolution, that gentleman, half-Tatar, half Turk, Muslim-born, wealthy but politically radical, had managed his family's factory, which made the gold cloth and "church accessories" for the entire Orthodox Church. With the Church now condemned, the factory was empty, though the family still lived in its five-story premises. But Zheverzheev had always cared more about art than business. He was an avid collector, like his Moscow compatriots Mamontov and Riabushinskii, amassing everything linked with the Russian avant-garde, especially theater. He'd gathered a treasure trove of sketches, stage décor models, paintings, sculptures, signed portraits, books about art, and other ephemera, all of which he'd presented in 1918 to the Bolshevik state. In gratitude, Lunacharsky moved Zheverzheev's "museum" to the former imperial theater office on Theater Street, and made him its director.[43] The old gentleman, of middle height, with curly dark hair, would come to "his" museum through the courtyard of the Theater School. Balanchivadze would meet him there, give him his arm, and the two would stroll and talk—the young heir to a pure imperial tradition, the old rebel who'd fought it all his life. Zheverzheev was Georges's next "father" in a long line of them.

Even with these extras in the relationship, Georges and Tamara always claimed they'd been in love. It's probably true: they matched eerily. She was a product, like Georges, of an exotic non-Russian father and a Russian-European mother, who'd come, as had Georges's mother, from the murky lower reaches of Petersburg society. Geva's mother was Swedish, and one of the city's former high-class courtesans. She'd married her husband after *his* disapproving father had died and their daughter was six, just as Balanchine's mother had (possibly) married Meliton Balanchivadze after her children were born.[44] Geva's mother brought her own mother to live with the family, as Maria Balanchivadze (probably) brought hers, and the grandmothers were kept in the background. Oedipal echoes were there too in the young peoples' liaison. In Georges, Geva found a younger version of her father, so ardent about art he couldn't quite muster a family role. In Tamara, Georges found his mother in younger form, silvery blonde, half-northern-European, as ambitious as Maria in the sociocultural sphere. And maybe Geva offered Georges something even more than a mother-replica. She had the same first name as his sister. She was a dancer, too, like his sister, and like her, not quite professional. Neither Tamara would ever have Georges's Theater School credentials. In dance, he would always be the master, Geva—or his sister—the pupil. Georges, that evasive, fragile, yet strangely sturdy psyche, had stumbled on exactly what he needed for the volatile NEP world: a wife who was twin and pupil, and a "father" who guaranteed immersion in Petrograd's postrevolutionary arts scene. At the Zheverzheevs', he would meet his idol, Mayakovsky. In March of 1922, ten months after his school graduation, he would solve his housing problem by moving in with them.[45]

For Lidochka and her girl classmates, maturing in the NEP was more complicated than for their male friends. The Bolsheviks had sent out confusing messages about femaleness. Women should be equal to men in the labor market and private life too. Once that was achieved, wrote the radical poet Ryurik Ivnev in 1919, "all complicated questions involving the interrelationships of the sexes (would) die out and fall away by themselves."[46] Some Bolsheviks proposed communal childrearing to spare the mothers bourgeois cares at home. And women were supposed to get the same chance as men to choose their intimate companions; divorce was made easy in Bolshevik Russia. Yet Lenin himself had trouble with the "free love" endorsed by two close female colleagues, Inessa Armand and Alexandra Kollontai. He thought the term was what bourgeois women used to justify adultery. The many memos exchanged between Lenin and Armand on this subject reveal Lenin's prudishness, and his aggressive use of relentless logic (from his point of view) to win a point.[47]

Then had come the Civil War, when both sexes were asked to sacrifice for victory. The marriage and love discussions had faded. But the NEP brought them roaring back, along with what seemed like a reversal of earlier ideology. Red Army soldiers returning to civilian life were taking over women's jobs, no matter what feeble directives came from the top, and most Bolshevik officials didn't seem to mind. But Kollontai and her colleagues at the Zhenotdel, the new government's Women's Department, felt completely betrayed. Kollontai, then perhaps the most visible female in Bolshevik high circles, wrote passionate editorials in the newspapers. If women lost their jobs, she argued, they would lose their newfound social status and their dignity. They would have to sell their bodies instead of their labor, or else slip back to male-dependence as wives and mistresses—"painted dolls," as she put it.[48]

Naiman in *Sex in Public* has mentioned a general fear during the NEP that society was sliding backwards into a state of bourgeois decadence, which would bring a "renaissance of the old female psyche."[49] This NEP-era fear generated an instant nostalgia for the supposed masculine-tinged unity of Civil War years. Sex was now seen as the Bolsheviks' main temptation. It was a powerful corrupter, and females were its embodiment. In Lenin's eyes, preoccupation with sex went along with bourgeois "decay and intoxication." "The proletarian does not require intoxication, which might deaden it or arouse it," Lenin told German communist Klara Zetkin in a pre-1925 interview. "It neither dares nor wants to forget the foulness, filth, and barbarity of capitalism. . . . Self-possession, self-discipline . . . these are essential in love, too."[50] A Marxist psychoneurologist named Aaron Zalkind published twelve "commandments" of proper behavior that included a ban on flirtation.[51] The result of this constant airing of sexual questions was to increase sexual awareness among young males, and sow confusion in their female counterparts. Official voices exhorted even girls to exercise a manly self-control, implying that their very femininity was part of the bourgeois contagion. Yet the NEP climate was signaling the opposite, that young women should dress up and look good. The result: a stark choice between self-denial and defiance, all but built into a female's NEP coming of age.

For Lidochka and her girl classmates, Olga Preobrazhenskaya's forceful daily presence in their ballet classes may have reinforced the Bolsheviks' original message, that women could be laborer-creators equal to men. They'd also learned Bolshevik comradeship in the school's daily life, sharing equally with the boys in the struggle to survive. School director Oblakov had encouraged gender equality without political stridency. And yet, ballet itself—its gestures, its attitudes—was sending the opposite message: that women should be adorned with jewels and shown off by their cavaliers. By tradition, a ballerina was herself a "painted doll," to be kept in high style offstage, handled like porcelain onstage. And yet under the painted-doll surface, she was a laborer too, at least in Bolshevik eyes, an athlete and sportsman—or this was one possible version of her, beginning only now to be explored.

Such confusions among onstage and offstage femininities can already be seen in Lidochka's young life. She'd been raised as a female prodigy, dressed for the part by her father, celebrated in paintings and photographs. She'd gone the other direction in the painful Civil War years, joining comrades in egalitarian school life. But now that the NEP had put the diva possibility back into the mix, Lidochka as an Ak Theater soloist was already on a social rung far above the mass of Russian women. She had friends in the arts world and fans in the audience, who acted like the old balletomanes and high-rank *chinovniki*, offering worldly temptations at every turn. On the other hand, what Lida wanted most passionately was something no ballerina had yet achieved: to matter to the people, to be "in tune" with the revolution.

Even as a seventeen-year-old just out of school, Lidochka was as much a loner as Georges, even if she looked mature and sophisticated. When she joined the Ak Theater, she shared a dressing room with the other youngest soloist, her friend Choura Danilova. Choura noticed her hard-to-find smart clothes, her numerous admirers (often the source of the clothes), her worldly air. Lidochka was already experienced in sex, Choura suddenly understood, while she, Choura, had admirers too but was still innocent.[52] Lidochka even had a boyfriend, Yelshin, an engineer, about whom little else is known. But even if savvy about clothes and boys, Lidochka talked only about the arts, which made most of her girl peers think she was putting on airs. When she'd come home from touring with Semenov at the start of the 1921 season, she'd asked a million questions about the death of Alexander Blok, the great symbolist poet whose mass funeral on August 10 she'd missed. A few friends like Kostrovitskaya understood; most were put off.

There seemed also to be a telltale schism in Lidochka's personality. Vaginov got this eerily right in his novel *Bambochada* when he named his fictionalized Lidochka Varenka. In real life, Lidochka had made up the alter ego whom she called Varotchka (another nickname for Varvara, or Barbara), about whom she told fanciful stories. Her peers found this unsettling. Adults like Zinaida Serebriakova found it entrancing. Serebriakova, then thirty-seven, was Alexander Benois's niece, and a modernist-realist painter specializing in female subjects, who'd studied with Repin. Serebriakova's daughter Tatiana joined the Theater School's evening ballet classes in 1921, which drew the mother into ballet's backstage life. Zinaida made arresting portraits of the youngest dancers in costume, especially Balanchivadze, Danilova, Geidenreich, Frangopulo—and Lidochka, to whom she related "with special tenderness," remembered Tatiana.[53] While Lidochka posed, Serebriakova listened entranced to her tales of her imaginary twin. She called her a gifted storyteller. But what did it mean that Lidochka had made up this twin? Did Varotchka help the real Lidochka cope with some unnamed emotional strain?

Lidochka was a complicated character. Even as she indulged her childlike side in story making, she showed adult concern about the future of her art. No one sought "the new" more than she, not even Georges. She read art books, attended exhibitions, usually with her father; she collected young writers, musicians, actors, painters at parties in her home, and more than anything else went to plays. She especially loved the Bolshoi Drama Theater (BDT), recently founded and directed by Blok, with a "heroic" repertory including Shakespeare and Schiller, meant to expose workers to masterpieces. Lidochka knew all the BDT actors, and they knew her.[54] She contrasted the theater's excitement with ballet's old-fashioned repertory. Georges had found his way to experimental art through Levkii Zheverzheev; Lidochka was making hers through new friends and play going. "Why can't *we* do that?" she would ask, about the impact of Petrograd's actors on their public.[55]

It's easy to forget that Lidochka and Georges had grown up among Russia's great theatrical experiments of pre- and postrevolutionary years, even if they'd been shut inside the Theater School. But if their school had closed off "real life" to them, it had opened the life of the theater. Both were exposed as early as twelve to the most dynamic theater figure of their day, Vsevolod Meyerhold: they appeared as small cupids in his staging of Gluck's eighteenth-century opera *Orfeo ed Euridice*. The dynamic director, with his rough-hewn face, had begun working in the St. Petersburg imperial theaters as early as 1909, when Imperial Theaters chief Colonel Teliakovsky had impulsively brought him in. Production after brilliant production followed, and not just drama. In 1910 Meyerhold collaborated with his dance counterpart Mikhail Fokine on the commedia dell'arte ballet *Carnaval*, which became a hit for Diaghilev's company in Europe. Meyerhold himself played Pierrot in *Carnaval*'s Russian performances, reprising his earlier Pierrot from the modernist (and haunting) Blok-Meyerhold *Balaganchik* (translated *The Fairground Booth* or *The Puppet Show*) of 1906. In 1911, Meyerhold and Fokine again worked together on an Isadora Duncanesque collaboration (stripped-down and "Greek") for Gluck's *Orfeo*, in which singers danced along with dancers, amid modernist decor. Only a thin curtain of tulle separated *Orfeo*'s underworld from its upper-world. This 1911 *Orfeo* was revived in 1916, just in time for Lidochka and Georges to appear in it. Everyone loved it—dancers, singers, art critics, musicians, even stagehands, and audiences on opposite sides of politics. And two onstage cupids would have understood, even if subliminally, that abstraction could open theatrical vistas closed to creaky old realism. Balanchine later said that Gluck's *Orfeo* had been important throughout his life. Fifty years later, he staged it himself as the neoclassical ballet-idyll *Chaconne*, set to *Orfeo's* ballet music.[56]

The controversial Meyerhold had begun his theatrical life as a student of an even earlier controversial director, Konstantin Stanislavsky. In 1898, Stanislavsky had lit the first fire under Russian drama by founding the Moscow Art Theater and discovering method acting. When the first of four experimental "studios" spun off from Stanislavsky's MAT, Meyerhold became its head. A few years later Meyerhold made his own studio-laboratory in Petrograd, on Borodinskaya St., a short walk from the Theater School, where he and his students reclaimed "all the principles of theatrical action lost to us today"—juggling, acrobatics, clowning, masks—from Italian popular comedy.[57] Meyerhold transformed even himself into a dapper alter ego named Dr. Dapertutto, after a character from his favorite commedia-infused author, E.T.A. Hoffman. Such *commedia* research bore fantastic fruit in Meyerhold's 1917 Alexandrinsky production of Lermontov's 1835 *Masquerade*, about love and murder in high society. After five painstaking years of rehearsal, it premiered in the very midst of the February Revolution, on the eve of Nicholas II's abdication.

When *Masquerade's* audience entered, the curtain was already raised, revealing a stage decorated by artist Alexander Golovin in gold-on-white, a mirror image of the Alexandrinsky's white-on-gold house. Throughout the play, shifting curtains at different stage depths were silently raised and lowered, seeming to dance themselves, even transporting a character in a monologue to a different "setting." Twice, for two ballroom scenes, the whole stage suddenly filled with the color, dance, and music of Lermontov's time. Glazunov had written *Masquerade's* score to "frame" a Lermontov-era waltz, *Valse Fantaisie*, by the great Russian composer Mikhail Glinka, which he echoed and refracted throughout. Theater School students, including Georges and Lidochka, came onstage as small gnomes, counting down the hours to the play's dread climax on a huge clock.[58] What Meyerhold's *Masquerade* did was etherealize the rococo trappings of the old regime, even as these were being torn down in the city outside. Echoes of *Masquerade* can even be found in Balanchine's own 1969 *Valse Fantaisie* (music by Glinka) and his exquisite 1960 ball-within-a-ballet, *Liebeslieder Waltzer*, with its semi-hidden currents of drama tucked into the waltzes.

Georges and Lidochka were bound up with Meyerhold's work in the Civil War years too, especially when that director got together with their poet hero Mayakovsky. On the Revolution's first anniversary in November 1918, the two staged Mayakovsky's *Mystery-Bouffe*, so outlandish in formal terms that the Alexandrinsky refused it, handing it over to the inferior Theater of Musical Drama. *Mystery-Bouffe* was the first major play in which "the people" figured as one unison character, billed as "The Unclean." The opposing "Clean" were cartoon villains: a Speculator, a German, an Australian, his wife, a Russian merchant, Lloyd George, etc. The Theater School children probably saw *Mystery-Bouffe*, which ran many times during the Civil War, pointing the conceptual way to the famous mass revolutionary spectacles staged then too, outdoors by Lunacharsky's Narkompros—*Towards a Worldwide Commune, Pageant of the Third International, The Storming of the Winter Palace*. These giant pageants used the city as a stage set for ritual reenactments of the proletarian victory, with its inhabitants as actors. In *The Storming of the Winter Palace*, for the revolution's 1920 third anniversary, 10,000 soldiers and sailors "re-stormed" the real Winter Palace or else repulsed the stormers, with an audience of 100,000 watching in Palace Square. All Mariinsky Theater artists performed, which would mean Georges and Lidochka too. Echoes of such pageants crop up in later Balanchine ballets such as *The Four Temperaments* (1946), when dancers in black leotards or black tights advance en masse in the final tableau toward the stage rim, signaling semaphorically with their arms—a revolutionary finale par excellence. These stripped-down "practice clothes" that Balanchine used so often as costumes could even be later versions of the everyman (and woman) *prozodezhda* workers' suits first designed for actors in Meyerhold's Borodinskaya St. studio.

Georges and Lidochka had learned in school that making theater was almost a religion. Now in 1921 they heard the message again from their theater friends, actor-turned-writer Yuri Slonimsky and stage artists Boris Erbshtein and Vladimir Dmitriev. The blond Dmitriev was the friends' leader: he'd been at Meyerhold's first Borodinskaya St. studio before moving to another Meyerhold studio for décor organized in 1918, where Erbshtein had studied as well. Dmitriev had already made a precocious professional debut designing Meyerhold's 1920 Moscow production of Belgian poet Emile Verhaeren's *The Dawn*, staged like a real political rally.[59] He kept his ballet friends abreast of inflammatory Moscow doings, but he adored his second city, Petersburg, especially Dostoevsky's seedy version of it, and the city as seen through Alexander Blok's modernist-Pierrot eyes. And he had a special reverence for Petersburg's old-fashioned ballet. He fell in love with ballerinas.

Maybe he encouraged Georges to do that too. He'd already had a hopeless affair with ballerina Olga Spessivtseva: his drawings of grieving ballerina figures lost Hoffmanesquely in Petersburg's streets and alleys attest to this.[60]

Dmitriev was interested in Lidochka too, though not romantically. She wasn't elusive, like his ballerina idol Spessivtseva, but impulsive and full of life. That was her newness. But she listened avidly to him and Erbshtein too, who became her special protector, quizzing them about actresses in Moscow, especially the vibrant star of Alexander Tairov's Kamerny Theater (and Tairov's wife), Alisa Koonen. Koonen's biggest hit so far was the 1919 production of *Adrienne Lecouvreur*, Eugene Scribe's nineteenth-century play about a young Parisian actress caught up in fatal political intrigues. Later, in May 1924, when the Kamerny Theater performed in Petrograd, Lidochka would meet Koonen in person and receive inscribed photos from her and her costar Nikolai Tsereteli.[61] Lidochka also admired the "free" dancer Isadora Duncan, who'd inspired not just Fokine and the ballet but Meyerhold and the other future great theater directors too. Tairov had told Alisa Koonen to study Duncan's "earthly gravitation."[62]

In the summer of 1921, as Lidochka and Georges had emerged from school, Duncan returned to Russia at Lunacharsky's invitation to teach the children of the revolution in a requisitioned Moscow palace. She gave solo concerts too, and in February 1922 she appeared in Petrograd, in three separate evenings on the ex-Mariinsky stage itself, dancing Wagner and Tchaikovsky. Georges and Lidochka of course went to see her. Georges reported much later his disappointment, even if she was too primal a figure to reject outright at the time. Lidochka, who attended all three evenings, continued to hold Duncan "close to her soul." More than anything, she wanted to understand how the barefoot dancer kept her public in thrall.[63]

In 1921–22 Georges, Lida, and the youngest dancers were still low in the theater hierarchy, not in a position to revitalize their art. The NEP's arrival, though, had intensified the questions they'd already confronted in the school. When would the ex-imperial ballet excavate its own roots, as the theater had done? When would it create its own experimental "studio"? Even its ex-imperial twin, the Alexandrinsky, had one. And where was the ballet's equivalent of a Meyerhold, a Tairov, or a Vakhtangov to head it? The newspapers were increasingly asking such questions, and so were Benois, Asafiev, and Cooper. That was why they were grooming Lopukhov. Even if Lopukhov's 1921 *Firebird* had fizzled, the triumvirate

Fedor Lopukhov.
Courtesy Saint-Petersburg State Museum of Theater and Music.

pushed him anyway. In January 1922, they made him an official ballet master. Leontiev was still in charge, but Lopukhov, his year-younger colleague, would be the one who oversaw the ballet's daily operations, and who would finally deal with its tattered imperial past and point the way to a revolutionary future.

The NEP Economy

Lopukhov threw himself into his new position, appearing everywhere—backstage with the artists, in the pit with the musicians, with seamstresses in the costume shop and typesetters in the printing shop.[64] But he made a special point of encouraging the younger dancers. Ballet was a young art, he believed, and the energy to move it forward "should come from the young of the company."[65] He urged his young favorites not just to dance but to go out and see concerts, plays, exhibitions. One of these favorites was Choura Danilova, rising fast after a year and a half in the theater. He gave her several new roles in the spring of 1922, including his own semi-acrobatic *Firebird*, which he thought she danced better than seniors Lukom and Vill. As for Lidochka, he singled her out too, giving her a solo in almost every ballet that went up in the ex-Mariinsky. Who wouldn't? Lidochka minutely prepared even the tiny roles. To be a lowly fairy in the suite of *The Sleeping Beauty*'s Lilac Fairy, she studied poses in old gravures; she thought out each gesture; she visualized the role in her mind. "Here are the *sirenki* [nickname for the Lilac's attendants, after the Russian word for 'lilac'-'*siren*'] lying in a line down a ramp, their right hands lightly touching their chins," wrote Kostrovitskaya, "and the public can't help but fix on one of them."[66] In the 1921–22 season's important last evening on April 30, Lopukhov put Lidochka and her already constant partner, Nikolai Efimov, into the divertissement collection that followed *Giselle*. The ballet master even pushed the earnest Mikhailov, giving him a bit part in *Daughter of the Pharaoh* but grooming him for *The Sleeping Beauty*'s prince. Lopukhov, Mikhailov wrote later, "prevented all my ardent young longing from dying at the root, without any soil to grow in."[67]

All the talented youngsters moved up when Lopukhov came in 1922—except Georges. He was featured only when Lopukhov wanted to showcase him as a young choreographer. Georges did dance with Choura and Mikhailov on that same April 30 season-closer as Lidochka, in his own new piece, *Valse*. But he was barely used in the regular repertory. "It was difficult for Georges in the theater," wrote Kostrovitskaya. "Lopukhov knew by the graduating performance [of 1921] that Georges was a good classical dancer and a wonderful [*velikolepny*] *caractère* dancer. But except for letting him choreograph independent 'numbers,' he was not in love with him. Stubbornly he set him in the remote corps de ballet, to hold garlands, move stools, stand in groups . . ."[68]

Such conduct by Lopukhov seems to confirm the personal authority Georges already wielded. Lopukhov was trying to master orchestral scores and set ballet alight, and here was this pale, proud youth already a real musician studying at the Conservatory and a real choreographer, whereas Lopukhov, twice his age, was just finding his own choreographic voice. And Georges was loved by his peers. It's probably not surprising that Lopukhov rarely cast him in the spring of 1922. In February, when Elizaveta Gerdt danced the faintly ridiculous Petipa ballet

Daughter of the Pharaoh, Georges played two bit parts: pyramid guardian and pyramid genie. On March 26, he finally got a bigger part, in a benefit for Elsa Vill: *The Nutcracker's* Buffoon. This was a hoop dance for a yellow-and-black-striped carnival figure together with four identically costumed little boys. Georges had often played one of those boys. Now he was their leader, in the part originated by Shiriaev. In his tight-fitting striped suit and a red wig, he flew across the stage with huge *saut de basque* leaps, holding a hoop behind his back. People broke into applause as he flashed by. And when he "jumped through the hoop repeatedly, tucking his legs under him" at the end, the audience went wild.[69] His friends thought this was the highpoint of Georges's performing career. To them he was dancing out all his frustrations at being held back in his career, his confusions about love, his longing to become something or someone in this volatile profession.

Georges's *Nutcracker* performance, the peak of his life as a dancer, was a wild declaration of longing, a cri de coeur.

NINE

The Young Ballet

Young artists from GATOB.
Seated: Balanchivadze; standing, Ivanova, Efimov, Kozlov, Danilova, Slavianinov, Vdovina, Nikitina.
Courtesy Saint-Petersburg State Museum of Theater and Music.

E ven if ballet master Fedor Lopukhov had treated him as a rival, young Balanchivadze willingly joined Lopukhov's first real revolutionary experiment, a plotless work set to Beethoven's Fourth Symphony that Lopukhov modestly named *The Grandeur of the Universe* (*Velichie mirozdaniya*), though everyone including him called it after its genre, *TanzSymphonia*. Despite its awkward name, this ballet stands out as probably the most radical dance experiment in the early NEP, maybe in the whole decade of the 1920s.

Lopukhov started rehearsing his eighteen volunteer boys and girls (nine of each) in spring 1922 and continued all summer, exploring this genre he considered new, "symphonic dance."[1] He'd first realized dance could mirror orchestral music in 1916, while watching a late Fokine ballet (from 1913), the almost abstract *Preludes*, set to Liszt. Lopukhov liked it immensely, even if others didn't. If plotless music could exist along with "plotted" music, he thought, why shouldn't plotless ballets cohabit with narrative ballets? "'Plotless' doesn't mean without contents!" he wrote in his 1966 memoir. "Plotless music has contents, and ideas, and themes!"[2] He settled on Beethoven's Fourth for his experiment, partly because Beethoven was ubiquitous then: his 1814 opera *Fidelio* about eighteenth-century Spanish political prisoners made him in Russian eyes an honorary revolutionary.[3] But the "contents, ideas, and themes" Lopukhov matched to the symphony didn't quite add up to a ballet scenario. They concerned life and death, growth and decay, and several varieties of energy, especially the "passively developing female principle" and the "actively pulsating male principle"—a scientific-sounding list worked out with his sister Evgenia's husband, a scientist.

Of Lopukhov's volunteer dancers, most were twenty or under. Only Lidiia Tiuntina was older, already twenty-five. Five came from the class of 1919, including Slonimsky's girlfriend Natalia Lisovskaya. Choura Danilova was alone from the tiny hardship class of 1920. Five more, including Georges and Lidochka, had graduated in 1921, and two, Georges's friends Piotr Gusev and Leonid Lavrovsky, had just graduated. This group worked patiently for Lopukhov as he fit steps to Beethoven's slow-building musical arcs. But even with Lopukhov's surviving diagrams and explanations and scenic artist Goncharov's drawings and silhouettes, it's impossible to tell what the ballet was like.[4] So much depended on the performers, who'd been partial creators too. "He really trusted the actors," remembered Gusev. "He gave us only a sketch of what he wanted. All the rehearsing, the working through and finishing, we performers did ourselves."[5]

TanzSymphonia was conceived in four parts to match Beethoven's four movements, labeled by Lopukhov "Life in Death and Death in Life," "Thermal Energy," "The Joy of Existence," and "Eternal Movement." A subsection of the first movement called "The Birth of Light" featured eight youths groping forward in blue light, overtaken by lightly running girl partners. In the longest section, the adagio, "Thermal Energy," Lidochka and Choura Danilova, alone onstage, mirrored each other in fifth-position *grand pliés* with arms joined crosswise. Then they stood and leaned out from each other, holding hands, in *passé* on pointe. Eventually, two partners joined them. In *TanzSymphonia*'s later sections, dancers evoked birds and butterflies, or imitated scythe motions in a field and Spanish dancing. Several squads feigned death or sleep, while others "woke up" and danced. The work's crowning point was a human spiral in a red spotlight. Those at the spiral's tail lay or sat, while at mid-spiral dancers stood and gestured upwards toward the highest central point—Lidia, lifted on the shoulders of a partner.[6]

Parts of *TanzSymphonia* were no doubt awkward. Danilova remembered being asked to move her legs on a two-count and arms on a three-count, challenging in those days. Kostrovitskaya, a witness, not a dancer, recalled Lopukhov counting wildly "10-13-6-6-2-5-11, etc." "He made the actors count, and not listen to the music!"[7] Nonetheless, the intent behind this work made it vitally important, at least for those in it. Here, finally, was that long-delayed search for the "pure" sources of ballet, uncolored by narrative tropes or dramatic attitudes. The theater's already decade-long quest for *its* sources had mined popular street forms like *commedia dell'arte*. Lopukhov and his brother-in-law went searching for ballet's in the realm of physics. Beneath any dance "surface," thought

Lopukhov, lay currents of energy, abstract but demonstrable. This was a very bold idea indeed. One contemporary Russian dance critic has called *TanzSymphonia* the "Black Square" of ballet, referring to the famous 1915 Kazimir Malevich canvas that pushed visual art into pure abstraction.[8]

At the very least, *TanzSymphonia* gave its participants, especially Balanchivadze, a switch in perspective they might not have encountered without it. Balanchine's later ballets turn on this belief that energy patterns can trump narrative in a dance construction. Lopukhov's emphasis on the ensemble also informs Balanchine's work. In many Balanchine ballets, soloists emerge from the corps de ballet and return to it, as they did in *TanzSymphonia*. Another Lopukhov feature in Balanchine's work is the idea that ballet's usually segregated "flavors," classical and *caractère*, can intermingle in plotless works. Lopukhov was also perhaps the first to make dynamic (rather than decorative) use of the lowest stage level, the floor, on which he had his dancers lie down and which Balanchine called on later (in the 1957 *Agon* pas de deux for instance). Lopukhov also pioneered a new pairing in "Thermal Energy": two girls together instead of a boy and girl (and two such important figures in Balanchine's life—Lidochka and Choura!), which could have inspired later female pairs in Balanchine's work, such as the two women mirroring each other, fugue-like, in Balanchine's 1941 *Concerto Barocco*. Even some of *TanzSymphonia*'s more contrived parts might have inspired young Balanchivadze. Watching Lopukhov earnestly plotting dance onto his precious orchestral scores, Georges might have seen that he could do that too, but without the fuss.

Lopukkhov's *TanzSymphonia* was never granted the serious public reception it should have had. Shown first in rough form to invited experts in September 1922, it sparked what Lopukhov thought "a profitable discussion." But by the time a real audience finally saw it, in March of 1923, an aesthetic war was raging behind the scenes, and Lopukhov's oddly gallant if maladroit experiment got caught up in this. Lopukhov's opponent, without his intending it, was the dance critic-philosopher who'd given frenzied voice in *Zhizn Iskusstva* to the old ballet's nostalgic defenders, Akim Volynsky.

Volynsky, then in his early sixties, was a frail, bespectacled, priest-like person. He had found his way to dance in the 1910s, during the culture-wide frenzy over Isadora Duncan's Russian appearances. Around this time, Volynsky became a "Hellenist," a believer in the ancient Greeks' "religion" of art that seemed to offer an antidote to Russia's casually anti-Semitic Orthodox Christianity. Volynsky had already had a major (though cantankerous) career as an advocate of the Russian symbolists. After he began to celebrate Duncan, a reverse epiphany hit him. He understood that Petersburg's own Franco-Italian-Russian ballet was even more "Hellenic" than Duncan's barefoot dance. It possessed a codified system like ancient Greek theater, and far more vocabulary for worshipping beauty and clarity than any free dance. Some say Kshesinskaya helped Volynsky toward this revelation by inviting him into her salon (or even paying for his praise). Whatever the cause, Volynsky's equating the imperial ballet with modernistic Hellenism was his great contribution to dance literature. From the time he discovered this synchronicity in the 1910s, he poured into his dance articles all the passionate erudition that had propelled him out of the Ukrainian Jewish pale where he'd grown up (as Chaim Leib Flekser) into the highest reaches of the imperial capital.

In the decade before the revolution, Volynsky, writing in *Birzhevye Vedomosti* (*Stock Market News*) was the first to really look at what ballet artists did onstage. He evoked what he saw through metaphors sometimes brilliant, sometimes over-effulgent. He was also the first to talk to the dancers themselves about their art. But one can feel in some articles an unsettling desire to get closer to his subjects than interviews warranted, especially to the ballerinas, and particularly the high and mighty Kshesinskaya. He had regular cozy lunches with her, as he reminded his reading public. Already in imperial times he'd crossed journalistic boundaries by instructing younger dancers in print how to remake their art to his specifications. With the February Revolution, Volynsky hardly missed a beat, writing repeatedly that ballet was the one art pure and noble enough to embody the solemn events of the day. But after October, the Bolsheviks closed down the whole bourgeois press, leaving Volynsky without a podium.[9]

When he returned to print in *Zhizn Iskusstva* in March 1922, he was no longer an armchair pedagogue—he had his own BaltFlot ballet school. His articles grew shriller on how the ex-Mariinsky should conserve its heritage: as literally as possible. He agitated for his colleague Nikolai Legat to become ballet chief, with him as Theater School head, a not-so-hidden agenda that drove his every piece. To this end, Volynsky belittled the ex-Mariinsky's reigning dancers, especially Elizaveta Gerdt for her "pure" classicism that fell short of former idols Pavlova and Kshesinskaya. He mentioned *them* in every article, which continually foregrounded his antirevolutionary nostalgia. He condescended to younger dancers, berating Choura Danilova for taking on a debased role like Lopukhov's *Firebird* and informing Lidochka that she lacked "the plantlike, picturesquely colorful substance of the theatrical adagio."[10] He even started a column with the title "Choreographic Advice," lecturing the ballet community on arcane technical points. He was ecstatically pessimistic about all of ballet. "Alas" peppered his columns. "My friend, classical ballet will last," he told readers brokenheartedly. "Its meaning is high and honest. It will last! It will last!"[11] When his campaign for Legat turned hopeless (Legat left Russia), he switched tacks and pressed for Nikolai Sergeev to be brought back, the hated ballet master who'd absconded in 1918 with notations of the whole repertory. Volynsky disapproved of actual ballet chief Leontiev. But his real wrath was reserved for Leontiev's assistant, Fedor Lopukhov, who'd meddled with the system of holy semiotics bequeathed by Petipa. The first thing he did on returning to print was lambast Lopukhov's *Firebird*, whose premiere he'd missed. And he stayed in attack mode for the next three years.

From on high, Lunacharsky tried to diffuse this feud in Solomonic fashion. In September 1922, he reconfirmed Leontiev as chief ballet master, with Lopukhov as assistant, but he also created a new government entity called Choreographic Advice, with Volynsky as head. In October 1922, an open meeting was held for ballet troupe, school, press, and public about Volynsky's attacks. But by year's end, these ballet "wars" were drifting out of public notice. A new social climate was abroad in the land. NEP-style cabarets had popped up all over the city; the first, Shkval (big storm), appeared in the dilapidated House of Arts, where recently the resident writers and artists had starved. Elaborate restaurant-cabarets followed: Slon (elephant), Monte Carlo, Taverna Maksim, In the Cellar, The Birzha (stock market), Donon's . . . Even the notorious Podval Brodiachei Sobaki (Stray Dog Café) reopened in its former cellar home across from the Grand Hotel Europe.[12] Dance acts sprouted to fill their stages, and *Zhizn Iskusstva* parodied them in constructivist-flavored cartoons.[13] Clothing for dancers and patrons also took a cue from the NEP. In October, a half page in *Zhizn Iskusstva* advertised a store called Petroodezhda (Petro-wear), the "source of art in the realm of clothes," offering "coats, costumes, dresses, underwear, headwear, fur stoles, neckpieces, boas, and muffs." The recovering city's citizens could finally give in to gaiety and self-display, just as the rest of Europe was doing in its roaring twenties. Nothing was unmockable, not even ballet. One of the cabarets hosted a show called "Archi-classical Ballet," featuring "The Swan Lake Fairy Doll, or The Little Humpbacked of the Sleeping Beauty."[14]

Real ballet artists spun off into lighter theater too. Lopukhov's sister Evgenia took a leave from the ex-Mariinsky to star in the sensation of fall 1922: a redone 1916 Viennese operetta called *Hanni Goes Dancing*, which poet Mikhail Kuzmin celebrated in a newspaper article. The "theater wars" happening all over Petrograd didn't concern him, he wrote, since over at the Musical Comedy Theater . . ." Hanni is dancing the Hop Sa Sa!" (whatever that was).[15]

The youngest Mariinsky dancers, not famous yet, risked less than their elders in cabarets, charity concerts, private soirées. For Balanchivadze, stalled at the bottom of the dance hierarchy, the cabaret scene offered a welcome way out. All who crossed from high art to *estrada* needed "numbers." Many asked Georges to make them, and he obliged, with a solo waltz here, an adagio there, a Dutch dance here, a fox-trot there . . . He was almost forced to turn away from dancing and think about dance making.

But he didn't have to think alone. His friends went with him to sample the new dance scene, not just his ballet companions but artist buddies Slonimsky, Dmitriev, and Erbshtein too. When Moscow's Kasian Goleizovsky brought his company to Petrograd in October 1922, the friends avidly attended. Goleizovsky wasn't just another theater radical who'd co-opted the ballet; he'd graduated from their own St. Petersburg theater school in 1909, and knew what to do with bodies. Yet he'd taken choreography out on a limb. He'd made boisterous works for children and erotically charged adult works, set to the "revolutionary-friendly" music of modernist composers Medtner and Scriabin. The Petrograd October audience saw the Goleizovsky suites *Medtneriana* and *Scriabiniana*, along with an explicit *Salomé*. Embedded in *Medtneriana* was a "Funeral March," which Balanchivadze eyed attentively—he would soon attempt his own. Afterwards, the whole group visited Goleizovsky in his hotel and talked through the night. Goleizovsky's ballets showed Georges that the classical vocabulary could be detached from its antiquated aura and retooled for audacious experiments. And his appearance—long hair, heavy earrings, finger rings—might have suggested the proper choreographer's costume.[16]

So far, the group was just a band of friends whose nucleus was Dmitriev, Slonimsky, and Balanchivadze, though girls—Lidochka and Choura especially—were important members too. Also key was the range of experience represented: ballet, art, criticism, history. A new member was the young Vitebsk transplant Ivan Sollertinsky, one of those surprisingly numerous postrevolutionary pundits who knew about everything *plus* ballet. Sollertinsky had learned early about dance at ex-Mariinsky dancer Presniakov's experimental Vitebsk studio, installed there in 1918 by Lunacharsky to complement that city's famous UNOVIS art studio.[17] Another new member was the dynamic young painter Solomon Gershov, from nearby Dvinsk. Many group friendships would later ripen to romance: Slonimsky would marry dancer Natalia Lisovskaya; Vera Kostrovitskaya would wed first Dmitriev, then years later, Gershov.

What made the friends unusual was not just their rebelliousness but their simultaneous reverence for old art. Figures like Dmitriev, Erbshtein, and Balanchivadze were, or would become, avant-gardists, yet they were also ballet history aficionados. Slonimsky, studying dance history at university, led the way. He was already working on his first book, a monograph on romantic ballerina Marie Taglioni and her first starring vehicle, the 1832 *La Sylphide*. He'd all but fallen in love with the pure and poignant Taglioni, and he made his ballet friends, especially George and Lidochka (the ones who would listen to him), read about her too. He probably deepened Lidochka's own Taglioni obsession—she always wore her hair pulled back Taglioni-fashion over the ears to a low bun. For the 1922 Theater School graduation, Slonimsky helped Shiriaev mount *La Sylphide*, about a young Scotsman in love with a forest nymph. Georges's best dance friend, Piotr Gusev, played the hero, James; Nina Mlodzinskaya was the sly Sylph, and Georges's first crush, Olga Mungalova, James' unhappy fiancée Effie.[18]

The group made a fetish of the old *ballet blancs*, *Giselle*, *Swan Lake*, and *La Sylphide*, even as they mocked ballet's more outlandish holdovers. Slonimsky, Erbshtein, and Balanchivadze liked to sing the most tinkly melodic of ballet scores, *Daughter of the Pharaoh*, out loud in the streets. Such a bifurcated approach puzzled many, but especially Lopukhov, who felt as they did but whom they treated as "an oldster." Some of the group, especially Georges and Erbshtein, would shout at him in rehearsal, "Not like before!" (a quote from Mayakovsky), meaning "Don't choreograph the old way!" Yet the simultaneous forward-backward glance was as important to the Young Ballet's aesthetic as the example of senior dance experimenters like Goleizovsky or Lopukhov himself.

Georges, though, wasn't only a group person. He had a private life with his paramour and dancing partner Tamara Geva. On October 24, 1922, he and Geva, eighteen and seventeen, officially married, or that's when they registered their marriage in Petrograd's Tsentralnyi Rayon (Central District) office. A ceremony may have occurred in the Theater School's chapel as well, presided over by Father Pigulevsky, as Geva claims. That's if Isaenko and Oblakov were able to get it reopened for the occasion as they'd done the previous March for Petipa's 100th birthday, with the help of a dancers' petition. Geva wrote later that Georges's father and brother traveled from Georgia for the wedding, though this seems unlikely given the distance, the ruined railways, and the Georgian Balanchivadzes' poverty. And where were Georges's mother and his friends in a school chapel wedding? No one has left an account of it except the bride. Georges's friends heard about it only afterwards; they'd barely known about Geva.

But for Georges, who did not advertise psychic events, this marriage was an ultraprivate affair, and in private terms a masterstroke. It paradoxically fixed his solo identity, shoring up his newfound independence from the Mariinsky complex that had been his world from childhood but had denied him a performance career. He still played the piano for school classes but didn't live there anymore. He also had a foot in the music world through the Conservatory, where he still studied. His choreographer's reputation was growing. And now he'd acquired the ultimate manly "accessory"—a wife, and a sophisticated one. Geva had intellectual proclivities, from her father's milieu. She managed a surface glamour too, even in scrappy NEP days when the people making the money weren't the dancers. Choura Danilova saw the "young and handsome" pair on the street after their wedding. Tamara was "beautifully dressed," she wrote. Choura herself felt dowdy, and hung back.[19]

It was probably in the fall of 1922 that Georges stopped going to ballet class. But he wasn't the only one detaching from the ex-Mariinsky. Dancers needed for cabaret concerts paid less attention than before to the serious stage. Audience attendance was falling off too, and not just for ballet. Officials from Lunacharsky down worried that popular entertainment was winning over highbrow.[20] Petrograd's great ballet troupe might have dwindled away amidst the frivolity if a grand event hadn't occurred in the fall of 1922. A magical Petersburg ballerina came back from abroad, to move audiences as they hadn't been moved since tsarist days. Olga Spessivtseva was twenty-seven, nine years older than Georges and Lidochka, a dark-haired languid beauty, inscrutable as a person but irresistible erotically to a succession of desperate souls, including Georges's friend Dmitriev. She'd been mostly in the West since 1918, recovering from tuberculosis, dancing for Diaghilev, studying with master ballet teacher Enrico Cecchetti. She had a miraculous technique that seemed to flow through her body and come out as spirituality. Shortly after Spessivtseva's return, the ever-alert Vera Kostrovitskaya watched her working with Vaganova through a studio door chink. The "pupil" was standing on pointe, yet she wasn't holding her arms up at the elbows as Vaganova always insisted. Her wrists were limp and her fingers "lightly hanging down." But "Vaganova did not correct this wrist!" wrote Kostrovitskaya, since on Spessivtseva it looked beautiful. Spessivtseva paused over a move that Vaganova had worked on with her students—"our" renversé from fourth arabesque to écarté. Then she got it, instantly and smoothly. As jumps neared, Vera feared she would falter, but she did them "lightly and quickly—naturally," as with everything. "And on the face of Vaganova," Vera remembered, "all the time, delight."[21]

Onstage, Spessivtseva rejoined her old partner, Viktor Semenov, he of the soft landings and smooth partnering, and the two raised ballet back to imperial heights. Spessivtseva made Giselle and Esmeralda even more tragic, and the India-themed Bayadère more unearthly. Even Don Quixote's audience wondered how such a creature could land in a noisy Spanish square. Volynsky's temperature rose in the pages of Zhizn Iskusstva: it was "his" prodigal who'd returned. Before her departure, he'd taken Spessivtseva under his wing and convinced her she had holy powers, which some thought contributed to her later mental instability. But in 1922, Spessivtseva offered the ex-Mariinsky not only balletic purity but an edgy glamour just right for the NEP. She and Semenov even got a jazzy caricature in the newspaper. At a charity concert, dance student Igor Schwezoff glimpsed the divine creature backstage, "standing on her toes—those fine, nervous points—admiring herself in the great mirror and being admired by some men who stood around. In one hand she held a tall wine-glass, from which she sipped; in the other hand a cigarette; while she took small, impatient steps on her points, made a few exercises to warm up her legs—a puff of smoke, a battement, a sip from the glass and a developpé that opened like a flower."[22]

Spessivtseva's return proved a boon for younger dancers. Her ease in the old roles raised their aspirations, and Lopukhov's own. He still hadn't had his audience response to TanzSymphonia, but he started now on his painstaking, exquisitely thoughtful, probably ultimately helpful refurbishing of the old ballets. They'd been mutilated by the hated Nikolai Sergeev, then shrunk and shuffled in the Civil War crisis.[23] Now he could "correct" them, and put a legendary ballerina in them too. And younger artists could grow in peace, without exceeding their skills.

During the winter and spring of 1922–23, both Choura Danilova and Lidochka matured into artists. They were paired onstage and in the public's mind. And in Volynsky's mind too, though he professed doubts about both, especially Lidiia, who'd "embodied hope" when she'd visited his school, but now, when she didn't come, coincidentally proved "disappointing."[24] Choura and Lidia danced the two key variations in *Coppélia*, "Prayer" and "Dawn"; the two chief Wilis, Mona and Zulma, in *Giselle*; companion sea creatures in *The Little Humpbacked Horse*; friends in *Corsaire*'s pas de trois; fairy soloists in *The Sleeping Beauty*. Lopukhov saw their rise as a "great event" for the theater. He and the older dancers had feared that stars were a thing of the past, but then the school sent them this pair, "antipodes" who completed each other. Ivanova "ruled 'in the air,' Danilova 'on the ground.'" Danilova was blond, pure, crystalline, even cold. Ivanova was dark, down-to-earth, and warm, even if her huge leap let her "hang in the air." But they're not quite equal in later memoirists' accounts. Choura, they wrote, was talented. But Lidia created something like a force field around herself, composed of emotions that can break the heart if embodied onstage. Anything she danced was imbued, said Lopukhov himself, "with some kind of inner holiness, urgency, ecstasy."[25]

It was this group of young people that trooped back to the rehearsal hall to reconstruct *TanzSymphonia* for its real debut on March 7, 1923, no longer just bright-eyed neophytes but stars in their own right. What did it mean to Lopukhov's grand experiment that it would finally be shown with a stellar cast? Not enough, it seems. *TanzSymphonia* failed, and it wasn't Lopukhov's fault. It had been put last on a special "jubilee" program of *Swan Lake* celebrating the ex-Mariinsky's longest-serving dancers. The audience had sat through ceremonial speeches and four *Swan Lake*

Alexandra Danilova as Veronika in Fokine's *Egyptian Nights*.
Courtesy Saint-Petersburg State Museum of Theater and Music.

acts before *TanzSymphonia* came on. As the curtain fell, there was no applause, no reaction. Or that's what the ballet master remembered. Kostrovitskaya wrote that half the audience left and the other half applauded. And Volynsky in his review went in for the kill. "It's both wildly funny and eerily sad," was his conclusion about *TanzSymphonia*.[26] Lopukhov had trouble hiding his grief even forty-odd years later. Just as he finished his 1966 memoir, the Paris Opera Ballet brought Balanchine's *Crystal Palace* (later called *Symphony in C*) to Leningrad. "Balanchine has invented a new genre of dance!" said young dancers. They didn't know, wrote Lopukhov sadly, about earlier experiments, not just his, but Gorsky's in Moscow and Fokine's in Petersburg. But Balanchine hadn't forgotten he was sure, that "in his young years he took part in Lopukhov's *TanzSymphonia*, and . . . supported my intentions to develop this genre."[27]

Maybe it was *TanzSymphonia*'s failure, plus the failure of an earlier dance experiment, Pavel Petrov's acrobatic *Solveig* of September 1922 (with Georges and Lidochka in it), that spurred the young people to take matters into their own hands. They started a small dance group, the Molodoi Balet or Young Ballet. Some witnesses credit Dmitriev or Slonimsky with the original idea. Georges's friend Piotr Gusev was the one who called the meeting of young dancers to see who was interested. But Georges, on the sidelines, was the "soul" of the group. When Gusev asked the small crowd what their *kredo* was, their first thought was that they didn't understand the question, but "Petya Gusev already seemed grown up and wise."[28] They answered anyway, "bravely," in a chorus: "We really want to dance. We will do everything that Georges finds necessary."

But Georges didn't begin with his own choreography. He asked his young colleagues first what they felt about the *old* repertory. "Each of the group, without being shy," Kostrovitskaya wrote, "said what he or she liked from the old ballets, and how (dancing them) we would infuse them onstage with . . . our own free artistic 'interior dance.'" They were supported in this belief by the special inspiration of their own mini-generation. Georges, Lidochka, and Choura were its "elders"; its "juniors" were the two-years-younger 1923 graduates, almost all of whom instantly joined the Young Ballet.[29] "Deep down, in our souls," wrote Kostrovitskaya, "several of us believed that with dance, one can do all: conquer evil—conquer evil in the whole world, and make people better and happier—and that dance should use a big space, and envelop a surface of many kilometers. Our dream was to cover the Field of Mars in the center of Petrograd ["it's now the Field of the Victims of the Revolution," she added in parentheses] with several *jetés*."

The Young Ballet

The Young Ballet began as a *kollektiv* in the pure revolutionary sense. Dancers picked their own numbers for its opening concert. Some chose new-made pieces, others old solos or duos—and this latter decision flew in the face of the hierarchy they'd grown up with. Choura and Lidochka were the only ones then dancing solos on the Mariinsky stage; the others hadn't yet earned that right.[30] The coming concert was to have two acts, with the shorter numbers, old and new, coming first. Many were Balanchivadze's: *Night* and *Poeme*, a Glazunov *Adagio* for Mikhailov and Stukolkina, a duet for Lidochka and Slavianinov, an *Adagio* for himself and Danilova from the music of *Javotte*, a sailor dance for himself and Geva, and a new *Dying Swan* "with Eastern coloration" for Stukolkina.[31] But other new numbers were the graduation pieces the dancers had made themselves, with school chief Oblakov serving as producer, choosing their music as he'd done for Georges and Lidochka. Tamara Masikova had made a small dance to Chopin, Veronika Faber a Beethoven polka, Mikhailov a pas de deux for himself and Vera Kostovitskaya, and Vera a solo for herself too, *Ekstase*.

It was the concert's second act, consisting of Balanchivadze's new group ballet to Chopin's *Marche Funèbre*, that would mark his breakthrough as ballet master. To make such a ballet was risky and ambitious, since recent group works by his elders had failed. Georges remained, though, ever modest and shy in rehearsals, just as the students remembered him from school. He rehearsed both parts of the upcoming show, making sure, as Kostrovitskaya noted, that his corrections weren't small or arbitrary but relevant to the "image" conveyed by the music.

For a performance space the Young Ballet had secured the hall of the former City Duma, a red brick building with a tower on Petrograd's main 25th of October Prospekt (formerly Nevsky Prospekt). Inside was an amphitheater with a half-circle stage facing audience bleachers.[32] Before opening as a performance space a year before, the Duma amphitheater had served as a lecture hall: Lunacharsky had given talks there on art and culture; Mayakovsky and Sergei Esenin had read their poems. The Young Ballet would be its first dance group. The hall was too small a venue to get its events advertised in newspapers, so Boris Erbshtein designed a big placard listing the dance numbers and placed it outside in front. "Evenings of the Academic Young Ballet," it said at the top in bold type, followed by a list of the seventeen participants and some of the numbers.[33] But the Duma hall already had a habitual audience, a rough crowd of Red Army soldiers, BaltFlot sailors, and the curious public from Nevsky Prospekt. Shows were free. Tickets were still handed out, to prevent a jam at the entrance. Even with assigned seats, the audience was noisy, freely shouting encouragement or disapproval. Once a major fight had broken out when Esenin was late for a reading.[34]

On June 1, the Duma was filled to the brim with its regulars and then some. The ballet crowd was out there too, as the nervous dancers backstage knew—Petrograd's balletomanes, as well as perpetual ballet students like Schwezoff who traveled from studio to studio with their "little ballet suitcases." From the Theater School, Oblakov and Isaenko had come to encourage their protégées. From the Ak-Theater itself, as Kostrovitskaya wrote pointedly in her notebook, *"no one came"* (she underlined this).

The lights went up. The pianist, the school's beloved Vassily Vassilievich Poliakov ("Uncle Vasya" to the students), struck up the first notes. The audience grew quiet. Numbers followed each other on the stage. Heartfelt applause met each. Lidochka's solo Rachmaninoff *Polka* was especially cheered.

Then came intermission. Backstage, the dancers changed into their costumes for the *Funeral March* and began to worry about it. Suddenly in swept Vaganova, their teacher. "You impudent girls! (*Nu, nakhalki*)," she said. "To dance what you haven't properly studied! And to choose ballerina roles!" "If I could have collapsed through the earth," wrote Kostrovitskaya, "together with the costumes, pointe shoes, makeup, and the whole thing . . ." Vaganova again eyed them sternly. "But on the whole, well done!" she said, breaking the tension, "especially your own numbers." Then "she snorted once more and escaped." The bell sounded again and put the dancers "literally in a fever." Balanchivadze said a few heartening words to them, "but he himself couldn't hide his nervousness," wrote Kostrovitskaya. The *Marche Funèbre* began to sound. Submitting to it "with our whole souls," the dancers filed onstage one by one.

According to Kostrovitskakya, Georges had made his composition with the Duma half-circle in mind, though without sacrificing internal coherence. Six dancers entered one after the other in a ray of light, slowly stepping on pointe, their heads inclined to one side, their arms crossed and stretched down in front of them. They wore pointe shoes, knee-length tunics of black and gray designed by Erbshtein, and little black caps with silver spirals on the ears. But no tights: their legs were daringly bare. At the center of the stage they dispersed into a circle, then dropped to one knee facing outside toward the hall, their bodies, arms, and heads bent low. On a new phrase of the doleful *Marche*, three men entered carrying a girl on her back in corpse position. They crossed the whole stage with big, grave steps, slowly raising her high above their heads. At stage edge they lowered her (Geva and Nina Stukolkina alternated in this role) to the same kneeling position as the other dancers. At that moment, the music swelled to Chopin's hopeful middle passage in a major key, and Danilova entered with light quick steps, crossing the stage. She went to each dancer, gently touching them, causing each to rise.[35] Gradually, the whole group returned to its feet, and then, "as if we were pure human souls waking from sleep," wrote Kostrovitskaya, began to move slowly forward in their circle. They kept arms crossed and down but gradually changed their expressions, as if they were dreaming of "something faraway, wonderful and full of light."

At the close of the *Marche*, when the slow drumbeats had sounded and the dancers had left the stage, the hall fell silent. It seemed to those backstage as if they were alone. "'Failure, failure, failure!' said the silence." Then there came from afar "a suspicious din." The audience was stamping its feet. They were whistling and clapping. Georges had captured something of the grief of their lives, the hope, the disillusionment, weariness and pain of revolutionary times. From the top of the house, the soldiers and sailors stamped and clapped even louder. Then came the unison shouts, "Go on, do it again!"

The Young Ballet's *Funeral March* was performed a second time.

TEN

The Last Year, Summer to Summer

Giselle rehearsal, Theater School.
In foreground, Makletsova and Dudko; far right, Lopukhov, Ivanova, Danilova. Courtesy Saint-Petersburg State Museum of Theater and Music.

Even in an incomplete description of the Young Ballet's *Marche Funèbre* of June 1923, one recognizes some motifs Balanchine would use in later ballets: the circle of dancers on the stage rim, energizing the now empty center; the solemn yet light steps on pointe for the female corps de ballet; the girl as "corpse" who's the focus of the mourning; a second girl acting as a kind of angel of grief; the sacrifice of someone who belonged to the group in life and is now part of its spirit. Such familiar motifs apparently present in this earliest group work raise the mysterious question of where a choreographer gets his or her "primal" material, those recurring compositional tropes that comprise a signature.

What did it mean that a circle (or half-circle) figured so prominently in Balanchivadze's first group work, and in later works too, especially this one's groundbreaking cousin, the 1934 *Serenade*? Did it come from the shape of the Duma theater? Or did it have a meaning in Balanchivadze's own psyche, related perhaps to patterns implanted during childhood? Did it stem from the ancient Georgian circle dances, especially a warriors' dance called the *khorumi*, which resolves momentarily into a circle and in whose climax one dancer is raised to the others' shoulders to "scout" the surroundings?[1] When small, Georges could have heard about the *khorumi* and possibly seen it with his father. But the dancer raised up in *Marche Funèbre* isn't "scouting," she's horizontal on her back, "dead," at least symbolically. One could answer that a funeral march required a corpse. But why did Georges pick a funeral march? Because of Goleizovsky's earlier funeral march? And whose funeral was it—a victim of the revolution? A primal figure from his imagination, forced to die so the living could go forward? To the *khorumi* must be added another possible source: the funeral-pageants of revolutionary martyrs held in Petrograd's Civil War years, with corpses in open coffins carried by solemn phalanxes of men. Balanchivadze's adolescence was filled with public funerals. Other key sources for *Marche Funèbre*'s funeral could be the ballet classics: the dead Wilis in *Giselle*, or the trance in *The Sleeping Beauty*. In that work's first act, sixteen-year-old Princess Aurora pricks her finger on a spindle (as foretold) and falls down in sleep, at which point attendant courtiers raise her above their heads and carry her offstage. Did *Marche Funèbre* consciously or unconsciously enact another funeral for the sleeping Aurora?

Virginia Woolf has suggested that one's earliest memory registers split-second impressions from preverbal shocks or revelations—"moments of being" amid dailiness. But the child choreographer would have had his senses open not only to stop-time scenes but also to moving ones. Are there such things as kinetic "moments of being?" If so, how early did they occur in Balanchine's life? In his first Petersburg years, when his father played Georgian music and possibly showed him the dances? Certainly, folk dance roots of all kinds can be found in Balanchine's later work. In the isolated country years in Finland, when the child practiced piano to a backdrop of forest, wind, and clouds? In his Theater School education, when the ballet vocabulary lodged in his body and the ballets he saw onstage "from within" gave purpose to his training? In postrevolutionary years, when his training merged with high drama in the streets? Balanchivadze's landing so early in the Theater School probably meant that theatrical events had as much "primal meaning" as real-life ones. Whatever the sources, it's clear that some of Balanchine's habitual onstage groupings and rituals were already in place in the summer of 1923.

So too was the nature of the Young Ballet as a company, that *kredo* Pyotr Gusev had asked the young dancers about. They'd put their trust in Georges because they believed, like him, that their dance was an art with a high purpose. Georges's friend Mikhailov clarified this view when he contrasted it to another notion of ballet, embodied in an Ak Theater event held in the spring of 1923. "Following the example of the Paris Opera Ballet, even our 'cathedral,' the Academic Theater of Opera and Ballet, was turned into a huge restaurant," wrote Mikhailov indignantly, probably referring to a famous NEP Mariinsky masked ball. The seats in the parterre were replaced by tables with white tablecloths, the tiered facades of the loges were hung with flower garlands, and dinner was served to Nepmen and Nepwomen dressed as Harlequin characters. On the stage, selections from the classic repertory were danced—as a joke. The pas de deux from *La Fille Mal Gardée* was performed by a man in a girl's tunic and a girl in male peasant drag. *Swan Lake*'s four "little swans" showed hairy legs beneath their tutus. And "the most popular ballerina" of the day and her partner performed a number that began with their running onstage in coats, hats, and felt boots, mocking (somewhat bitterly) their recent artistic lives.[2]

The Young Ballet was a response to such blasphemy, offering something like a corrective to the official "academic ballet," itself struggling to stay alive in the cruel new economics. The young dancers wanted to reinsert ideals back into art the way the Kronstadt sailors had tried to put the revolution back on course. In doing this, they were also reaffirming the artistic education their mini-generation had received from school director Oblakov and his staff. The Young Ballet gave its dancers something they'd counted on finding in their own theater but hadn't. "Moral satisfaction," Mikhailov called it, and the enviroment for that. "The Young Ballet gave us an 'air vent,' through which an influx of free thoughts about art came to us," he wrote.[3] The little company wasn't only about experimenting, but also about preserving an idea of true art in the face of NEP bourgeoisification. One could call it reactionary. It even practiced a kind of social welfare that the NEP had made obsolete. When the group found itself with leftover money from concert earnings, this was offered, at Georges's suggestion, not to everyone equally but to members who were sick or weak and needed food for strength. That's how young Vera Kostrovitskaya remembered the procedure. She, with her chronic tuberculosis, might have benefited.[4]

But if the Young Ballet was conservative within the freewheeling NEP moral climate, it was radical in terms of the theater itself. There, the old ritual hierarchy still reigned, even if the directors were scrambling to make money. Young dancers still waited for years for even small roles, as in tsarist times. It was this hidebound tradition that had prompted Agrippina Vaganova, backstage at the Duma, to call the young dancers impudent. The Young Ballet had set itself up as a collection of equals without ranks or "stars." Everybody worked together. All performed corps de ballet parts, but even the youngest got to express themselves, alone onstage or with a partner. In this sense, the new company was in tune with other cultural forces still fiercely holding onto revolutionary purity. Radical theater directors, for instance, weren't ready to give up the idea of equality. In Yevgeny Vakhtangov's groundbreaking 1922 Moscow production of Gozzi's play *Princess Turandot*, the actors in evening dress processed to the footlights and donned "costumes"—a turban, a scarf, etc.—in full view of the audience. In Meyerhold's 1924 Moscow play *D.E. (Give Us Europe)*, the actors outdid each other in quick costume changes and mask exchanges.[5] Rank and status are theatrical illusions: that was the message these auteurs wanted the audience to get. In the music world, too, the early NEP years saw a series of conductorless orchestras. The ensemble could be the conductor.[6]

So, too, in the Young Ballet, Georges went out of his way not to be dictatorial but to let the dancers suggest some of the repertory, and compose it too. This helped ensure their dedication. It wasn't easy for these young dancers in the NEP to give away their time. At GATOB they received "miserable salaries" for dancing constantly. They had to race around after hours to make extra money, in cabarets, movie houses, and restaurant floor shows.[7] Devoting hours to the Young Ballet was no small thing, but with the "no stars" credo they could show an audience their art. That went even for Georges. In the fall of 1923, he was still on the Mariinsky-GATOB payroll, at the back of the corps de ballet.

Two Young Ballet members, though, were heading fast up the theater's hierarchical ladder, Choura Danilova and Lidochka herself. What did dancing with the little company offer them that GATOB couldn't? No doubt the same "moral satisfaction." Old ties of friendship also bound them to Georges and to what he did. Perhaps even more important was that the Young Ballet kept them in their school group, sharing, as in the cold and hungry years. That was the spirit that the young company had institutionalized, along with the intense enjoyment of working together now threatened by NEP competition. A snapshot shows Young Ballet members in summer clothes in front of a stage curtain.[8] It could be summer 1923, after the Duma concert. Balanchivadze sits on a stool. Behind and above him stands Choura in a white dress, probably on another stool. Lidochka to his right, also in a white dress, is next to Efimov and G. Kozlov; on his left stand Vdovina, Nikitina, and Slavianinov. All look happy and easy together, especially the two "stars" among their equals.

By the summer of 1923, Choura Danilova had been in the theater for three seasons. Already in her second, she'd been entrusted with the acrobatic bird of Lopukhov's *Firebird*. True, there was a gap in the ranks right above Choura and Lidochka caused by civil war hardships, which meant that the youngest ones with talent were likelier to get bigger roles. But even with a smaller company and this personnel gap, Lidochka's and Choura's rise was a phenomenon. With no new repertory aside from isolated experiments like *Firebird*, the senior dancers held tightly to their old star turns in the old Petipa ballets and the slightly newer Fokines, not just to leads but to the solo variations that offered the way up.

Choura was ahead of Lidochka in conventional terms. After her *Fire-bird* lead, she'd received in spring 1923 the coveted Veronika in Fokine's *Egyptian Nights*, the temple dancer who loses her slave "husband" to Cleopatra's amorous greed, just before Mark Antony arrives in chariot to claim Cleopatra himself.[9] Choura danced it whenever it ran. In the fall of 1923, she was given a chance at *The Sleeping Beauty*'s Lilac Fairy. Choura, it seems, was respected by both older dancers and critics, including Volynsky. He proved his special interest in late October 1923 by chiding her again in print, this time for dancing half-nude in Veronika's costume (as if it were the dancer's choice).[10] Choura had her own admirers too—Nepmen, high Bolsheviks, and foreign diplomats posted in Petrograd who kept her and others supplied with the silk stockings they couldn't afford. "I was always invited to the theatre, to the opera, to all the new movies, to late-night restaurants with live music," she wrote later, remembering especially one candy shop owner who took her on sleigh rides.[11] In October 1923, Choura got her own cartoon in *Zhizn Iskusstva*: a constructivist Veronika in scanty striped Egyptian triangle. At the end of the 1922–23 season, she was clearly on the way up, not as a soubrette but as a classicist in the tradition of Elizaveta Gerdt, who also taught her privately.

Lidochka's rise was different. After two seasons, she didn't dance principal roles yet, but she'd gotten an unusual number of lesser fairies, frescoes, and sea creatures; a duet in *Egyptian Nights*; *Swan Lake*'s Pas de Trois; two parts in *Carnaval*. Nothing on the scale of Danilova's *Egyptian Nights*, yet from these small roles she'd made a colossal personal reputation. By the summer of 1923, she'd become the favorite dancer of a broad spectrum of Petrograders, from literati to BaltFlot sailors.[12] When the Pavlovsk summer theater opened on June 24 with a ballet evening instead of the usual music concert, only three dancers were advertised: "E.I. Vill, V. Semenov, L. Ivanova, and others," read the announcement.[13] Her pictures were in shop windows. "From every shop window there was smiling a child in a tutu," said the writer Nikolai Nikitin. When Lidochka went to Pavlovsk to dance, people got up from park benches to see her walk by. They went to the station to find her train and crowded around her car. "Let's go to Lidochka," people would say when they went to the theater. Such attention, Slonimsky noticed, was not the usual ritual fuss around a theater diva. It came from spontaneous affection for Lidochka's onstage persona, so joyful it made her seem like family.

What were the mechanics of this persona? First, there was Lidochka's famous jump that carried her halfway across the stage. It wasn't a light jump; she wasn't sylphlike but a little plump. It was a mighty jump, a heroic jump, like "a bird with a wide wingspread," wrote Mikhailov.[14] She launched herself and rose to a high place—and stayed there. A high jump and the staying power usually didn't come together in one body, as Kostrovitskaya explained. And Lidochka gave her elevation a special accent by splitting her legs wide as she went up (before her, dancers kept their legs decorously closer together, even in leaps) and moving forward at the same time. "No one taught her this," wrote Kostrovits-kaya; "she thought it through herself and used her possibilities from nature."[15] Nowadays Lidochka is considered the inventor of this split-leap that became key to Soviet ballet style (and American ballet style too, through Balanchine), and of its cousin, the wide-open version of the *pas de chat* ("leap of a cat"), which takes a huge gulp of air.

Onstage, Lidochka deployed her jump in a number of ways. In *cabrioles*, she brought her "standing" leg high up to meet the other in the air, an exciting effect usually reserved for male dancers. As the fourth of four Moorish "Frescoes" who step from a tapestry in *The Little Hump-backed Horse*, she entered last, to a welcome burst of brass in a fussy violin and flute waltz. She was supposed to leap up in *écarté* (profile to audience), describe a double *rond de jambe* with the leg in the air, then land, and push onto the other leg into an *attitude* (bent arabesque) pose—then repeat the maneuver five more times. Instead, Lida's first mighty leap, with her air-leg describing two leisurely circles, seemed to propel her in one fell swoop into her *piqué attitude*, as if she'd not landed at all but flown down from that huge first leap into the final proud pose. "The whole theater resounded with shouts" the first time she did the step, and she repeated it five more times.[16]

But it wasn't just the jump that excited fans. Lidochka had unusually strong pointe work too, say witnesses, and an expressive face with "huge, huge eyes," conductor Mravinsky remembered. Lida's slanted eyes seemed to open wide in charged moments and shine on the audience "like searchlights."[17] She put this passionate craft to the service of anything she danced, highlighting steps no one had noticed before, small details, modest transitional passages. In Fokine's 1916 *Eros*, about a girl torn between the pagan god and a Christian angel (the angel wins), Lidochka played one of nine nymphs dancing the traits of romantic love in front of the statue of Eros. Lida's nymph was Jealousy. The music was Tchaikovsky's *Serenade for Strings*, which Balanchine would later use for his first American ballet. The *Eros* nymphs danced to the sweeping waltz that would become the Balanchine *Serenade*'s second movement (perhaps with the ghost of Lidochka still in it). Mikhailov didn't remember each separate step, but he vividly recalled the end when she ran zigzag on pointe from upstage to down. "With unbelievable lightness, sharply accenting the rhythms, she rushed to the footlights, her body pitched forward, her arms held in a halo above her head, her huge black eyes shining. This run was so full of sparks that the whole hall spontaneously broke into applause (and usually this part of the dance didn't make any impression at all)."[18]

Others remembered Lidochka's "Dawn" in *Coppélia*, when she gradually opened her body on the musical arc from despondency to vibrant hope; or the "Crumbs" Fairy of *The Sleeping Beauty*, in which she seemed to spray precious stones of happiness into the air; or the last-act Diamond Fairy, when she crossed the stage in two leaps and in that urgent music "shone—shone more than anything, so that everything glittered before and after her."[19] All memoirists mention the waves of applause. Lidochka's impact was enhanced by a kind of revolutionary aesthetic that seemed to cling to both her dancing and her life. She was known to be impatient with the old ballets' silly plots and tinkly scores, to love instead the deep lyricism of Tchaikovsky and the even more modern composers: Rachmaninoff, Sibelius, Scriabin. These offstage preferences merged with her stage persona to convince people that Lidochka had stumbled on ballet's missing revolutionary agenda.

Lidochka's mischievous defiance was seen especially in a small role in *Le Corsaire* in spring 1923. The ballet had been restaged several times by Petipa (from 1868 to 1899) after the 1858 original by Joseph Mazilier, itself loosely based on Byron's poem about shipwrecked Greek pirates rescuing Greek slave girls from Turks, all to the oompah-pah sounds of various old composers. Lidochka played a slave girl shown off to lascivious pashas. But she galvanized the role, displaying her scorn for it even as she danced it to the hilt. This was a slave girl refusing to cower in sad captivity, teasing her owner-merchant, the comical buyers, and by extension the old ballet itself. "It seemed as if she was ready to burst out of confinement, and with one jump, cross over the footlights and orchestra pit into the audience and there wake *it* up with her pranks," wrote Kostrovitskaya.[20] At last, someone had figured out how to bend an old plot to revolutionary ends without even changing the steps. The slave wins out, thirty-three years before Spartacus hit the Soviet stage! Lidochka's antics even momentarily sidelined the tragic Olga Spessivtseva, onstage too as the heroic Medora. Slonimsky emphasizes the contrast: Spessivtseva in her otherworldliness summed up centuries of the old imperial ballet; Lidochka with her vividness announced the new.[21]

And Lidochka's "new" meant not just political but emotional. Her memoir-writing "witnesses" didn't just list her roles but described them minutely. Each went on for pages, as if swept by memory back into the dance. Lidochka made audiences feel she was saying something, something vital. "There—that's all that I can bring her for happiness," was what Kostrovitskaya heard her "saying" at the end of her *Sleeping Beauty* "Crumbs Fairy" variation. "Just dare to sell me to that old Graybeard! I'll just run away!" Mikhailov heard in her *Corsaire* slave dance.[22] The excitement further built from Lidochka never saying what was expected. "Ivanova rarely danced the same way twice," wrote Slonimsky, "believing that changing every number from one time to the next brought to old dances new features."[23] Sometimes she came onstage with no advance idea how she would proceed, Slonimsky said, even if she'd usually fixed dance textures in her mind. "Mood, inspiration—call it what you will—directed her every gesture, step, body movement, giving her audience the precious impression that she was improvising the dance, pouring it out of her very soul."[24] She was a dancer "in the moment," the phrase Balanchine used later as a mantra for his NYCB dancers. It seems Lidochka invented this mock unpredictability, out of sheer high spirits and acute musicality, just as she'd invented the split-leap. Or else she'd extended her teacher Preobrazhenskaya's improvisatory musicality. "You receive pleasure when you listen to the music and see an artist onstage also listening nicely to the music," wrote Kostrovitskaya. "But has it happened to you that you didn't even listen to the music as you watched, because the whole body of the artist, her whole being, has *become* this music? That miracle occurred in my life twice. The first time—Lida; the second—Alicia Alonso."[25]

Lida's compulsion to reach audiences seemed to come from deep inside. Sometimes she'd leave the stage and say that "it didn't work tonight," meaning she hadn't fully reached them.[26] But holding an audience was difficult as the NEP entered its third year. Dance venues multiplied. Besides Petrograd's twenty-odd "state", "government," and collective theaters, there were movie houses, miniature stages (where dance divertissements were mixed in with "small songs," wrote Mikhailov), workers' clubs, art exhibitions, even the Circus, plus the after-hours cabarets, restaurants, and casinos. The official casinos, ironically, proved the superior venues, even becoming "hotbeds of culture," as Mikhailov remembered. Their shows occurred at a reasonable hour before patrons hit the gambling tables. This allowed for complete pas de deux or trois, with variations, like the *Paquita* Pas de Trois Mikhailov remembered dancing with Lida and Choura at "Casino," at 96 Nevsky, near Fontanka.[27]

More taxing were the flash appearances in cabarets, nightclubs, movie theaters, and party meetings that could happen at any hour. Cabarets, especially, kept late hours. "In front of couples heated up with wine, dressed in fancy Nepman clothes," wrote Mikhailov, "together with distinguished dancers (and me only a boy) we had to appear after midnight." The most popular spots were Taverna Maksim, the Letnii Bouffe, Donon's (with its prerevolutionary red velvet curtains and secluded alcoves), and the Hotel Europe's roof restaurant. "To the sound of glasses and ceaseless talk, serious songs were heard, and soul-pinching romances and mood songs, along with salon dances like the Death Tango and the One-Step. Among them appeared me, with a partner, in, for example, the classical duet *Night* made by my comrade and friend Balanchivadze." Many dancers used *Night*, courtesy of Georges. How did they know not to perform the same dances? In fact, the most popular dancers booked themselves for multiple nightclubs on the same date, then ran from one to another, not even removing makeup and costumes, just throwing on coats and hats. After one number, they would jump into an *izvozchik* horse cab waiting at the stage door and emerge into the next theater's wings "straight from the street, from the frost and snow," wrote Mikhailov. "They'd cast a businesslike peek at the audience, checking that they'd gotten the right place; then they'd take off coats and hats to reveal a Greek tunic, and, assuming the look of ancient Hellenic youth, urgently ask the conductor to move them up in the line of numbers so as not to be late for the next engagement."[28]

In the NEP years, there was a bureau, a part of the Union of Workers in the Arts, known as Posredrabis (acronym for Intermediary [Bureau for] Workers in the Arts), which helped match theater artists with venues. Its director liked dancers. "But the way to his heart was not always easy," wrote Mikhailov mysteriously, perhaps referring to some service that assured his good graces. Every dancer had a series of "numbers" in readiness—short solos, pas de deux, pas de trois—which could be quickly performed on small stages. It's hard to pinpoint the style of these; in the volatile NEP climate, commerce, art, tradition, and experiment were all mixed together in both venues and dances. The experimental dance scene was even more vigorous in Moscow than in Petrograd: Goleizovsky injected sex into ballet steps; Nikolai Foregger had dancers impersonate machines; a certain Lev Lukin propagated *his* "free dance." . . . But the Moscow groups often hit Petrograd on tour. On one June evening in 1923, Petrograd's Free Theater offered Foregger's *Machine Dances*, a *Foxtrot Macabre* by a Russian pair, and a potpourri of comic songs including *Okuli Pokuli*.[29]

In Petrograd, many of the floor-show numbers were Georges's, though not all. Mikhailov made up his own number to a Chopin étude, *Perpetuum Mobile*, which he danced in a tight costume adorned with a spiral. He flew around at presto tempi in various jetés, fast turns and big pirouettes, impersonating the new energy. Lidochka had an *Italian Polka* by Rachmaninoff that she'd probably choreographed herself (always bravoed and repeated); also a "heartwarming" *Valse Caprice* by Rubenstein, a dance to a Schumann piano song, a spicy number to Glinka's *Venetian Night*, and a gentler *Spring* set to Grieg's "Spring," all by her or unknown others.[30] She'd earlier danced *Spring* at the winter opening of an exhibition of nineteenth-century landscape painter Arkhip Kuindzhi, and received three little paintings in payment (not by Kuindzhi): an autumnal cabin, a house on a peninsula, and a sailboat on the open sea. On the back of the cabin is written in her round, vertical hand: "5 February Monday 1923. For a concert at the Exhibition of the Kuindzhi. I performed Grieg's *Spring*."[31] She also danced two pas de deux by Georges. One, to a gypsyish waltz by Fritz Kreisler for herself and her usual partner Nikolai Efimov, was "unveiled" at a July 31, 1923, evening of "Dancers from the Ak Theater." The other, *Enigma*, to Arensky's music from Fokine's *Egyptian Nights*, she performed barefoot with Georges himself (who later danced it with Geva). *Enigma* was one of only two of Georges's numbers to make it to the ex-Mariinsky's stage. It used the latest, most chic acrobatic steps around, including a "bridge" backbend done by Lidochka that attracted a storm of protest from the powers that be. The "bridge" reappeared later (in Balanchine's 1972 *Stravinsky Violin Concerto*, for instance).

There was also Lidochka's somnambulist solo, like a short story by Poe, set to Sibelius's brooding mini-masterpiece *Valse Triste* and constructed intentionally in the "plastic" style of Isadora Duncan. Kostrovitskaya remembered Lidochka making it herself while still in the school, but it evolved after that in consultation with Georges. Kostrovitskaya puts *Valse Triste* in some Young Ballet concerts. Mikhailov claims, more plausibly given its shock power, that it wasn't seen till a May 1924 Ak Theater evening, when it eclipsed all else shown. From the depth of stage left, Lida entered in a ray of light, wearing, in Kostrovitskaya's words, a "smoky" chiton, her back to the audience, face hidden in her arms, long black hair loose (it fell to below her waist). She walked backwards on a diagonal from the upstage corner to the footlights. "But it was the kind of walking that made the hall freeze; they didn't breathe," wrote Kostrovitskaya. The rest of the dance was so "sharply emotional" that Kostrovitskaya says she can't describe specifics. "From far away, darkness, suffering approached, and threatened death, in the fight with which it won," was how she put it. The dance was about "the pure and strong soul of a girl [*chistaya i silnaya dusha devushki*]," which couldn't prevail in the struggle. Mikhailov remembers virtuosic turns and pointe work and a series of leaps rising "from piano to fortissimo." Near the end, Lidochka ran in ever-narrowing circles as though driven to center stage, where she shuddered as if caught like a wounded bird, and in a last gesture, threw her hands forward to protect herself from an engulfing wave. "But in its onrushing force," he wrote, "she fell as if dead, with no more force to resist."[32]

Where did this harrowing dance come from, when the others were so joyous? What was the fear that propelled it? All the young dancers were living fast as the NEP reprogrammed a whole city's behavior, but Lida's pace was breakneck. It was a rare Mariinsky ballet she didn't dance in, remembered Mikhailov. Daily rehearsals came with these performances. She also took regular classes with one of the great figures of Mariinsky history, the seventy-five-year-old Ekaterina Vazem, the first Nikiya of the 1877 *La Bayadère*, still teaching a daily class to dancers who wanted it. Lidochka made sure to attend, though she didn't always attend other official ballet classes. There were also Young Ballet rehearsals when an engagement loomed, plus countless nightclub gigs. On her own and with partners, Lidochka was one of the most popular on that circuit. Besides all this, she'd started serious work on her singing, studying privately with a Conservatory professor, Josif Shvarts, preparing the role of Tatiana in Tchaikovsky's *Eugene Onegin*.[33] And she didn't stop attending the concerts, readings, art exhibitions, and theater performances that filled Petrograd in those years. She was seen constantly about town.

As if this wasn't enough, Lidochka was hired in fall 1923 to dance in a movie made by the local Petrograd branch, SevZapKino (Northwest Cinema), of the newly nationalized (in 1919) Russian film industry. The once robust prerevolutionary industry was still recovering from inactivity during the Civil War, when film stock and projectors couldn't be had. Revolutionary subjects were finally finding their way into the movies. Lidochka's, called *Dvorets i krepost* (Palace and Fortress), was a costume drama about mid-nineteenth-century radicals and their mortal enemies, tsars Alexander II and III.[34] At one point in the film, the younger tsar (the older has been assassinated) attends a ballet performance in the Winter Palace's Hermitage Theater that features Lidochka with a corps de ballet, dancing a *Chopiniana*-like ballet. She looks pretty and vivid in a long romantic tutu for literally a second, before the film cuts back to the star prisoner being laboriously fitted for leg irons. Then the tsar and all his court leave the theater in a lengthy procession. *Palace and Fortress* may have brought prerevolutionary history back to life, but it missed its chance to do that with Lidochka. Still, by December 1923 *Palace and Fortress* was running in two big Petrograd movie theaters, the Parisiana and the Picadilly, and in spring of 1924 it was one of the first Soviet movies exported to Germany.

Lidochka, not surprisingly, was late to almost everything. It was as if *she* were a *perpetuum mobile*, and sometime that year, says Slonimsky, she veered toward recklessness. A photo of a ballet rehearsal in spring 1923 shows visiting Moscow ballerina Ksenia Makletsova reaching down toward Mikhail Dudko on the ground. Behind them stands a line of corps de ballet in tights, leggings, and tutus with one arm raised, and at the end of the line, next to Choura, stands Lida, her arm raised too. But she's wearing a street dress and high heels, as if she'd come in late and hadn't changed. Natalia Lisovskaya's iconic memory of Lidochka is also a breathless one. Lisovskaya was waiting backstage with two other Frescoes of *The Little Humpbacked Horse* for the fourth Fresco, Lidochka, late "as always." Just when the waiting Frescos panicked and decided to costume the understudy, Lidochka flew in like a whirlwind, full of impressions about something she'd just seen and wanted to talk about. "Quick, quick, Lida, get dressed! We're late!" they all cried. Without a pause Lida began to put on her costume and limber up at the same time, but then veered toward the mirror and her own reflection. "Look! My eyes have gotten bigger!" she exclaimed. "They've grown!" Her fellow dancers were called onstage; now the dressers hurried Lidochka. But suddenly "her" music sounded from the orchestra pit and she "flew like a bullet" out of the dressing room. "Huge applause met her first step," wrote Lisovskaya. "'Bravo, Ivanova, bravo!'"[35]

The story suggests mood swings, self-dramatization, maybe even the cocaine present in high Bolshevik circles. But Lidochka didn't slow down to rest, she just went faster and faster. And her pace seemed to generate in her an undercurrent of dread, perhaps the dread that powered *Valse Triste*. It seemed the stage was the only place where Lidochka could unleash all that was in her psyche. There alone she seemed to find the wholeness that eluded her elsewhere in life. She still lived at home with her parents. Alexander Ivanov had been demobilized from the Red Army in the summer of 1922. A few months later, he became chief of repairs in one of the Soviet Union's first massive plants, Svetlana, that made light bulbs. The family apartment at the corner of Sotsialisticheskaya St. and Pravda St. (formerly Ivanovskaya and Kabinetskaya) had a room for Lidochka where she made a shrine to ballet with engravings of her idol Taglioni and other romantic ballerinas. She even had a private phone, with a separate number from her father's.[36]

But she was rarely home. Her parents worshipped her, but they pushed her, or her father did. He told her to go to Ekskuzovich and demand bigger roles. Slonimsky saw that the parental pressure plus the constant attentions of fans was obscuring Lidochka's judgment. She wasn't always given good advice. Danilova and Geva, writing later and out of range of Soviet censors, report that Lida didn't just dance in nightclubs, she attended them with high-ranking Chekists. Lidochka was seen at the secret police club at 1 Gorokhovaya St., across from the dread Cheka/GPU headquarters at 2 Gorokhovaya (the Cheka had been "reformed" in 1922 and renamed).[37] She enjoyed in fact much of what of this uniquely promiscuous moment in Soviet history could offer a young ballerina, including the intimate attentions of the Bolshevik elite. Balanchine remembered that one Party boss especially courted Lida and used to kiss her white shoulders. Slonimsky's belief that Lida grew more nervous in late 1923 rings true, if paired with a review Volynsky wrote in November chiding her for a lackluster performance as the *Corsaire* slave girl. Lida had impossible standards for herself, and her whirlwind life didn't help her meet them.

This crisis didn't occur in Lidochka's life alone. The NEP's second full year produced a society-wide identity crisis, especially among youth.[38] They'd lived through four stern Civil War years, suffering in the name of the Revolution. Now they'd been flung into a different time when ideals were fading, nightclubs flourishing, and Nepmen and Nepwomen flaunting fancy clothes, liquor, even cocaine. Such a high life was beyond most Petrograders, but the dancers on the *estrada* circuit saw it nightly while performing for this NEP elite. And they were still so young! Lida had been pushed from childhood to be a ballerina, which meant going out on the town with whoever were the higher-ups. If such behavior accompanied a gradual pulling away from parents, especially from a father who'd been too close to his daughter, internal turmoil would result. In 1922, Lidochka had inscribed a *Chopiniana* photo of herself, "to my close one, from his very warmly loving daughter, Lidiia Ivanova." Was it meant for her actual father? If so, did she still feel that way a year later? Had something in their relationship pushed her to become "Varotchka" as well as Lidochka, to split internally and imagine an escape route? The carousel that was Lidochka's life was turning faster and faster.

Georges was going fast, too, though with his reticence, the opposite of her theatricality, he didn't betray the tension. True, he'd eased his schedule by making what must have been a painful decision: to abandon his music studies at the Conservatory just short of a piano diploma (as his father had done). But he still played three hours a day for the Theater School's midlevel ballet classes, he rehearsed daily at the Ak Theater, he danced twice a week in its ballets (Wednesdays and Sundays were still ballet days), and he staged numbers for his friends and performed in nightclub and cabarets with his wife. When Tamara branched out as a cabaret *diseuse* in French and German, he went to those jobs too, as her accompanist. The summer of 1923 gave him a respite from his school job, but the Young Ballet, whose June 1 Duma concert had been a hit, stepped up its claims. Its repertory fit well with the NEP's fragmented concertizing; it could offer an evening-length show or a few short dances, depending on the needs of the small *estradnye* stages. Amateur producers didn't want the old variations, only the group's new *Marche Funebre* and the short numbers by Balanchivadze and the others. The summer of 1923 was when Georges switched his inner focus from dancing to choreographing. And by summer's end, his Young Ballet work paid off. He was invited to choreograph at a real theater, the former Mikhailovsky. The introduction was probably made by an influential theater critic who'd gravitated to ballet, Alexei Gvozdev, another mentor for Georges, and who would shortly replace Volynsky as dance critic at *Zhizn Iskusstva*.[39]

The Mikhailovsky was the old tsarist French and German theater that Lunacharsky and Ekskuzovich had been reinventing since 1917. Lunacharsky in particular wanted it to be Petrograd's second opera theater, which it became from 1918 on. But its new identity was wider too. It hosted experimental plays with the *feel* of cabaret, becoming a second, freer stage for both other ex-imperials, the Mariinsky and Alexandrinsky. In 1921, the Mikhailovsky was renamed the Maly (small) Academic Theater, or "Malegot" for short. People soon realized this neoclassical hall tucked behind the Hotel Europa was "listening closely to its time." Celebrities from both opera and drama performed in it, including the great bass Feodor Chaliapin.[40]

Georges's task, starting in August of 1923, was to make the dances for the Maly's coming season opener, a new production of Rimsky-Korsakov's 1907 *The Golden Cockerel*. It was Rimsky's last opera, composed at age seventy-one, a year before his death, when the conservative backlash to the 1905 revolution had compelled him to one more effort. In 1914, Diaghilev had staged a shortened *Golden Cockerel*, but in France, not Russia. Now the Maly took on Rimsky's (actually Pushkin's) fable about a stupid king, conniving queen, and wicked sorcerer, to retool its satire for a new time. This was the first collaboration of the soon-to-be-legendary duo: conductor Samuil Samosud and director Nikolai Smolich. Samosud in 1923 was a Mikhailovsky theater veteran who "not only heard the music but saw it" and matched it to actors' movements—a useful example for a young choreographer. Smolich, who'd been an Alexandrinsky actor and director, also revealed a musical flair. Artist Vladimir Shchuko clothed *The Golden Cockerel* in Russian-miniature style: red, yellow, and black, with the enemy kingdom in ancient-Persian lilac. But modern technology figured as well. The second-act dance for the Queen was filmed and shown on a movie screen. Georges made the steps for the movie as well as the live dances in the first act.[41]

The aim of this *Golden Cockerel* was to bring the theater's revolutionary-experimental spirit into the seemingly resistant art of opera. Ballet, opera's sister art, was even more stubborn about resisting experiments. But Georges had landed in one of opera's breakthrough moments: *The Golden Cockerel* was an opera parody with a serious end. It would run throughout 1923–24. And at a time when the Revolution, even diluted by NEP, was still spawning attempts to reconfigure the classics as contemporary texts, the Malegot's production upped the ante. It reimagined Rimsky, while staying "in the frame of the composer's stylization," as the critic Elena Tretiakova wrote later.[42]

By the time *The Golden Cockerel* opened on September 13, 1923, Georges was already at work on his next Malegot project, a production of George Bernard Shaw's 1901 *Caesar and Cleopatra*. Petrograd theater experiments had always showed a heightened sensitivity to theatricality beyond text. Since Stanislavsky in the late nineteenth century, plays had been staged with specially written music, and specially made dances. This practice had culminated in Meyerhold's great 1917 *Masquerade*, with its Glinka-centered score by Glazunov. The Maly's 1923 *Caesar and Cleopatra* continued the trend, featuring strident music by the future movie composer Yuri Shaporin, tailored to the raucous treatment of the old Egyptian-Roman tale by the no-nonsense Shaw and then by his Petrograd interpreters. Georges's society dances took their cue from the Prologue's cabaret setting. Playing free and easy with history distinguished this particular picture of Roman Egypt from the others available at the time. In fall 1923, Petrograders could choose Fokine's *Egyptian Nights* at the Mariinsky, Shakespeare's *Antony and Cleopatra* at the Alexandrinsky, or the Malegot's *Caesar and Cleopatra*—which was more a bacchanal than a history play.[43] Shaw's Maly hero, wrote one reviewer, was ready to don any mask needed, including the ultracontemporary. But in the NEP, contemporary bourgeois decadence could be displayed only if it was condemned before the curtain fell. Under the circumstances, Georges was almost forced to master those scandalous foxtrots and shimmys.

His next Maly project made use of this mastery: the first Russian staging of the German expressionist drama *Hinkemann, the German*, premiered only a year before in Germany, now renamed in Russian *Eugen Neschastny* (*Eugene the Unfortunate*). Its author, Ernst Toller, was a World War I veteran and the ex-People's War Commissar in the short-lived Bavarian Soviet Republic of 1918–19. His hero Eugen was also a vet, one who'd returned from the war a "hidden" cripple, castrated, and convinced his wife would stop loving him. The play's setting, Berlin, allowed the Maly to once more put the criminal social indifference of the West on display. "Armless, legless, blind . . . prostitutes calling their clients in harsh despairing voices . . ." began the excited Russian reviewer when *Eugen Neschastny* premiered on December 15, 1923, "and right next to them, indifferent messieurs, fat gendarmes, sated policemen keeping order—and cafes, music, dances!"[44] The play's director was Sergei Radlov, a former Meyerhold disciple who'd specialized in freewheeling topical drama with his Theater of Popular Comedy ((in the Iron Hall of Petrograd's Narodny Dom) that included a famous clown and some jugglers. With *Eugen Neschastny*, he crossed over to serious theater, but retained his expertise with crowds. Georges's dances enhanced these crowd effects, especially in a scene where the suffering proletariat gathered below a two-story café whose lit upper windows showed the silhouettes of dancing couples. Georges had probably taken the idea from the famous moment in Nikolai Evreinov's 1920 pageant *The Storming of the Winter Palace* when hand-to-hand combat was silhouetted in the Winter Palace's windows. He was praised by name for his dances in *Zhizn Iskusstva*

Eugen Neschastny gave Georges his first chance at high-level theatrical collaboration. The play's haunting music was by Mikhail Kuzmin, Petrograd's great and notorious homosexual poet, composer, and dandy-about-town.[45] Georges's young artist friend Vladimir Dmitriev did the cubist-expressionist decor. Altogether, the Radlov-Kuzmin-Dmitriev-Balanchivadze team transformed a little man's cri de coeur into an almost too lascivious display of capitalist Europe's decadence. The *Zhizn Iskusstva* reviewer wasn't sure the text could bear it. Still, *Eugen Neschastny* sparked newspaper debates long after it opened and must have boosted Georges's self-confidence.

By 1923's end, he'd choreographed three important productions at the chic Maly and countless nightclub and Young Ballet numbers. Sometime that winter, Georges also made another ambitious group work (now lost) for the Young Ballet's second concert in the Duma Hall, set not to music this time but to a vocal chorus from the Institute of the Living Word reciting Alexander Blok's 1918 verse epic *The Twelve*. The long poem, written in rough rhyming couplets, charts a tale of twelve Red Guards marching through revolutionary Petrograd on a winter night, with Christ at their head. It's monumental and humble, and heartbroken. Blok had merged his own poetic voice with the voice of the people, capturing the new language of his transformed country. It would be thrilling today to know how Georges moved his dancers to Blok's sounds. But the fact that Georges engaged with the poem at all shows how intensely he was bound up with his time, with revolutionary emotions and the theater's refractions of them. Young Balanchivadze wasn't a Bolshevik; deep down he was still the boy drawn to the rituals of the Orthodox Church. But in the winter of 1923–24, as he approached twenty, he was alight with new ideas, part of an adventurous group of youth just like him. Culturally, they lived almost in an idyll. Russia hadn't yet closed in on itself. The vision hadn't faded of a vibrant Bolshevik arts milieu in dialogue with the rest of the West.

Georges even worked with the most antic cultural force in the city, the ad hoc group calling itself FEKS (Factory of the Eccentric Actor). Two friends had made FEKS, Leonid Trauberg and Grigory Kozintsev, twenty-one and eighteen. They also counted in their circle the even younger Dmitri Shostakovich and the slightly older Sergei Eisenstein. In 1923, FEKS was still a theater group; later it would progress to wildly innovative filmmaking. In theater, FEKS took up where Radlov and his Theater of Popular Comedy had left off, with rowdy commedia improvisations barely tethered to text or structure. After the NEP forced Radlov to close his theater, he accused FEKS, only half-jokingly, of stealing his patent. Georges advised FEKS on the choreography of their popular "play," *The Wedding (not according to Gogol)* that ran in 1922–23 in Petrograd's Experimental Theater. The play *was* mostly choreography, but with a crazy newsreel flavor. *Wedding* captured the fascination of Petrograd youth with the surreal new world of machines, cities, cinema, and celebrities, whose shorthand name was "Amerika." Charlie Chaplin, Albert Einstein, several robots, and three suitors on roller skates were some of its characters, yet it also drew on anthropological studies of real peasant weddings.

By the winter of 1923–24, Georges had become the city's go-to guy for new choreography, or one of them. As always, though, the pull towards experiment was mixed in his psyche with loyalty to the ballet traditions he'd trained in. Buoyed by his reputation, he chanced a very public gesture in late December 1923, which both defied and embraced these traditions. The elderly Volynsky was still attacking the Ak Theater's ballet in the newspaper, maligning present-day dancers and directors and invoking past paragons. Volynsky's targets grew increasingly irritated, especially Leonid Leontiev, still head of Ak Theater ballet, and his assistant Lopukhov, whose *TanzSymphonia* had earlier been trashed. Volynsky, however, was a prestigious figure, probably protected by Lunacharsky. But in mid-December, he put himself in a risky position, presenting a class demonstration of his BaltFlot School students and a *Nutcracker*. Volynsky's enemies seized the moment to move in, but it was Georges who "fronted" the attack in a full page article in *Theater* magazine. "If you'd read the majority of Volynsky's articles," writes the young choreographer, "in which he reveals all the unfortunate features of our ballet, you would expect from his 'Choreographic Technicum' [the fancy new name Volynsky had given his school] a renewal of classical ballet." That wasn't what you got. "How awful!" (*Kakoi uzhas!*) was the gist of his reaction. If the students had studied for only a year, that would be ok, but they'd studied for two. "Backs—they have none; their feet don't point; their movements are coarse; their flexibility [*plastika*]—is nil; their technique is simplified; their turnout—not especially; their mime is impossibly faint." Here, by negative example, Georges reveals the principles that would guide him all his life: innovation, yes, but based on rigorous training. In the midst of possibly the most confused moment in history for Petrograd's ballet, the winter of 1923, George stood up and said what *he* thought should be its future.[46]

Still, it was risky to put his name on such a prominent attack. Volynsky, never strong on objectivity, responded in January 1924 by heaping shame on "people who take the trouble to attack children on the stage." Then came a broadside against Georges himself. "So far the theatrical biography of Balanchivadze doesn't amount to much," he writes. He remembers that Georges had danced quite nicely *The Nutcracker*'s Trepak (as the Buffoon) two years ago (in 1921), "and was praised by me in print." But since then the young dancer has been "almost extinguished" on the Mariinsky stage. In fact, writes Volynsky, Balanchivadze has left ballet for the popular stages and for the "piquant and unbridled" genre of cabaret dance. "This is also a road to fame," Volynsky mock-concedes, "on which Balanchivadze can thrive, in any case in the material sense of the word . . . But now this young man thinks he can distinguish a battement from a glissade, an arabesque from an attitude . . . !" Volynsky even attacks Georges's writing. "Choreography is saved, but where is orthography?"[47]

How peculiar it must have been for Georges to be known citywide, even infamous, but to be obscure in his own Ak Theater. On December 22, 1923, the theater renewed his contract, confirming him as an "Artist of the Ballet Troup of the State Academic Theater," but at the bottom of the scale, the thirteenth rank, and "receiving compensation accordingly . . . that is, 2,745 rubles subject to taxes" (not a lot—the wildly inflated ruble was about to be replaced in February 1924 with gold-backed *chervonets* notes).[48] Even if Georges didn't want to dance at the ex-Mariinsky, he wanted to make dances there. But his enemies wouldn't let him. His immediate superior Lopukhov wasn't the problem. It was his old teacher, Semenov, soloist and partner of reigning ballerina Spessivtseva, who thought Georges's fledgling choreography irreverent, even blasphemous. Matters weren't helped when Tamara, Georges's wife, heard from Mikhailov that Semenov had called her a tart and Georges hadn't defended her (Semenov had taken Geva on a summer tour as he'd earlier taken Lidochka). Exhorted belatedly to act, Georges went back the next day and punched Semenov in the jaw.[49]

Had a gap begun to show in the young marriage? Tamara had found her own stardom as a European-style singer-dancer even before she'd finished her courses at the Theater School (she would graduate to good reviews in May 1924). Georges was her pianist. She was already a woman of the world. He, for all his professional authority, was still a boy, at least physically. His body hadn't filled out; at nineteen, he looked fifteen. In the winter of 1923–24, he and Tamara moved out of the Zheverzheevs' quarters to their own apartment at 8 Griboyedov, the corner of Griboyedov Canal and Italianskaya St., not far from the Russian Museum.[50] Georges was working on choreography, spending his free time in rehearsal rooms. Tamara served as "material." They probably had fun outside the studio, too. But being a husband wasn't Georges's forte. In the evenings, he was often too tired to squire his young sophisticate about town.

Lidochka too was caught up in her own conflicting desires. She was waiting for a lead role, but she was hard to cast. She was too vivid onstage, and offstage she made no secret of scorning the old conventions. "Be patient, the roles will come," she told her parents when they urged her to act. But perhaps inside she was afraid of being stalled. Georges and Lidochka weren't alone in their anxiety about where they were going in the NEP. Capitalism had arrived, but no one knew the rules. As 1923 became 1924, the opacity of the future prompted frenetic living. Could the NEP last, or would the arts change again? In late November 1923, the Ak Theaters' director, Ekskuzovich, took a month-and-a-half off, his first break since 1917. The city erupted in rumors: Ekskuzovich was out; Gorky's wife Maria Andreeva was in; Moscow's theaters were tired of supporting Petrograd's; the Petrograd Ak Theaters would be shrunk and put in control of a Moscow office. . . . Ekskuzovich's second-in-command M. P. Kristi did his best to quash the rumors: his chief deserved his holiday. But suddenly, on the evening of January 21, 1924, a huge change did occur, with serious consequences.

Lenin, the inventor, defender, and helmsman of the revolution, died. He was only fifty-three, but he'd had three strokes and he'd been a walking corpse since spring 1923.[51] Still, his end was a massive shock. Enormous crowds gathered on Nevsky Prospekt and in the Field of Mars with the revolutionary martyrs' graves. Resolutions were passed asking that this mighty figure too be buried in Petrograd, the site of "his" revolution. One was penned by the workers at the Red Guard Factory. Lenin had gone to Moscow "only temporarily, on a business trip," they wrote (they meant the 1921 transfer of government from Petrograd to Moscow). "Give him to us to bury, here where he worked and where he lit the flames of revolution!"[52] But this was not to be. A compromise ensued; three days after Lenin's death, the St. Petersburg of Georges and Lidochka's youth, and the Petrograd of war and revolution, got its third reincarnation: Leningrad.

The tremors were felt city-wide. A slow-motion struggle for power had gone on in the Party for over a year, out of the public's view but not beyond its radar. Marshaling their forces were two men at the top, Stalin and Trotsky, based in Moscow but eyeing Russia's second city too. Dangling uneasily between them was the Petrograd/Leningrad Party boss, Grigory Yevseevich Zinoviev, convinced that parts of the government would now move back to Leningrad; not powerful enough to make this happen. But with Lenin dead, the gloves were off. Stalin won the first round in the deadly game, as he would win the others. He'd sent Trotsky in November to Abkhazia in the North Caucasus for a rest cure (Trotsky's weakness was his hypochondria). Now he sent him a telegram about Lenin's death, but "mistakenly" advanced the funeral date so Trotsky would have no hope of getting back to Moscow. Trotsky probably couldn't have traveled anyway: Stalin's Abkhazian crony Nestor Lakoba was watching over his cure. A nationwide cult of Lenin had begun spontaneously, but Stalin had coopted it. Stalin's "Lenin" would dictate much of the Soviet Union's later aesthetic face: the Mausoleum shrine in Red Square, the badges and uniforms, the heroic paintings and giant statues.[53]

Now in the aftermath of this death, the editorials that opened each weekly edition of *Zhizn Iskusstva* began to shift their tone. "Art should become a carrier of the ideology of the proletariat!" said the one on February 19, 1924. In March, Lunacharsky stepped out of his usual anonymous place in "his" newspaper to sign a two-part editorial on the "Art Policies of the Soviet Government." "It's entirely obvious," he wrote, "that the government can't brush aside the duty of subsidizing those big artistic treasure-houses that retain the serious artistic traditions of establishments which the proletarian government has received from previous epochs." But the government expected something in return. What? "We're already on the road to a real proletarian theater," Lunacharsky affirmed, but then he throws around so many terms like "mass" and "artistic-industrial" that a reader feels even the buoyant commissar sliding into doublespeak. Of course, it's tricky to read policy from editorials. One wonders, though, whether this shift in the political climate had affected Georges's employment chances. Or maybe it was his recent attack on Volynsky. After being ultra-busy in the fall of 1923, Georges got no choreographic engagements at the Maly or anywhere else that spring of 1924. His old teacher, Alexander Chekrygin, who'd been the Maly's and Alexandrinsky's nominal chief of choreography since fall 1923, took over its hands-on dance making. Georges's two-years-older school comrade Vasily Vainonen was hired that spring as dance master for the Theater of Free Comedy.

Georges was in a bind. In April 1924, he was asked by prima ballerina Elizaveta Gerdt to make a variation for her benefit performance. Three years before, in Pavlovsk, he'd failed her as a partner; maybe this was her gesture to him as a choreographer. But hers seems to have been his only spring commission. For obvious reasons, the Young Ballet now became vital for Georges, providing his only forum. He worked all spring on its forthcoming concert, scheduled for May 1924, in the Troitsky Theater on Troitskaya (now Rubinstein) St. It had earlier been the private theater of Fokine's brother Alexander, then was managed for a while by dancer-impresario Lidia Pavlova; now it had become the long-awaited studio for the ballet (and drama too). The Young Ballet belonged there. But the May 24th concert was not a success, at least not to the critic most important to Georges, Gvozdev, the thirty-seven-year-old professor and theater critic who'd taken over in March 1923 for Volynsky as dance critic for *Zhizn Iskusstva*. The new critic's succinct and thoughtful prose offered a welcome corrective to Volynsky's lengthy missives. He'd pushed hard for ballet to have a studio like the theaters, and he'd encouraged Petrograd/Leningrad dance experimenters, especially Georges. But the Young Ballet's May concert fell short of his hopes. The repertory, as he described it dismissively, contained "flirtatious things from Arensky and Rubinstein. There was a polka by [Evgeny] Vilbush-evich and some homemade foxtrots. In a word," he writes, "the show strays somewhere beyond 'artistic culture.'"

On the surface, Georges was undeterred. He'd started an even bigger project for the Young Ballet, a staging of Stravinsky's *Pulcinella*, com-missioned by Diaghilev in 1920 for a ballet by Massine. It was based on *commedia*-flavored works of the opera buffa composer Giovanni Per-golesi and other Italians, rearticulated with modernist vigor. *Pulcinella* offered Georges an ideal mix of tradition and experiment; a 1924 ballet by him might have put onstage *his* version of all the masked Pierrots, Harlequins, and Columbines of Petrograd's haunted modernism, or their spirit. According to Kostrovitskaya, Georges was completely engrossed in it and expected to finish it in the fall of 1924 when his dancers returned from summer break.[54] Vera herself had to leave re-hearsals early, in April, to go to a Caucasus sanatorium; her tuberculosis had worsened. Georges was onstage the evening she left, but sent a friend to tell her she must "get better and save her strength for the coming autumn's work on *Pulcinella*." (Later, in 1927, Lopukhov would take over the project and make *his Pulcinella*. Much later, in 1972, Bal-anchine finally made his with Jerome Robbins.)

Ambitious and inventive as they were, such speculative projects couldn't earn Georges a living. In the faint impression comes through historical documents that he'd hit a wall. And Lidochka too. That spring of 1924, she made new friends in prominent positions. She met the bril-liant Mikhail Chekhov (nephew of the playwright and actor-hero of Moscow's Vakhtangov Theater) and began a series of intense conversa-tions with him. She started a correspondence with the writer Mikhail Zoshchenko, author of beloved stories about the absurdities of postrev-olutionary life. She'd met him at a party and written him a fan letter. He answered in his deadpan literary voice, saying he was glad to hear from her but found ballet unnatural and silly. She wrote back (on March 12, 1924) that he'd read her mind. She suffers too from ballet's foolishness. "I have a worried nature," she continued, "and I'm more worried now when you say that ballet is stuck in a routine. Sometimes I can't bear it and I go out to another theater," she added. Both Chekhov and Zoshchenko contributed to the commemorative booklet Lidochka's father commissioned in 1927.[55] Zoshchenko quoted their correspon-dence in it but left out the end of her last, May 1924, letter, which suggests a needy frame of mind. "I love your eyes they're wonderful (*chudnye*) eyes," Lidochka wrote longingly (and without punctuation) to the older writer, "And if our correspondence can continue I will be grateful."[56]

One could say that both Georges and Lidochka harbored inner long-ings both private and professional that couldn't be satisfied under present conditions. When the chance came for a summer tour that would take them beyond Russia's borders—beyond the borders of what had just been officially renamed the Union of Soviet Socialist Republics—they both leapt at it. They'd been shut inside their slow-motion revolution since 1917. Neither had been out of Russia, only to Finland when it was part of the empire. But such a tour wouldn't have seemed as cataclysmic to them then as to us now. Olga Spessivtseva had gone out on tour and come back several times; Elena Lukom had often toured abroad. Dancers' tours were periodically announced in the newspapers,. In summer 1923, *Zhizn Iskusstva* had written that both Choura and Lidochka would soon perform in Germany with Lopukhov. Important figures like Alexander Benois, Alexander Glazunov, and Ekskuzovich went abroad regularly for business.

"Before Lenin's death," as Balanchine once reminded Taper, "there was freedom to criticize; the students spoke their minds freely."[57] Balanchine told Taper too, firmly, that he didn't leave Russia "out of moral principle, in the sense that he had wanted to do some great work which had been censored or prevented." He left because, in the early spring of 1924, someone offered to pay for a tour. The someone was an acquaintance from the opera world, a man about forty years old, who seemed to embody the NEP's extremes.

His name was Vladimir Dmitriev (the same name as Georges's younger artist friend Vladimir Dmitriev, though with the patronymic Pavlovich instead of the artist's Vladimirovich). He was an opera singer. In the 1922 city directory, he's on the roster of the Maly, which is probably where Georges had met him. In 1924, he's missing from that roster, though he's still listed as "artist" in that city's directory, *Ves Petrograd* (All Petrograd). Earlier city directories show no trace of him, at least as a singer; he could be the 1916/1917 Vladimir Pavlovich Dmitriev listed as a lowly *praporshchik* (ensign) of the Russian army, though people who knew him later in America mention an aristocratic background. After the revolution, many people reinvented themselves radically, and not just once. But even if this Dmitriev had already switched from army officer to opera baritone, by 1924 he'd switched again. He'd lost his voice, say both Danilova and Geva in their memoirs. So he'd waded into the NEP and became a croupier at the government-regulated gaming tables, probably at the casino called "Casino." He liked ballet and pretty girls. He'd amassed a lot of cash that he wanted to spend on this tour, perhaps insuring himself a way out of the country as well. He asked for

Georges, Lidochka, Choura, and Efimov, and of course Geva was part of the package. Dmitriev's first choice for a destination was the Russo-Chinese city of Harbin in the southern Far East, on Russia's busily commercial Chinese border. The tour would include musicians as well. On April 4, 1924, all its proposed members signed a contract with Dmitriev, naming him their agent. Ivanova's up-and-down signature is the biggest and boldest; Balanchivadze's is fancy, its letters diminishing to form a cone on its side, enclosed in an oval made by the last stroke of the pen. And their destination had already changed. Visas to Harbin and China took too long. They would try for Finland, and maybe Sweden.[58]

The five friends planned in secret, away from even close comrades (no one could afford to take the whole Young Ballet on tour) and the risky notice of ballet elders. They met at Georges and Tamara's apartment. In late May, Lidochka pulled out of the tour: a fortuneteller had told her she would die on water. Then she rejoined. On June 10, *Zhizn Iskusstva* stated in its events listing that "Five Soviet dancers are slated to dance 'Russian numbers' in neighboring Finland," and listed their names with the musicians'. But before they left, they had to finish the theater season and dance its remaining *Swan Lakes, Esmeraldas,* and *Pharaoh's Daughters.* On June 15, the day it ended, the five appeared in a concert at the Pavlovsk Concert Hall, together with the All-Russian orchestra and two opera singers from their theater, in what was probably a tour rehearsal. They danced numbers they'd done on the *estrada* circuit, many by Georges, conducted by the conductor, Vladimir Dranishnikov, who would tour with them. Afterwards the group took the train home and reconvened at Tamara and Georges's apartment.

In June in Leningrad/St. Petersburg the summer light never completely darkens, but only fades to midnight blue, bathing the great Neva River and its palace-lined canals in a blue light. Wandering at night provokes dreamlike thoughts. Having returned from their Pavlovsk concert, the five wandered from the Vitebsk Station up Vladimirsky Prospekt to the Nevsky, then along it to Georges's and Tamara's Griboyedov Canal apartment. They drank tea in the kitchen and talked through the night, about practical matters and dreams too: what they would do when they got to the West, what they would buy and see. One small worry was the still-missing exit visas.

Can we imagine them there? Georges, leaning against the wall, listening but unmistakably in charge; Tamara handing teacups to her guests; Choura making a wide-eyed, emphatic statement; Efimov the wonderful partner, nodding agreement (he was Kolya, short for Nikolai); Lidochka laughing, gesticulating, seizing on one idea after another, spilling over with vitality . . . At dawn, they dispersed to their separate homes to rest before the working day. Choura, Lidochka, and Efimov were supposed to dance again that evening (the Pas de Trois from *Paquita*) at the Izmailovsky Garden summer theater on the Fontanka. Lida was going out earlier on a canal boat excursion with some of her admirers, two men from the Ak Theater administration and their friends.

What's known about Lida's motorboat excursion companions comes mostly from later newspaper accounts. The trip's host was a man named Kelmet or Klement (depending on the newspaper), apparently an engineer connected with the 2nd Labor Collective, whose motorboat it was. He brought along "a sailor," Rodionov. The other two men were key to Lidochka's agreeing to come—Andrei Yazkykov, then the Komendant of the Mikhailovsky Theater (a glorified janitor in charge of the physical plant), and Grigory Golshtein, administrator of the former Troitsky Theater, now the experimental studio for the ex-Alexandrinsky and the ex-Mariinsky. Golshtein especially would have been important to Lidochka's and the others' futures.

At the Ismailovsky Garden theater that evening, Choura and Kolya Efimov, who were backstage, got worried first. They knew that Lidochka had gone on this motorboat trip with fans. Choura had been invited too, but she'd declined. But now their *Paquita* Pas de Trois was imminent and Lidochka wasn't there. That wasn't unusual, but as the minutes passed and no Lidochka rushed in brimming with news, their worry deepened. They finally told the theater manager they couldn't go on. The orchestra should skip their music.

Georges and Tamara, in the audience, saw that the Pas de Trois had been skipped when the next part of *Paquita* came on the stage. Concerned, they walked toward the park gates, hoping to spot the dark-haired Lidochka rushing in with apologies. Instead, there appeared a man from their theater, wearing an incongruous winter coat and hat and walking stiffly, heading for the stage door. They followed.

This account comes mainly from Geva's memoir, *Split Seconds*, which contains so many questionable details and blurred contexts that we can't know if it's accurate. Writing of Georges punching Semenov, Geva fails to say he was Georges's teacher. She's indignant that schoolmaster Isaenko was jealous of her but doesn't mention that he'd looked after Georges since he was nine. She's usually the wronged party in the book. Still, this Party man, who she says was Adjutant to GATOB's Commissar (a Party watchdog), didn't engage with her, so maybe she described him accurately. Every institution now had a Party overseer who made sure Bolshevik ideology was daily put into practice. If he was that, his name was Rubezhov, Yakov Ivanovich. His face under the hat, Geva writes, was "rutted with hatred and torment and self-doubt, the lips trembling and the eyes glistening with fever." He told the four to "stay out of this . . . ," that Lidochka "won't be back."[59]

The manager of the Summer Theater overheard and offered to drive the four friends to the port in his government car, along with Lidochka's boyfriend, the shadowy engineer Yelshin, who'd turned up too. They drove across the Neva to the city's maritime quay on Vasilievsky Island's Nevsky Embankment (today it's the Lieutenant Schmidt Embankment). They split into two groups, to pace the Embankment in both directions and try to discover what had happened. What were they looking for? They didn't know.

As the light sky darkened to midnight blue, Balanchivadze and Geva, in Geva's telling, came upon a double-decker ferryboat, the *Chaika* (Seagull), tied up at the docks. The other group joined them. Barely visible roped to its rear was a smashed motorboat, almost split in two. The five shouted up at the *Chaika*, rousing a watchman who sent them to a cabin nearby where its captain lived. They found him, an old Finn named Heinonen at his worn kitchen table, hunched over coffee, muttering that it wasn't his fault, a motorboat had been in his path and he couldn't stop; that he'd seen some men fall out and get hauled up with ropes tossed from his decks. But he was vague about the missing young woman.

Behind them appeared again the tormented Party official in his coat and low hat, causing the old captain to fall silent. In Geva's account, this Rubezhov was saying crazily that someone had to tell Lidochka's parents she was dead, and it was probably him. The young people were horrified. How could a motorboat get into the path of a ferry? Why hadn't its occupants jumped out? Lidochka was a good swimmer.[60] What had really happened? What should they do?

They'd known her since childhood, all of them but Geva. They'd grown up with her, danced with her, joked with her, loved her. How could she be gone? For the rest of that night they walked through the city in the ghostly daylight of the midsummer night.

The next day their exit visas arrived for Germany.[61] Was there a connection between the visas coming through and Lidia's drowning?

ELEVEN

Death and Life

Lidochka with cat.

Author's collection.

"Death of the ballet artist Lidiia Ivanova," proclaimed a headline in the evening *Krasnaya Gazeta* (Red Gazette) the next day, June 17. There'd been a collision at the mouth of the Fontanka River between a motorboat and a passenger ferryboat, the *Chaika* (Seagull), heading to Kronstadt. Three of the motorboat's passengers had survived, Yazykov, Golshtein, and Rodionov; the other two, Klemet and Lidia, had not. The paper quoted one of the survivors, Yazykov: "We entered the motorboat at the Anichkov Bridge and went down the Fontanka to the Kalinkin Bridge. Paying attention to the motor that had overheated we tried to cool it down, and two of us tried to row. Suddenly a whistle sounded and our boat found itself under the steamship, with its nose broken off."[1]

It seems that the motorboat had reached the Fontanka's mouth at the city's port, where the Neva River's several branches empty into the Bay of Finland among small islands. It's a tricky place, full of shoals and currents. The motorboat's stalled motor prevented it from moving away from the Kronstadt-bound steamer bearing down on it from the Neva's main mouth. Yazykov said he didn't remember his own rescue by a government tugboat; he'd regained consciousness in his apartment where he was brought. He reported that Lidochka had been in a wonderful mood, urging her companions toward the open sea even if motorboats weren't supposed to go there. (It seems he blamed the victim.) The newspaper suggests that she could have fallen between the two boats and died instantly, adding that the Marine Department of the GPU secret police was searching for her body. But because the collision occurred at the intersection of two currents, she would probably be carried in to one of the Neva's banks, said the Department, or else swept out to sea. Theater director Ekskuzovich added his comment.

He'd received a midnight call and had instantly gone to his office to deal with this "nightmarish" event. "With this loss the Mariinsky Theater has lost one of its best . . ." etc.

The next day's *Krasnaya Gazeta* printed an interview with the *Chaika*'s captain, who'd "noticed a small sloop without motion" about 100 meters from his ship, which he took to be a fishermen's rowboat whose passengers weren't responding to his whistle. He gave more whistles but couldn't stop his ship in time and hit the right side of the motorboat, which broke and sank. One of the passengers caught its nose and was pulled up to the deck of the ferry. The other two were thrown life preservers, and another motorboat behind the *Chaika* saved them. A tugboat named *Moriak* (Sailor) was also on the scene.

More details trickled out over the next few days, plus a small flood of information about searches for the bodies——maybe too much to be believable. The first search took two full days and yielded nothing. Another search was conducted, then another, according to a June 24 article in *Zhizn Iskusstva*. The Marine Department of the GPU was still in charge of the case, but afterwards it would go to the Accident Commission and then to the *prokuror* (public prosecutor). On July 2, *Krasnaya Gazeta* reported that the motorboat was eight years old and not seaworthy; also that the drowning Klemet had swum to Ivanova trying to save her, but she'd grabbed him around the throat and they'd both gone down (the source *here* was "as they say"). And furthermore that many barges had sunk in this tricky place between channels, and both missing bodies could have gotten tangled up in one. The diving technician in charge, a Comrade Bobrovich, thought that "with vigorous efforts," the divers would find her.

A July 8 *Zhizn Iskusstva* article belatedly quoted a passenger on the *Chaika* deck (coincidentally, the boss of the diving base, Eilov), who claimed to have seen a man in the water grasping a life preserver and a woman who couldn't reach one. Two teams of divers had again searched for the body, voluntarily, again concluding it was snagged on a sunken barge and could only last ten days anyway. The motorboat, apparently, had first tried to sail *up* the Fontanka toward the Summer Garden, but barges blocking the way had caused it to turn around and sail toward the port, where motorboats didn't usually go. The body search was reported over on July 2. But on July 8 another search was undertaken, though a subheading in this article reads "A Watery Grave."

The shock of Lidochka's death hit people on the street the next day, even before the newspapers reported it. According to the young writer Nikolai Nikitin of the Serapion Brothers literary band, groups around the city would be talking and someone would interrupt: "Yesterday Lidochka died." "Which Lidochka?" "Lidiia Ivanova." "*Died, how?*"[2] That same evening, everyone at a Communist Party gathering in the former Mariinsky Theater stood up "in memory of the dead artist L. Ivanova."[3] Then the rumor mill started up. Mikhail Kuzmin questioned the official reports in the June 18 *Krasnaya Gazeta.* "An innocent excursion on the water, a ruined motor, a collision with a steamship, the rest murky. Two dead, three saved. Ivanova dead. An accident?" Twice he repeated the newspaper's words, "the point where two currents meet," implying a meaning beyond the literal. On June 19, Lidochka's face, drawn icon-like with huge eyes and smooth black hair, filled the cover of *Zhizn Iskusstva*. Inside were tributes from arts luminaries Volynsky, Gvozdev, Kuzmin, Nasilov, Storitsyn, and one G. M-v. Volynsky entitled his "Adrienne Lecouvreur," after the 1849 Eugene Scribe play that Moscow's Kamerny Theater had brought to Leningrad that May about a real eighteenth-century Paris actress caught up in political intrigues (played by Lidochka's favorite Moscow actress, Alisa Koonen). On June 21, Alexander Benois noted his shock in his diary, especially since he'd just seen Lidochka at his theater office looking pretty in a striped summer dress, even if she was clowning around as usual and screwing her doll-like face into silly expressions. "She went off in a motorboat with some kind of Communist boys," he writes, adding that she had an inclination for this kind of thing. But with the body not found, he can't help having nightmarish visions of it underwater, "executing a last eccentric dance."[4] A few days later, on June 25, Benois writes that there's no news about Lidochka's death, but Ekskuzovich and his assistant Darsky are being "strangely silent" about it, even if Ekskuzovich is "indignant about that communist who was in the motorboat and then two hours later was sitting at the operetta" (was this Yazykov or Golshtein?). Furthermore, people are saying that this same "hooligan" (the one at the operetta) has boasted of kicking away someone in the water when he or she grabbed hold of him. "Maybe this was Lidochka?" Benois asks.[5]

It was Nikolai Nikitin's mock-parable in *Zhizn Iskusstva's* July 1 edition that best summed up Leningraders' feelings about this death.[6] On the "third day" after the death, he writes, a flurry of "sightings" occurred of a laughing dark-haired girl in a checked gingham dress. She was seen at a movie theater for a children's showing and an artists' studio on Basseinaya St.—in a hurry, as always. The people who saw her, says Nikitin, were not fancy folk but the simple people "who can't write articles but who can become enchanted, people who are wise maybe in their simplicity, like the restless fishermen of Nazareth, people who followed after her, as after happiness, so they could bring that happiness home to a quiet room and keep it to themselves, in the quiet."

For Nikitin, Lidochka is a kind of savior who stood for something unregulated and joyous in a time when joy was decreasing and regulations increasing. She was a child, he writes, yet already a wonderful artist, and she was theirs—she belonged to the city. As a child, she would of course agree to a boat trip with men who appeared to be "real sailors." When the boat capsized, though, those "'real sailors' decided to save themselves," he adds dryly.

At the end of his article, Nikitin returns to the day after Lidochka's death. But he takes us now to the city's dark outskirts on Vasilievsky Island (Lidochka's childhood neighborhood), where under the porch light of an obscure café called Olimp (Olympus) the ladies of the evening have gathered. One says to the other, "Did you hear . . . today?" "I heard," replies her neighbor grimly. He ends the piece in a nearby *traktir* (workingman's pub) called the Golden Anchor where an orchestra of blind musicians usually plays, where screaming and scandalizing goes on and no strangers come, just "our own"—sailors from the port and even bandits. A sailor with medals on his chest (implying he's served the Revolution) approaches the orchestra and says to its blind conductor, "Comrade, play 'You Fell As Victims' [the revolutionary funeral march]. The conductor with his unblinking white eyes asks, 'It's about that artist who died, right?' The sailor answers curtly 'Yeah,' as if on the deck of a ship. 'So I'll play you Chopin.' 'Suit yourself,' the sailor says, then shouts to the patrons, 'Shut up. They're gonna play now for the artist who died.' And the crowd silently listens to the *Marche Funèbre*."

This is politically risky stuff. Lida's death in Nikitin's article seems to be mixed up with some horror lurking beneath the NEP surface that everyone knows about but can't name, and a stubborn defiance that's there too. Nikitin seems to imply that the real spirit of the revolution has survived only on the margins, among the "real people"[7] who'd truly loved both art and this dancer "with the checked dress and the child's loud laugh." They're the ones feeding the rumor mill, repeating the tales about the three survivors supposedly seen in a restaurant the night after the accident, toasting one another. Or about the diver who's found Lidochka's body with a bullet hole in its head. Or other divers who've been called off the search by higher-ups. Or Lidochka's suddenly aged father telling people in the streets that foul play killed his beloved daughter.

The uneasy feeling that Lidochka had died violently coalesced into two possible dark narratives. One held that prima ballerina Olga Spessivtseva had ordered her killed out of jealousy. This was Lidochka's father's view, or rather Vaginov's rendition of his view in *Bambochada*, and Vaginov implies Volynsky was guilty too for incurring Spessivtseva's wrath by praising Lidochka.[8] Spessivtseva had friends in high places, especially Bolshevik functionary Boris Kaplun, who'd taken her (and her mother and sister) into his home in the hungry years. Spessivtseva and Kaplun had had an affair, possibly not serious. Spessivtseva at any rate was an exotic flower who depended on the kindness of strangers, and Kaplun was in a position to offer it. He was the nephew of ex-Cheka chief Moisei Uritsky, the Uritsky who'd been assassinated in 1918 (and had Palace Square named after him), and also the tutor to party boss Zinoviev's children. Kaplun had been involved among other things with building and opening Russia's first crematorium, in Petrograd, and he'd given Spessivtseva the honor of choosing the first corpse to burn.[9] Had Kaplun acted on Spessivtseva's suggestion and had Lidochka disposed of? Such insinuations surfaced in a cloak-and-dagger poem Kuzmin wrote about Lidochka's death. "An aging Persian woman entered,/Holding in her hand a forged document, /And something sweet—vengeance!—reverberated . . ."[10] Yet by June 1924, when Lidochka died, Spessivtseva had already left Leningrad for an Italian tuberculosis sanatorium, and Kaplun, whom many remembered as a kind man instead of a Bolshevik villain, had helped her leave. It seems unlikely that Spessivtseva would have sent back a request to eliminate a rival dancer who was coming to Europe.

The other version holds that the GPU/Cheka secret police had ordered Lidochka killed because she'd overheard something dangerous in her evenings with Chekists. "The circumstances of her death were suspicious," wrote Danilova many years later. "How does a motorboat manage to hit a ferry hard enough to knock people overboard? People speculated that she somehow knew some secret information and that the accident had been carefully arranged."[11] Balanchine thought the same. "They shouldn't have collided," he later told told Volkov. "The ship had time to turn. And then, Lida was a marvelous swimmer. . . . I had heard that Lida knew some big secret, and they didn't want to let her out to the West. They wondered how to get rid of her and, apparently, decided to fake an accident." There wasn't even a proper investigation, Balanchine remembered—the case was hushed up.[12] He thought that the Cheka big shot who used to kiss her shoulders was behind it. "He had an affair with her—not love, just a balletomane intrigue. It's so easy, after all!"

Death and Life

This version of Lidochka's murder calls for a deeper look at the men in the boat and their possible connection to the GPU/Cheka. Who were they beyond what the newspapers say? About Klemet and Rodionov, nothing further can be known. Klemet was dead (according to one source, his widow later received compensation from the government). Rodionov, the sailor, doesn't show up in any city directory.[13] But more can be gleaned about the other two from their TsGALI personal files. Andrei Alexandrovich Yazykov, the Mikhailovsky/Maly Theater's manager, was probably from Moscow. Two months earlier, in March, he'd received official permission to visit his ailing mother there. In April, when he got back, he got a promotion within the Ak Theaters—50 percent more duties and 50 percent more money. When Lidochka died, he was on his way up. But Yazykov doesn't seem to have profited from engineering a murder (if he'd done it). In October of 1924, he was relieved of his duties, or at least of caring for the Maly's building, and he lost his two-room apartment there. He was reduced to managing a movie theater in the theater's basement (Kino Teatr LaSallia, at 1 Ploshchad LaSallia); that's how he's listed in the 1925 city directory. In 1928, Yazykov was still in living in Leningrad, but with no profession indicated. By 1935, he's gone.

About Grigory Yakovlevich Golshtein a bit more is known, since his Ak Theater *anketa* has survived, the lengthy questionnaire that all Soviet citizens filled out at their workplaces.[14] In 1924, Golshtein was twenty-eight years old and a Communist Party member. He'd come from Kherson in the Ukraine, son of Yakov Semenovich Golshtein and Raisa Iosifovna Golshtein, both "workers." During and after World War I, he'd served as a noncommissioned "motor" officer in the Baltic Fleet—a sailor—but he'd also been involved in "various theatrical enterprises." Since September 1923, he'd been a theater director and administrator within the Ak Theaters. He too seems to have received money (45 gold rubles) in March of 1924 and a salary increase in April, then a salary doubling in late May. But in September of 1924, according to a Finance Control certificate, he too lost his job. "Citizen Golshtein is not listed in the service of the Ak Theaters," attests another document eight months later. He was still living in the same place (10 Sapiorny Pereulok), but his profession now was harness maker. In May 1925, he was summoned to a salary dispute hearing (did it also have something to do with Lidochka?).

If Yazykov and Golshtein had carried out a murder on someone's instructions, they hadn't done it very well. Maybe they'd boasted too early or left too many loose ends. But were they in fact working for the

GPU? Here we enter a murky world that eludes most researchers, at least in the West. Since late 1917, when Lenin founded the All-Russian Extraordinary Commission for Combating Counterrevolution and Sabotage (in 1918, Profiteering and Corruption were added), known as the Cheka, Russians had been living with fear, no matter how distant. The Cheka answered to no other legal bodies. It had various incarnations from 1917 up to the NEP years (Cheka to GPU to OGPU, though people still said Cheka), but during the summer and fall of 1923, when the first constitution of the USSR was being adopted, the Cheka shed its pretense of being a temporary body and emerged as permanent. A "lid of secrecy was clamped on it" too.[15] Its staff hovered between 100,000 and 150,000, but appendages included army units, border guards, concentration camp guards, foreign espionage detachments, and, during the NEP, a section combating "economic counterrevolution," that is, "bribery, speculation, and malfeasance."[16] In short, the GPU had the power to have anyone arrested and shot for being an enemy of the state. There's a vacuum in literature, though, about how it overlapped with other parts of life, especially the theater. Some historians, like Donald Rayfield, Sheila Fitzpatrick, and Leslie Chamberlain, have touched on the shadowy ties between Chekists and artists.[17] The Cheka chose the best-educated from the employment pool at a time when, as Rayfield put it, "there was a desperate shortage of competent leadership."[18] Some Chekists thought of themselves as *intelligents* and liked to keep company with artists and literati.

Naturally, this new elite gravitated to the ballet as well, the art that had been the special playground of the old elite into whose shoes they'd stepped. Enough anecdotal evident exists—if only from dancers' memories—to put many Chekist fans at the Petrograd-Leningrad ballet. The young Ak Theater dancers were offered precious food by these privileged Chekists, as well as flowers, alcohol, luxury clothing. They were invited to parties and squired about town. A very few novels of the time explore the temptation that someone like Lidochka would have offered Chekists trying to maintain the "cool heads, warm hearts, and clean hands" that their chief Felix Dzerzhinsky (paraphrasing the Gospel of Matthew) wanted for them. The 1922 novel *Chocolate*, by Alexander Tarasov-Rodionov, features a ballet dancer, Yelena Varts, who gets arrested by the Cheka in an unnamed city, then reprieved by local Cheka chief Zudin. Zudin is so charmed by Varts's beauty, perfume, and seductiveness that he makes her his secretary. He becomes obsessed with her, contrasting her in his mind to his stolid comrade of a wife, who unwisely accepts Varts's present of chocolate for their children

(Varts had gotten it from a British embassy official). Zudin resists temptation to the end, but he's brought down anyway by Varts, who's also started a corrupt side business selling "reprieves" to the relatives of prisoners. Zudin manfully takes the blame and goes off to the firing squad.[19]

A female dancer, supposedly corrupt to the core just by who she is, made a good scapegoat. And what man could resist being distracted by such a creature? Were Yazykov and Golshtein men like this, visionary Communists who'd succumbed to temptation in the person of Lidochka, or were they acting for someone higher up? Maybe Lidochka was inappropriately pregnant, though there's no proof of this. The problem with such assumptions is that Yazykov and Golshtein already had jobs, in the Ak Theaters. Were they also secret members of the Cheka? How did that work anyway? "Not members, agents," was the correction offered in summer, 2012, by the present director of Petersburg's Museum of the FSB (first the Cheka, then the KGB, before it became the FSB), Liudmila Mikhailova, small, sixty-something, gruff, disheveled, savvy, disillusioned. Even if they weren't agents on the books they could have been agents anyway, since "Cheka agents had their own agents, who in turn had *their* agents," she says, describing an underground bureaucracy with multiplying tentacles. Mikhailova had heard the Lidocha story years before and was sure the men in the boat were drinking—why else would they not hear a ferry whistle several meters away? The Cheka, she added, wouldn't have needed to warn off divers searching for a body; diving bases were already Cheka cells. Technology belonged to the Cheka. Mikhailova also flagged Vladimir Dmitriev, the croupier sponsor of the proposed summer tour, as a likely target for Cheka surveillance. "The Cheka followed the money." Does this thought pertain to Lidochka's death? If the Cheka was following Dmitriev, (while also accepting his money under the table to permit the tour), they would have known that Lidochka was planning to leave the country. Once she was out of the way, they could grant exit visas to the others, which in Balanchine's memory is what happened.[20]

Two other witnesses, who waited to speak until they emigrated, believed that Golshtein and Yazykov were Cheka or Communist Party golden boys who'd killed Lidochka. Semion Rogov published his article in 1928 in the Paris émigré biweekly *Teatr i Zhizn* (Theater and Life) under the title "The Murder of the Ballerina Lidiia Ivanova."[21] He spiced it with the anti-Bolshevism that played well in émigré circles, claiming that Lidochka hated Bolsheviks and told friends "how awful it was to work in the atmosphere of everyday arrests and executions." That doesn't sound like our flower-child Lidochka, but some of what Rogov writes rings true. Rogov knew Lidochka because his wife, Lidia Pavlova-Rogova, was a dancer in the ex-Mariinsky (she's listed on the ex-Mariinsky roster in 1923) and also the impresario who'd booked acts into "her" theater on Troitskaya St., the one Golshtein now ran as the official experimental studio.[22]

Rogov, himself a high factory official, says that he ran into Lidochka at noon on the day of her death on Troitskaya St. with Yazykov and Golshtein, heading to the boat ride. She was embarrassed, he says, since she knew *he* knew she was engaged to Yelshin the engineer. But she explained sotto voce that she couldn't turn down an offer "from the bosses." That evening Rogov ran into Golshtein again calmly drinking a beer at the *Letnii Bouffe*, where Lidochka was supposed to dance but hadn't appeared (could that be Benois's guy "sitting at the operetta?"). When Rogov heard a minute later that Lidochka had drowned, he couldn't believe it. He'd just seen her that morning—and here was Golshtein. He rushed to the Ak Theater for information and found Lidochka's shocked father, whom he escorted home. At 3 AM, Golshtein himself appeared at the Ivanovs', forced to pay a visit by the alerted Bolshevik command at Smolny. "Why aren't you sleeping?" Golshtein asked the parents. "Drowned is drowned—there's nothing you can do." But a "private investigation" carried on at the same time (by Rogov himself?), established that neither the *Chaika*'s captain nor its passengers had actually seen Lidochka in the water; they'd seen only two figures, Golshtein and Yazykov. And Yazykov, Rogov further claims, had earlier wanted to marry Lidochka but he'd been rebuffed. Also, the motorboat's motor and steering wheel looked deliberately broken, and Lidochka's journal was in the boat, which wouldn't be the case if it had capsized. The "private investigation" concluded that Lidochka had been hauled off the boat into the woods somewhere on the shore southwest of the port, raped and killed, then buried in that woods, at which point Golshtein and Yazikov returned to the Fontanka to stage a collision with the *Chaika*.

There are too many mistakes in this account to swallow it whole, and the other émigré account gets facts wrong too (the year of the accident, Lidochka's theater, etc.). This was a book, *Likhie Godi* [The Evil Years] 1925–41, published in Paris in 1977 by ex-church official Anatoly Krasnov-Levitin, who asserts that Lidochka had a Chekist "uncle" protector, and that Petrograd Cheka chief Bakaev also fancied her. Krasnov-Levitin implies, like Rogov, that the Bolsheviks had Lidochka raped and murdered and then covered it up, since many Bolsheviks used women badly and an investigation into one affair might expose all.

But something does ring true here. If a crowd of people saw the motorboat collision from the *Chaika*'s deck, why weren't more interviewed? A diver supposedly on that deck, contacted *three weeks later*, is the only eyewitness who claimed to have seen a woman in the water—besides Yazykov and Golshtein themselves. Not even the *Chaika*'s captain was sure a woman was in the water. Neither Golshtein nor Rodionov was ever quoted. The father was never interviewed. No body was found, despite all the searches (though Lida's "little red purse" floated up and was returned to her parents). No conclusions from investigations were published. Either incompetence was rife among reporters and investigators, or Lida *was* killed elsewhere and wasn't even at the ferry collision, and newspapers were told to print and substantiate Golshtein and Yazykov's versions.

Vera Kostrovitskaya, the most consistently trustworthy of this book's eyewitnesses, wasn't in Leningrad when the accident happened. She'd been sent away to a Caucasus tuberculosis sanatorium. She writes about Lidochka's death much later in a 1970s letter to Slonimsky, who'd asked for help on his memoir. To him, she repeats some of the rumors—the overturned motorboat, the kick to a drowning Lidochka, the divers warned off. The whole ballet world was thinking up "a thousand explanations, conjectures." But she herself believes it was murder, premeditated murder. "Three strong men, who could swim, couldn't save a miniature girl, who could also swim! In our youth," she writes staunchly, "there occurred a dark death, awful [*strashnaya*] in its incomprehensibility." She adds something more too, or she almost does. "Thirty years later, suddenly the curtain that had fallen on the mystery of this murder lifted slightly." Artist Boris Erbshtein, of the Young Ballet's circle, she writes, had come back from the Siberian camps (he'd been arrested, as were many of their circle) and revealed something he'd learned about Lidochka's death. "But I'll tell you this in person, or convey it through Galya T.," she says, ending the document abruptly (and leaving a researcher almost in tears). "She was afraid to write it down," says Tamara Fedotova-Gershova simply. Fedotova-Gershova is an atomic scientist and the much younger widow of Vera's husband Gershov (Kostrovitskaya died of cancer in 1979, Gershov in 1989). That more was known about this accident is also Danilova's conclusion. "It was years before we understood what had gone on [in Lidochka's death]," she says in her memoir. "The extent of the tragedy dawned on us only later. In a sense, she [Lidochka] was a casualty of the revolution."[23]

If this book were a novel, it would describe a rape, then a corpse buried or hidden, followed by a faked accident. The scene would be brutal, and inexpressibly tragic. But the only thing certain about Lidochka's death is that it was caused by some young Bolsheviks. Whether they acted carelessly or malevolently can't be determined. Lidochka's own character may have made whatever they did easier. The faintest of impressions comes through history of a hugely gifted young woman too much adored by her father, of psychic confusion resulting from that adoration that may have contributed to both her brilliance onstage and her appetite for risk. Lidochka, though, did not cause her own death. Her innocence, in fact, made her a symbol for her city, then and later. Lidochka was a woman in a female-identified art at a time when femaleness was thought to lead to temptation and corruption. However she really died, she was indeed a victim, perhaps not so much of the revolution as of the confusions generated by Lenin's sudden move away from "revolutionary purity," into the many "impurities" of the NEP.

Just seventeen days after Lidochka's death, on July 4, 1924, her four friends plus conductor Dranishnikov and ex-croupier Vladimir Dmitriev reassembled at the same Nevsky Embankment port where they'd found the broken motorboat. Would they be allowed to leave? They were still in a state of shock. Georges, Choura remembered, had seen Lidochka in a dream, saying "I am so lonely," and reaching out to her, Choura. In the dream Georges pulled Choura back to safety.[24] After a scary delay at Russian customs, they boarded the German steamship *Prussia* and set sail for Germany. All remember their amazement at the baskets of bread sitting "unguarded" on tables in the ship's dining room. Sixty-some hours later they landed on July 7 in Stettin—now Szczecin, Poland, but then the port for Berlin, and the next morning arrived in Berlin by train. Dmitriev, though, had no real plans for them—more indication that his primary aim had been to get himself out. Some Russian immigrant friends helped them obtain a shabby Berlin booking, then Dmitriev scrounged up some spas on the Rhine where they could finish out a summer tour.

Dranishnikov had by then returned to Russia, but the other five elected almost unthinkingly to stay in Europe, though Danilova, then Efimov and Balanchivadze together, wrote letters back to their theater asking for their places to be held for their return. For now, though, none wanted to give up on seeing the world—or on eating.[25] In October, Dmitriev got the four booked into a London music hall where they performed for several weeks but were in the end let go. With no visas for Germany, they ended up in the only place that would take visaless Soviets: France. Miraculously, Diaghilev found them in Paris.

In Europe, Georges with Tamara Geva on his shoulders.
In foreground, (possibly) Nina Nikitina. Courtesy, Vaganova Ballet Academy.

He auditioned them, and after he'd learned that Georges could choreograph opera ballets quickly, he took them into the Ballets Russes. On January 12, 1925, they arrived in Monte Carlo, the company's winter home.

What a balm for these bedraggled young refugees to find themselves in this mimosa-scented city-kingdom on pine-covered hills above the Mediterranean, with a miniature ornate opera house and casino on the sea. The emotional darkness left by Lidochka's death must have seemed to dissolve in the sunlit air. Georges loved the place.[26] He'd already put several variations of the past out of his mind. Now he shut out the most recent. He got a new name, adapted from his old by publicity-wise Diaghilev: Balanchine. But even if Georges thought he'd left the bleakness of Soviet Russia behind, he'd arrived in one sense right back in Russia. Diaghilev's company, even with its international artists' gang in attendance—Picasso, Matisse, Cocteau, Coco Chanel, Stravinsky—was still a Petersburg enterprise.[27] Its language was the language of ballet nurtured by the imperial court. Its esprit de corps was the Petersburg intelligentsia's old stock in trade: mixing the audacious and the spiritual. Balanchine couldn't have dreamed up a better situation for addressing his heritage. Between January and March, the young choreographer created the ballets for nine operas. Most important for him, though, was the carnivalesque modernism that permeated the very air of the Ballets Russes, emanating from its self-dramatizing impresario, Diaghilev.

Balanchine's first original ballets for the Ballets Russes were not ostensibly linked to St. Petersburg. Between 1925 and 1928 he choreographed, besides the nine opera ballets, two fairy tales (*L'Enfant et les Sortileges* and *Le Chant du Rossignol*, both 1925), a comic Italian nursery rhyme (*Barabau*, 1925), a mock-English pantomime (*The Triumph of Neptune*, 1926), and a futuristic Aesop fable (*La Chatte*, 1927)—all with different music by various adventurous modernist composers. But as productions they all exuded that special Petersburg stylization whose genius lay in finding a meeting place onstage between the traditional and the avant-garde. Diaghilev even made a point of enlightening Balanchine on theater's ancient roots by taking him to Italy in 1926, together with his young Russian secretary Boris Kochno, Balanchine's age, and his one-year-younger favorite dancer Serge Lifar. They viewed Renaissance paintings, and made a special detour to Naples so Georges could see "the last remaining *commedia dell'arte* troupe." (Georges, as he claimed in the long-ago interview with me, was more interested in learning how to make fettuccine Alfredo.)[28]

In 1928, Diaghilev entrusted Balanchine with a major new Stravinsky score, *Apollon Musagète* (Apollo Leader of the Muses). Stravinsky, wanting a classical subject, had fixed on Apollo, perhaps because Apollo was Petersburg's special god. He stood for grace and restraint. An influential literary journal had flourished in the city from 1909 to 1917 called *Apollon* (considered the continuation of Diaghilev's own *World of Art*), guided by quintessential Petersburg artist-critics like Blok, Benois,

Gumilev, Bakst, Meyerhold, and Volynsky, devoted not just to belles lettres but to all the arts, including dance. And besides literary Hellenism, any city flaneur would have met up daily with the embodied kind. Everywhere in Petersburg, classical personages of stucco adorned—still adorn—the facades of palaces, "holding up," on backs and necks and shoulders, the windows, balconies, and balustrades above them. They're called *atlantes* if they're male figures, *caryatids* if female.[29] In the city's semiformal Summer Garden, which young Balanchine had frequented and young Stravinsky before him, marble Apollos and muses mark the intersections of allées.

Balanchine's task was to find dance material to fit not just the music and subject but the needs of the company and its performers. He has said that *Apollo* marked a turning point for him, and indeed, in its capaciousness and high spirits, it goes far beyond what he'd made so far. Stravinsky's music, as he famously remarked, taught him to discard ideas and use only dance steps with "family relations" that belonged together within the musical framework.[30] But judging from the ballet's content, he learned something else too: how to please and entertain himself; how to play with the steps' private meanings, even translating secret sense memories into dance moves. The resulting work is about Stravinsky's musical Apollo, and also about the Ballets Russes dancer who would play him, Serge Lifar, who'd worked hard to make himself a classical dancer; and about the ballerina dancing Apollo's chosen muse Terpsichore, Choura Danilova, with whom Georges had fallen in love, even as he'd fallen out of love with Geva (she left the company in 1927).[31] But it's especially about Georges himself, learning to be a choreographer.

There's a platform onstage at the start of the ballet (or there was, before Balanchine revised it, and *it* had replaced Mt. Olympus). On top of it a kneeling woman gives stylized birth. Out hops Apollo from under the platform in swaddling clothes, his arms wrapped at his sides. Two handmaidens run around him unwrapping the cloth and sending him into a pirouette. He has a fit, like a rebellious boy, or a jazzman, or a Harlequin who doesn't know he's supposed to be on a classical stage. The handmaidens put a lute in his hand. He learns to strum it and listen to it, as *The Sleeping Beauty*'s Aurora listens to her lute-playing pages. Then the three muses of the ballet join him from three corners of the stage.

In 1979, when Balanchine taught the ballet to Mikhail Baryshnikov, he dropped the birth and the boy-tantrum, removing the messy human stuff that had worked on Diaghilev's stage (orgasms, births) and perhaps removing material connected with Lifar, who'd become a professional rival. Nowadays the ballet opens with Apollo alone posing with the lute, already a god, which deflects attention from his "biography" and highlights his relations with his muses. He sorts them—"you two go left and you go right." He auditions them. Calliope and Polyhymnia, muses of poetry and mime respectively, can't master their genres well enough to please him. The first falls prey to pangs of inspiration; she mimes cramps in her solo. The second, forbidden to speak—she mostly holds a finger to her lips—finally opens her mouth as if to shout. Apollo chooses the third, Terpsichore, muse of dance, whose solo shows her not just expansive and classical but modern and jazzy too. She whizzes through space and winds herself around and through it. Having chosen her, the god exults alone: "I am Apollo, cornerstone of this ballet." In a lovely pas de deux with Terpsichore, he explores some of the shapes he and his chosen muse can make together, especially the biggest shape in a ballerina's arsenal, an arabesque, which in the person of Terpsichore he turns upside down, pushes forward, pulls back, makes fly as he spins her while holding her off the ground. The two "own" the stage, holding hands and leaning apart, mirroring each other in frisky steps. At the duet's climax he puts her on his neck and supports her in a swimming motion, the way the *atlanti* hold up beautiful architectural details. Then the other two muses rush back onstage to join them in the ballet's playful but serious enterprise.

And what is that enterprise? Surely it's building something: a classical edifice, a lost St. Petersburg—a ballet as classical city. Dance has more three-dimensional volume than poetry or mime. There's even a piece of London added, as Balanchine once confessed. A blinking sign in Picadilly Circus inspired the moment in the ballet when Apollo pauses, opening and closing his fists. The muses act as "raw material" for the god, then as partners. They sit, kneel, intertwine their arms with his to make complex shapes. Two at a time hang from his biceps, like flying buttresses. All four flow together down a stage diagonal, one being lifted, the other two swirling at his sides—the river in the center of the city? They clap their hands and Apollo rests his cheek in their cupped palms. They become the horses of a chariot with Apollo driving, like the chariot atop the Alexandrinsky Theater that Balanchine saw every day from the age of nine (though that one has four horses). In the end, they make a sunburst wheel of arabesque "degrees" which Apollo supports—the city's midnight sun; Apollo's sun. This Apollo is not just Stravinsky's creation or Lifar's, he's Master Builder, god of the dance. He's Georges himself, with his ballerinas.

Death and Life

Has Lidochka disappeared? She could be a subliminal model for *Apollo*'s muses—Georges had choreographed on her already, as he had on Danilova. But perhaps Lidochka had receded in the demands made on Georges by the Diaghilev enterprise, whose underlying narrative featured the male dancer, not the ballerina. In 1929, though, Diaghilev unexpectedly died in Venice, scattering his still stateless and now "fatherless" dancers. Each had to improvise a new life. Georges's worsening tuberculosis led to lonely months at a Swiss sanatorium. Then he became a journeyman around Europe, making ballets to order in London, Denmark, Monte Carlo. He and Danilova split, though Dmitriev remained with him as agent and father figure for this part of his journey. Georges also reunited briefly with his friend Boris Kochno, Diaghilev's secretary-scenarist. A rich backer funded their joint season in Paris, *Les Ballets '33*, consisting of Georges's ballets, one of whose stars was the black-haired, fourteen-year-old, reportedly half-Georgian Tamara Toumanova, a Preobrazhenskaya Paris student (and perhaps a reminder to Georges of both his sister and Lidochka). It was during this Paris season that the young arts-mad American Lincoln Kirstein found Balanchine and issued the invitation for him to start an American ballet. Georges and Dmitriev arrived in New York on the *Olympic* on October 18, 1933. Another steamship, to another new world.[32]

Here, despite the grim financial odds of the Depression, Balanchine finally turned to his own narrative within ballet, starring not the male dancer but the female. This is the narrative he'd been handed at age nine when he'd stepped into the life meant for his sister. He started in with his first "American" work, *Serenade*, feeling his way towards another version of classical ballet.[33] It plants the unevenly trained Americans as quickly as possible in the haunted world of the Russian ballet. Seventeen girls in its opening pose wear long romantic tutus (at least starting from the 1950s, when short costumes were discarded), like the Wilis of *Giselle*. They stand with feet parallel and one hand raised, as if shielding their eyes from the moon.[34] Then they open feet into first position, the foundation of ballet. Throughout the ballet they skip and run and swoop around the stage like ghost-*Wilis* set free, sometimes quoting *Giselle*, other times channeling Isadora Duncan. Just "a dance in the moonlight" was how Balanchine described *Serenade*, which was named after its music, Tchaikovsky's *Serenade for Strings*.[35]

Yet even if *Serenade* has no story line, its creator went to specific lengths to give it a narrative shape. He reversed the order of the last two of Tchaikovsky's four movements, so the third, an elegy, comes at the end, and the ballet itself becomes an elegy. On the way to this elegy's raison d'être, the dancers enact some scenes that seem particular and deliberate. A woman comes in late and tries to find her place in the corps de ballet. The same woman later trips and falls to the ground. (Both events really happened in rehearsal and went into the choreography.) A man enters after the girl has fallen and walks toward her, with another girl hugging his back and shielding his eyes—so he won't see the fallen girl? So he can't help her? The two pause behind the fallen girl, and the walking girl, now hidden by the man, flaps her arms like wings to the music, as if giving wings to the fallen one. She and the man continue walking offstage, then the fallen girl gets up and runs to another tall dancer on the other side of the stage (as Giselle runs to her mother at the end of her mad scene). In her embrace, she slips down and is lowered to her knees. Has she died? She's preparing, at any rate, for the next phase of her destiny, which will transpire in heaven.

Here is the subject of *Serenade*'s elegy: another victim, another ballet corpse like the one in *Giselle* or *The Sleeping Beauty*, or in Georges's own *Marche Funèbre* for the Young Ballet. But the corpses in earlier ballets rise again to dance. *Serenade*'s corpse doesn't. She's lifted instead still in a standing position by four men who come onstage for this purpose, then carried across the stage into the upstage right wing. Her raised face meets a ray of light. A train of *Serenade*'s corps de ballet follow, their faces raised too, and arms stretched forward in supplication.

Is she Lidochka? Who can know? Whoever she is, she's spared the indignity of being carried horizontally. She enters heaven vertically, in a ray of light, like the ray of light Lidochka once died in onstage in *Valse Triste*. And *Serenade*'s music is the same that Fokine used for his ballet *Eros*, in which Lidochka danced so memorably. One more clue links Lidochka with *Serenade*. When Choura Danilova performed *Serenade*'s fallen girl in a later Ballet Russe de Monte Carlo production, she asked Balanchine what the role meant. "The girl in the ballet, who leads the boy to the girl on the floor, is his wife," Balanchine told Choura. "And together they pass down the road of life." "I, the girl on the floor," continues Choura, "was pitied by the man, but I was a frivolous girl who had one affair after another. Then I was left alone."[36] Lidochka in life had "fallen" into a dangerous milieu and been left very alone, in death. But in the ballet, the fallen girl seems to acquire wings from the man and his "wife," so as to be lifted up to heaven. There's an almost religious tale of comfort being told here. And all of Lidochka's friends knew how she felt about Tchaikovsky. "Sometimes I would like to be one of the sounds created by Tchaikovsky," she once wrote on a picture for a fan, "so that sounding softly and sadly, I could dissolve in the evening mist."[37] In *Serenade*, she does that.

Other corpses in Balanchine's American ballets may also contain the ghost of Lidia. In the 1951 *La Valse*, a young girl at her first ball leaves her partner to dance with Death (a Chekist in eighteenth-century black garb?) to Ravel's haunted waltzes, and ends up as a corpse held on high as guests rush in a circle underneath. Most of the corpses in Balanchine ballets die in ballrooms or while dancing. In what may seem a trifle but isn't, Balanchine's 1975 *The Steadfast Tin Soldier* (made for his later Columbine, Patricia McBride), the ballerina doll dances for the toy tin soldier, then is blown by a gust of wind into the burning fireplace and disappears. We know she's dead because the soldier finds in the ashes the tin heart he'd given her. If these corpses exist partly in homage to Lidochka, they also testify to other elements bequeathed by history to Balanchine's psyche, especially the narrative tropes he and she knew intimately from the great Russian classical repertory (*Swan Lake*, *The Sleeping Beauty*, *La Bayadere*, etc.), about innocent maidens destroyed or entrapped by worldly people around her. Innocence (and love) menaced by evil was the primal narrative of Petersburg classical ballet. In the Silver Age this narrative trope merged with the city's favorite Hoffmanesque literary myths, which posit a frightful ghost-world breaking without warning into the coziness of everyday. Lidochka was simply the last, and "realest," in a long line of balletic Deaths and Maidens.

But not all Balanchine's corpses are ballerinas. Two are male, though related somehow to the dead ballerinas. In the 1946 *The Night Shadow*, revived in 1960 as *La Sonnambula*, a poet arrives at a masked ballet, dances with a Coquette with whom he seems to have a past history, then encounters in the now deserted ballroom a woman in a nightgown who's come sleepwalking from an upper room, holding a candle. She's another dead yet not-dead spirit who entrances soulful men. (She also reminds every woman in the audience of Bertha Rochester, roaming the attic above Jane Eyre's head.) The Poet dances with her, then follows her upstairs. He's stabbed up there, offstage, by the castle's jealous proprietor (her husband?), but he staggers back onstage and dies—and is placed in the arms of the Sleepwalker, who's returned as well. She backs offstage, holding him curled in her arms. The audience gasps: the cradled male corpse merges subliminally with the ballet's male creator. What we think we glimpse is a moment of intimate vulnerability.

The other male corpse appears in a later ballet, but he doesn't die onstage. He's one of four men dancing with their partners in the ballroom of Balanchine's 1980 *Robert Schumann's Davidsbündlertänze*. The women wear diaphanous dresses and hair ribbons; the men have eighteenth-century jackets over their tights. But in an interlude near the end, one man runs terrified around the stage as green lights flash and four top-hatted gentlemen holding quill pens appear silhouetted in the wings—the Grim Reapers. In the end, the terrified man backs off the stage, leaving the woman he's danced with alone, her face in her hand. Three years after this, Balanchine himself would die of a then undiagnosed disease, later identified as "mad cow disease" or Variant Creutzfeldt-Jakob Disease. The Silver Age's "Death in the Ballroom" trope had become personal.

Death or the threat of death occurs often in Balanchine's ballets, as do ballrooms and masked balls with a *commedia dell'arte* spirit: in the 1920 *Le Bal* and the 1932 *Cotillon*, and in later works, *The Nutcracker, La Sonnambula, La Valse, Liebeslieder Walzer, Valse Fantaisie, Brahms-Schoenberg Quartet, Harlequinade, Vienna Waltzes, Davidsbündlertänze*, and even one of Balanchine's last full ballets, *Mozartiana*. These balls-within-ballets are descendants of the masked balls of Petersburg's Silver Age, during which things both transcendent and awful happen. In hindsight, the masked ball can be seen to presage the catastrophe coming to the city, revolution. The balls Balanchine created much later in America also contain, like their Petersburg precedents, a quickened if dangerous vitality. If one peers into Balanchine's repertory, all the haunted musics of the ballroom ballets seem to play in a magic cacophony, and visions of masks flash before one's eyes along with the sly dance gestures Balanchine so often put onstage implying quick secrets exchanged amid *commedia* grotesqueries. When Silver Age material appears in a Balanchine ballet, it seems to signal his conversation with his lost Petersburg past, and perhaps with Lidochka too. But with which part of that past?

Much has been written about Balanchine's return to the classical symmetry and precision of nineteenth-century Petersburg ballet master Marius Petipa, and to Petipa's habit of privileging the ballerina over the male danseur. But Balanchine never knew Petipa in real life. The old Frenchman and his story ballets—*The Sleeping Beauty, Swan Lake, La Bayadere*—constituted his mythic past. His actual past contained another towering figure, the vigorous, opinionated, reformist choreographer Mikhail Fokine, and both Georges and Lidochka need to be placed in the world that Fokine created on Petipa's foundation. Lidochka, who performed wonders with many of Petipa's variations, was even more a Fokine ballerina, a creature of drama and masks and the alchemy of musical phrasing. There was talk just before her death of her being cast as the ballerina doll in Fokine's *Petrushka*.[38]

As students, both Lidochka and Georges watched the talented and arrogant Fokine choreographing the 1915 *Eros*. They became his actual material in the 1916 *Jota Aragonesa*. As young dancers, they also performed in his *Les Sylphides, Petrushka, Egyptian Nights, Polovtsian Dances,* and *Carnaval*. Balanchine got his Petipa not just from Petipa's ballets, but also from Fokine's conversation with *his* Petipa. In later interviews, Balanchine tended to be dismissive of Fokine. But he often threw interlocutors off the scent, perhaps so that he could continue conversing with his past without audiences overhearing. All the ballrooms Balanchine put onstage seem to stem from Fokine's own haunted ballrooms—in *Carnaval*, with its *commedia* types in their carnival costumes; in *Le Spectre de la Rose* and *Eros*, where the memory of the ballroom shapes the action; in *Petrushka*, where the "ballroom" is a crude city fair and the dancing puppets are in thrall to a magician. We could also label this inherited landscape "Fokine-Meyerhold," so as to factor in the effect on young Georges, and Lidochka too, of Fokine's and Meyerhold's 1911 *Orfeo* and Meyerhold's 1917 Fokine-scented *Masquerade*.

Looking closely, we can catch Balanchine speaking with "Fokine-Meyerhold" in a number of ballets, starting with the 1934 *Serenade*, which dresses its dancers (at least after 1948) as Fokine costumed his in *Chopiniana/Les Sylphides* and which uses the Tchaikovsky music of Fokine's *Eros*. Balanchine's 1980 *Davidsbündlertänze* is another nod to Fokine. It could be called his *Carnaval*, since he choreographed it to a Schumann *commedia*-flavored piano cycle as Fokine did with the real *Carnaval* (though not the same cycle). A mid-repertory ballet like Balanchine's 1966 *Brahms-Schoenberg Quartet*, set to Schoenberg's orchestration of Brahms's G Minor Piano Quartet No. 1, also touches on Fokine's *Les Sylphides*, whose "meaning," according to Taper, the young Georges often pondered.[39] Commentators have treated *Brahms-Schoenberg* as an example of Balanchine gone slightly mad. "A large, almost over-lush work in dusky ball gowns," writes critic Nancy Reynolds, and quotes Balanchine himself saying the ballet was like a television ballroom with "too many voluminous drapes."[40] But in the ballet's first and third movements, one can see something like the opening (and closing) tableau of *Les Sylphides*: a male "Poet" encircling two muses with his arms, another muse group kneeling in front with more muse-groupings on the sides. At the end of the First Movement, the three "extra" male soloists even tiptoe backwards out of stage corners so as to leave the "correct" single man for Fokine's quintessential scene. In the third movement, corps girls ripple their arms like their sister sylphs from *Les Sylphides*—another quote. *Brahms-Schoenberg* is over-the-top in its romantic texture and fraught movement, but if the music is a clue, Balanchine was pumping up Fokinesque steps here the way Arnold Schoenberg had pumped orchestral steroids (raucous brass and a million strings) into the already lush Brahms piano quartet. And *Sylphides'* score was already an orchestral augmentation of Chopin's piano, by Glazunov and Stravinsky.

Balanchine's iconic 1946 *The Four Temperaments* set to Hindemith's majestic-dissonant score looks, on its stripped-down surface, as far as possible from a purposefully theatrical Fokine-Meyerhold landscape. Yet who are *The Four Temperaments'* two male soloists, the sad and drooping Melancholic and the suavely nonchalant Phlegmatic, but Pierrot and Harlequin "camouflaged" in practice tights and T-shirts? The ballerina leads, Sanguinic and Choleric, seem more removed than the men from their creator's Fokinesque heritage, though Balanchine's forceful Choleric could be Fokine's fitful Columbine grown to a giantess. Balanchine's ballerinas seem in general to be bolder, newer versions of their Fokinesque predecessors than his male leads. (In their vitality, they spill out of the ballets like Lidochka did, though Balanchine's choreography invites them to.) Even Balanchine's 1963 *Bugaku*, a slow-motion rendering of a Japanese wedding/defloldering, dressed up in Noh theater clothes and inspired by Japan's Imperial Gagaku troupe, looks more like the erotic machinations of Cleopatra and her slave in Fokine's *Egyptian Nights* than anything Japanese. And it treats the woman's surrender Fokinesquely, as both triumph and horror.

In many Balanchine ballets, such themes are found alongside many other themes and other kinds of dance: the romantic-lyrical, the Petipa-imperial, the jazzy angular, the surreal, the all-out joyous. Balanchine was ballet's great synthesizer. He drew on stimuli from his contemporary life—his dancers' personalities, American popular dancing, the very pace of New York—mixing these in with evocations of his own "lost" dance theater and lost city. In America, Balanchine constructed a great company with a mighty repertory. Helped by impresario Lincoln Kirstein, he reproduced the apparatus of the Imperial Mariinsky, but without the monarchy and the protectors, balletomanes, and higher-ups courting ballerinas. It was just him. He was ballet master and teacher to his ballerinas—and tsar and suitor and balletomane and mischievous companion, all at the same time. But in his private life, Balanchine himself sometimes fell under the spell of the enchanted ballroom, reenacting "his" part inherited at the beginning of his stage career, the Pierrot/clown.

Death and Life

Even outside the theater, he exuded that Pierrot quicksilver aura. He delighted in costumes. As Diaghilev's choreographer, he sported cane and spats. In America, he wore the cowboy gear with string tie "inherited" from his third wife, the American Indian ballerina Maria Tallchief. Throughout his life he fell in love, Pierrot-like, with a succession of ballerinas, most of them cool leggy creatures who couldn't quite reciprocate the abject-yet-mastering love offered them. Or if they did, they seemed to set in motion a cooling of the suitor's affections.

At times, this master of his own large-scale ballet world, with his mostly unfailingly polite exterior, seemed to lose control of himself in a private orgy of grief. This happened several times in his career, but especially in 1969 when his young inamorata Suzanne Farrell married a New York City Ballet dancer her own age and left the company. Those close to Balanchine feared he'd entered a downward spiral, but he eventually recovered his polite and balanced manner again, as he'd done before. He found new ballerinas to work with, notably Patricia McBride, Kay Mazzo, Gelsey Kirkland, Karin von Aroldingen, Merrill Ashley, and the very young Darci Kistler, and to create even more monuments-in-ballet to his longing—for a muse or a mother, for beauty or peace. He found, as before, a way to live with those unrequited fires in his heart that could be stilled only in music and dance.

The depth and breadth of Balanchine's inner landscape informs one of the last full ballets he made before he grew too ill to choreograph, the 1981 *Mozartiana*. It's mostly a new work, not the 1933 ballet he'd made earlier to this music (Suite No. 4, *Mozartiana*, Op. 61).[41] *Mozartiana* was special to Tchaikovsky: he wrote it in 1887 for the hundredth anniversary of his beloved Mozart opera *Don Giovanni*. And he wrote it in Tiflis, which was perhaps important to Balanchine. But here again, the choreographer switched musical parts to fit his own agenda. He moved Tchaikovsky's third movement, the *Preghiera* (prayer, based on Mozart's *Ave Verum Corpus*), to opening position. The ballet starts with this prayer, danced mesmerizingly by Suzanne Farrell, the ballerina who in her concentrated and intimate performing style seems most to resemble Lidochka. Four little girls dressed like her in black gauze knee-length tutus accompany her like small angels of grief, framing her as she bourrées back and forth and raises her face. She even sinks to one knee and opens head, chest, and arms to the sky, reprising the surrender of the girl at the end of *Serenade*.

Surprisingly, this lush prayer is followed by an up-tempo syncopated male solo to Tchaikovsky's *Gigue*. This *Gigue* dancer in black satin knee breeches and jacket is the odd man out, not anyone's partner but the ballet's master of ceremonies, or its Pierrot, or its Death (as in *La Valse*). He might be equated with Balanchine. Some of his steps quote from Balanchine's own greatest role, the Buffoon of *The Nutcracker*. This eccentric *Gigue* male summons four tall corps girls onstage dressed like the earlier child dancers. Then the ballerina comes back with a partner-cavalier in white tights rather than black. This odd grouping of archetypes offers all the human furniture of a choreographer's life: the female corps, little, then grown; the ballerina-muse; the muse's cavalier-partner—and the animator of them all, their Coppelius doll-maker. The contrast of tones and textures is striking, from the prayer to the eccentric Gigue to the turnings and posings of the corps de ballet. But the ballet's glory lies in an intricate theme-and-variations pas de deux, in which the ballerina especially "speaks" in delicate and filigreed fashion of the beauty, gravity, surprise, and humor that can be unearthed in superbly musical ballet steps.

And in this glory, Lidochka is present. It was she who in Balanchine's youth opened the enchanted ballroom to the vital drama of her time. She showed her audience a living personality inhabiting a passionate musicality: the real girl breaking out of the dancer's mold. She pioneered Balanchine's favorite instructions to his dancers, to "be in the moment," and she did that all by herself on a stage where cool stylization reigned. The mature Balanchine wanted just this for his ballerinas, this entering the music and swimming out in it. Many of Balanchine's great ballerinas have tested their limits onstage so daringly that they've lost their stage "selves" and revealed that most precious of theatrical offerings, "the pure and strong soul of a girl," as Lidochka once revealed hers in her collaboration with Georges, *Valse Triste*.

The miracle of Balanchine's rich and volatile life, full of triumph yet infused with longing, is that he stayed true to the vision of ballet that he and Lidochka were searching for—a ballet that rose above imperial court intrigues and NEP squabbles to embody the utopian ideals they'd learned to hold sacred: transcendence, beauty, purity, excitement. Balanchine in his choreography rode the currents of whatever time and place he was in and still paid homage to the disparate layers of his past.

Twice, in 1962 and 1972, Balanchine went back to Russia, to the St. Petersburg that must have seemed like a dreamscape for him, to show off his New York City Ballet. The first time, he got so agitated he could only stay a week in Leningrad. He flew home to New York, missing the company's Kiev stop. But he rejoined his dancers a week later in Georgia, seeing his father's homeland for the first time and reuniting, uneasily, with the brothers he'd lost when he was handed over at nine to the Theater School. How could he not be affected by such a return—first to the scenes of his growing up, then to the mythical country of his father?

And in Leningrad itself, how could his old comrades not be affected by the resurrection of this figure from their old life? Balanchine had wanted most to see Levkii Zheverzheev, his wife Tamara Geva's father. But Zheverzheev had died of starvation in his own Theater Museum during the Leningrad blockade of World War II (the city's second interlude of material and spiritual agony). He did manage to meet his old friend Mikhailov, but only late in his Leningrad week. Mikhailov had sent flowers to the theater but was shy about meeting in person. "What's with you? I've waited to see you for five days!" Balanchine said when he finally ran into him. But when they sat down together, the impulsive and earnest Mikhailov couldn't believe that this very type of the old reserved Russian intelligentsia was his long-ago comrade Georges. Mikhailov had seen Balanchine's class demonstration and was excited to talk pedagogy. But maybe because Georges was so detached, Mikhailov also blurted out his doubts about the ballets. He'd liked *Serenade* but not the abstract *Agon*, and not the "art for art's sake" credo Balanchine had explained in the newspapers. (Poor Mikhailov. Poor Balanchine.[42])

Balanchine also met up in a more relaxed way with Vera Kostrovitskaya, who'd loved and admired him and Lidochka, who'd mourned them both when she'd come back from her tuberculosis cure in the fall of 1924 to find one dead and the other gone. Maybe Vera's grief for Lidochka was even more bitter, since she knew that somewhere Georges was alive. ("When we returned that fall of 1924 to the rehearsal hall, she'd written, I kept thinking that familiar head with its smooth dark hair was just about to appear, and that fervent laughter.")

Now here was Georges, recognizable at the end of a hall in the Theater School. Balanchine knew her too, and they kissed in greeting. "The flexibility of youth was in his gait, in his steps . . . and still that familiar shyness, from his youth," she wrote later. She too saw his demonstration class with his dancers. She noted his "peaceful, quiet corrections" and their quiet responses, such a contrast to a snobbish and arrogant class shown the year before by the visiting American Ballet Theater.

Kostrovitskaya also watched the ballets carefully and came to a different conclusion from Mikhailov, which she wrote about later. "What's so special about these ballets of Balanchine?" someone had asked her. "Interesting, many-imaged, musical, showing symphonic development," she'd answered, but then concluded that such words weren't enough. The important thing, she writes as if figuring it out for herself,

Vera Sergeevna Kostrovitskaya.
Courtesy Saint-Petersburg State Museum of Theater and Music.

is that "Balanchine doesn't expect, in fact doesn't let his artists be 'emotionally expressive.' They don't show off in performance or put fake smiles on their faces or act coquettish the way dancers do even in "*very good* troupes" (she underlines the "very good.") Sometimes for a ballet master," she writes ruefully, "it's easier to teach artists to move correctly than to clean up the soul-essence of each of them." She concludes that Balanchine intends to show just that: dance, technical perfection. "And what do you get from that? You get of course dancing, but you get also some kind of impression of the absolute high internal purity of the dances and the nobility of the performers. The idea of this purity, I think, is not simply the refusal of a subject, but the refusal of jaded, everyday, debased, and predictable dance and musical work."

Russians believe, she writes, that the duty of art is to show life as it should be. Watching the Balanchine ballets, she sees that classical dance "may also take on the job of showing some wonderful maybe inner life of a person. Isn't this the unspoken credo of Balanchine? You have to look at his childhood, his school years, and the years of his youth, and try to remember him as a person making his first small dances here, in Leningrad."[43]

Vera Sergeevna, my companion of the archives, you were there when Georges and Lidochka were young. You saw how he kept alive their dreams of an art that was honest and that spoke to its time.

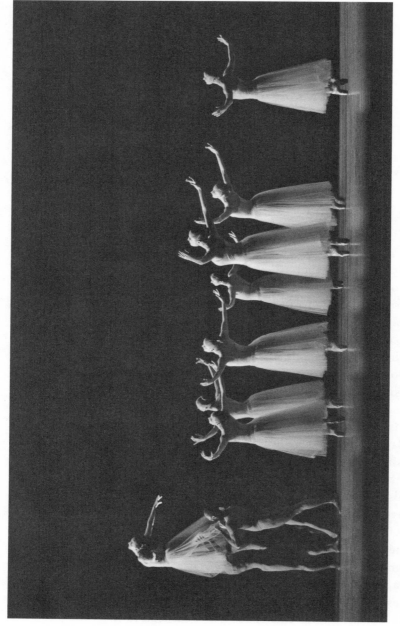

Serenade.

A Note on Sources

NEWSPAPERS AND JOURNALS

Birzhevye Vedomosti (Petrograd)
Krasnaya Gazeta (Petrograd, Leningrad)
Zhizn Iskusstva (Petrograd, Leningrad)

MAIN ARCHIVAL HOLDINGS
United States

New York Public Library, Slavic and East European Collections and Microform
  Reading Room (NYPL)

Russia

Gosudarstvennyi literaturno-memorialnyi muzei A.A. Akhmatovoi v Fontannom
  dome (MA)
Institut russkoi literatury (Pushkinskii Dom) rossiskoi akademin nauk (IRLI RAN)
  St. Petersburg
Mariinsky Theater archives, St. Petersburg
Rossiiskii gosudarstvennyi istoricheskii arkhiv (RGIA), St. Petersburg
Rossiiskii gosudarstvennii voenno-istoricheskii arkhiv (RGVIA), Moscow
Rossiiskaya natsionalnaya biblioteka (RNB), St. Petersburg
Sankt-Peterburgskii gosudarstvennyi muzei teatralnogo i muzykalnogo iskusstva
  (GMTMI), St. Petersburg
Sankt-Peterburgskaya gosudarstvennaya teatralnaya biblioteka (SPb GTB),
  St. Petersburg
Tsentralnyi gosudarstvennyi arkhiv literatury i iskusstva (TsGALI), St. Petersburg
Tsentralnyi gusudarstvennyi arkhiv Sankt Peterburga (TsGA SPb), St. Petersburg
Tsentralnyi gosudarstvennyi istoricheskii arkhiv Sankt-Peterburga (TSGIA SPb),
  St. Petersburg
Vaganova Academy of Russian Ballet, St. Petersburg

Finland

National Library of Finland, the Slavonic Library, Helsinki
Provincial Archives of Mikkeli, Mikkeli

Georgia

Central Historical Archives of Georgia, Department of Literature and Art, Tbilisi
Georgian State Museum of Theater, Music, Cinema and Choreography, Tbilisi
Kutaisi State Historical Archive, Kutaisi

Notes

Note: *Fond* is the number of the collection; *opis*, the subseries within the Fond; *delo*, the individual file. To clarify: a document is in a delo, which is in an opis, which is in a Fond.

INTRODUCTION

1. Mikhailov, 1978, p. 107.
2. Baedeker, p. xv.
3. Shklovsky, p. 175.
4. TsGALI, F.259, *opis* 2, *delo* 1.
5. Mikhailov, 1978, p. 107.
6. Shklovsky, p. 177.

CHAPTER ONE

1. Gorokhovaya 53, apt. 61, lay in the Third Ward of the Spassky borough, then containing the highest number of brothels in the city. Bater, p. 204. See Khuchua.
2. Ancient Georgian guitar-like instrument with four strings.
3. Information on Anton Balanchivadze, Kutaisi Central Archive, Fond 21, delo18071.
4. Conversation with Djarji and Tsiskari Balanchivadze, Tbilisi, 2006.
5. See Khuchua, pp. 9–24.
6. Here are buried generations of Balanchivadzes, including Anton and Evelita.
7. State Museum of Georgian Theater, Music, Film, and Choreography, Fond Meliton Balanchivadze. Documents #30, 39, 71.
8. A few years after Meliton's time, a student would fatally stab its Russian rector. In 1899, Stalin would be expelled for revolutionary activities.
9. Russia occupied different parts of Georgia at different times. See Ronald Grigor Suny's classic history.
10. Khuchua, p. 10.
11. Suny, ch. 4, pp. 63–95. See also Kuchua.
12. Khuchua, pp. 19–20.
13. Her 1930s letters explaining this can be found in the Pension Department, Georgian Central Archives, Tbilisi.
14. In her late 1930s petitions to claim Meliton's pension from Maria Balanchivadze, Gayane writes that Meliton had helped her financially all her life, even sending her to health resorts.
15. Khuchua, p. 26.

16. See n. 7 above.

17. Mandelstam, p. 69.

18. Quoted from the memoirs of Nikolai Malko in the excellent Rimsky-Korsakov Wikipedia article.

19. Khuchua, p. 32.

20. Meliton Balanchivadze brief autobiography, Georgian State Museum of Theater, Meliton Balanchivadze file, Document #30.

21. Khuchua, pp. 46–47.

22. Information kindly furnished by Ralf Stullich of "Beyond History" (www.beyond-history.com).

23. Her patronymic, Nikolaevna, shows that her father's first name was Nikolai. Information on Russian Almedingens comes from a paper given by genealogist Vadim Rykhliakov at a "Germans in St. Petersburg" conference, published in 2003 by the Museum of Anthropolgy and Ethnographics of the Russian Academy of Science (kunstkamera); also see Nikolai Almedingen *lichnoe delo* at RGVIA, Russian State Military History Archive in Moscow.

24. Sources untraceable. The most specific: a teacher at the Georgian Theater Museum, Rusudan Solomonovna Mikhailadze, who had spent time in 1920s Petersburg at a stenographers' course, told her Tbilisi students that "Meliton's wife had a Jewish mother."

25. Khuchua, p. 49.

26. Five hundred to 600 rubles a year were needed to maintain a tolerable standard of living for a family. Bater, p. 256.

27. Meliton's name appears for the first time in 1902 in *Ves Peterburg*, which gives his address as Kirochnaya 23; his wine importing office is also listed.

28. The sons remembered a Georgian restaurant instead.

29. See note 31. Meliton's own ranks were *potomstvennyi grazhdanin* (distinguished citizen) and *svobodnyi artist* (free artist).

30. Razed by Stalin in 1934.

31. Metricheskaya Kniga Khristorozhdestvenskoi tserkvi na Peskakh, Fond 19, opis 127, delo 1317.1902, pp. 71–72. Borisoglebskoi na Kalashnikovskoi pristani, Skorbiashchenskoi na stekliannom zavode, pri Mariinsko-Sergievskom priyute, pri Aleksandrovskom dome prizrenia, 1902, pp. 117–18. Schot rodivshikhsia muzha polia.

CHAPTER TWO

1. Kelly, p. 301. Several maternity institutions vetted peasant wet-nurses and matched them with families. The sum for this service was a steep ten roubles.

2. Metricheskaya kniga Khristorozhdestvenskoi tserkvi na Peskakh, Fond 19, opis 127, delo 1586.1904, pp. 71–72. Schot rodivshikhsia muzhskogo pola.

3. Apollon Balanchivadze, Archive of the Georgian Patriarchate, documents of Kutais-Gaenati Eparchy, pp. 56–57.

4. Certificate # 5055, a 1920 copy of a birth certificate filed in 1913 at the Imperial Theater School, asserts that Georgi Balanchivadze was born to legally married parents. The fact that his christening records indicated otherwise possibly points to documents falsified at a high level. Source: G. Balanchivadze *lichnoe delo*, RGIA, copy from SPb Theater Museum. tk

5. 1902: Kirochnaya 23; 1903: 4th Rozhdestvenskaya, 18–4; 1904: Baskov Pereulok, 23.

6. In 1908, St. Petersburg had seventeen *kontory* (agencies) for "Rented Governesses, Nursemaids and Servants," most run by foreigners.

7. Volkov, 1985, p. 59; Taper, p. 29.

8. Nabokov, p. 25.

9. See Taper, and Volkov, 1985.

10. Mason, p. x.

11. Volkov, 1985, pp. 40–41.

12. She died during World War II on a train from blockaded Leningrad to Georgia, near the Sea of Azov. Interviews, 2006–2011, with Balanchivadze family, Tbilisi.

13. His brother Andrei, by contrast, remembered a communal childhood that included Georgi in various units—"the family," "the children," "the two little boys."

14. Volkov, 1985, p. 39.

15. Andrei Balanchivadze, "My brother, George Balanchine," interview by Nona Lomidze in *Samshoblo* (*Homeland*, a Georgian periodical), no. 4, February 1990. The flavor of the Christmas parties may infuse Balanchine's *The Nutcracker*.

16. Including later revolutionaries Mamia Orakhelashvili and Shalva Eliava. *Samshoblo*, See n. 15 above.; Khuchua, pp. 50–51.

17. For this philanthropic act, plus a gift for melody, Meliton became known as the Georgian Glinka. Khuchua, p. 51.

18. Tamara's "thesis" at the Tbilisi Arts Academy was a large (and beautiful) oil painting of a robed old man holding a jug.

19. See Don C. Rawson, *Russian Rightists and the Revolution of 1905*, Cambridge, UK: Cambridge University Press, 1995.

20. Velichko lived in Tiflis from 1896 to 1899, editing the pro-Russian, anti-Armenian *Kavkaz*, until ousted by Armenian city fathers.

21. Balanchine called him an uncle, though he was not a brother of Meliton.

22. Taper, p. 34. Confirmed in Georgia. Another small Petersburger who'd played at the priesthood earlier was Tsar Nicholas II.

23. Their first names appear and occasionally their patronymics (Vasilievna and Yakovlevna, respectively), but no family names. A collection of fourteen Balanchivadze family letters dating from 1910 to the late 1930s in Andrei Balanchivadze's personal archive at Tbilisi's Georgian Historical Archives were kindly made available to the author by the Balanchivadze family.

24. Taper, p. 32. Sophia Almedingen information from Nikolai Almedingin's *posluzhnoi spisok* (service record) in the military-historical archive, RGVIA, Moscow, and *Ves Peterburg*.

25. This was confirmed in interviews with the Tbilisi Balanchivadzes, 2006–11. In 1909 Chumbadze was the bookkeeper of the Petersburg Fourth Mutual Credit Union when Meliton was a board member.

26. *Samshoblo*. See n. 15 above.

27. Volkov, 1985, p. 185.

28. Balanchivadze family letters, Andrei Balanchivadze personal file, Georgian Central Archive, Tbilisi. By family permission.

29. *Samshloblo. See n. 15 above.*

30. Information from Balanchivadze family archive, Georgian State Museum of Theater, etc., Document #93.

31. See Elizaveta Fen, *A Russian Childhood*.

32. St. Petersburg was considered the least healthy European capital. See McKean; also Lovell, ch. 3, p. 58.

33. One Russian source says workers possibly used the site for meals when they built the railroad.

34. Records from Finnish Karelia, Finnish National Archives, Mikkeli, Finland.

35. The Balanchivadzes' plots were called Sosnovka ("little pinewoods place" in Russian), Puisto ("park" in Finnish), and Tasanko ("plains" in Finnish). Mikkeli Archives. See also Balashov, *chast* 3.

36. Lounatjoki, since 1948 called Zakhodskoe, contains moss-covered dacha foundation ruins and one intact marble staircase. It's reachable by commuter train from St. Petersburg.

37. Volkov, 1985, p. 83.

38. *Ves Peterburg*, 1908, 1909.

39. The factory was probably in provincial Ostashkov, center of the Russian leather-tanning industry. The Ostashkov Savin family holdings also included a roof-tile factory. Major-General Vitmer, Meliton's wine-merchant colleague, is listed in *Ves Peterburg, 1914* as Petersburg representative of all Ostashkov industries.

40. *Samshoblo*, see n. 15 above.

41. Le Clercq, p. 57.

42. Volkov, 1985, p. 104.

43. Volkov, 1985, pp. 104–105.

44. Bolshaya Moskovskaya 1–3 was replaced in the 1950s by the Vladimirskaya metro station.

45. Andrei Balanchivadze once remarked later that Georgi as a child was "closed in, and dry." Interviews with Balanchivadze family, Tbilisi.

46. Taper, p. 32.

47. Volkov, 1985, p. 39.

48. Volkov, 1985, p. 58. Old Finnish saying: "A Russian is a Russian, even if it's fried in butter."

49. Ivan Balanchivadze was dismissed from his Simferopol Prison command on suspicion of aiding an imprisoned assassin's escape but later cleared of blame. This prompted his 1908 return to Petersburg. TsGIA SPb, Fond 1c/569, opis 28, delo 22.

50. *Samshoblo*, see n. 15 above.

51. D.A. Zasosov and V. I. Pyzin. *Iz zhizni Peterburga 1890–1910-kh godov*, St. Petersburg: Lenizdat, 1999, p. 36.

52. Theater Street (now Rossi Street) is wide as it is high (22 meters) and ten times as long, Rossi, 1775–1849, son of a ballerina, and court architect under Alexander I and Nicholas I, built some of the grandest, severest, and most graceful Petersburg public spaces.

53. See n. 15 above. A photo from Lounatjoki suggests that her ankles were slightly thick.

54. Taper-Balanchine interview 9/19/61, kindly shared with the author September 2009.

55. An August 13, 1913, letter petitioning for Georgi Balanchivadze's entrance to the Theater School, signed by Meliton, survives in Balanchine's *lichnoe delo*, RGIA, ond 498, opis 1. It's either written after the fact or the parents knew they would audition Georgi but omitted to tell him.

56. Taper notes, 9/19/61.

57. See Fen, pp. 286–87 for a similar scene.

CHAPTER THREE

1. Founded as Her Highness the Empress's School of Dance, it became the Imperial Theater School under Empress Elizabeth I (1742–62), adding actors, musicians, and

singers. In 1888, a commission decided that actors and musicians didn't need child-hood training, leaving again just dancers.

2. This move partly reversed Peter's vision of a civil service drawn from all classes, with advancement based solely on merit.

3. Pleshcheev, p. 130.

4. Rossi planned Theater Street in 1828 as a replica of Paris's commercial Palais Royale. Because of nearby rival street markets, it was converted in the mid-1830s to bureau-cratic and educational use by architect A. K. Cavos. Fomkin, pp. 30–35.

5. The author thanks Alexei Fomkin for a fascinating historical tour of the Theater School, now the Vaganova Ballet Academy, and for much else besides.

6. Andrei Balanchivadze, *Samshoblo*. See n.15, ch. 2.

7. Balanchivadze later compared notes about the jangling nametags with a younger student. TsGALI, Vera Sergeevna Kostrovitskaya *lichnyi* Fond #151, opis 1, delo # 26, 20.

8. The logbook begins on August 20, about a week after Georgi arrived.

9. Taper-Balanchine interview 10/20/61.

10. Among older boarders in 1913–14: Anatoly Vilzak, 17; Andrei Lopukhov, 15; Vladimir Tomson, 13; Boris Shavrov, 13; Vassily Vainonen, 12; Mikhail Dudko, Kiril Zhuralev, 11; Alexander Sakselin, 11.

11. Mikhailov, 1966, p. 18.

12. Volkov, 1985, p. 62.

13. In 1913, the monarchy was on the verge of instituting compulsory elementary education, plans derailed by World War I and later realized by the Soviet state. See Alston's wonderful book, especially the last chapter (243 ff).

14. Mikhailov 1966, p. 19.

15. Mikhailov, 1966, p. 27.

16. Volkov, 1985, pp. 62–63.

17. Mikhailov, p. 63.

18. Volkov, 1985, p. 42.

19. Roné, p. 137.

20. This nickname is usually written "Shura" in English. But Danilova became "Choura" in France in 1924, and she purposely kept the French spelling, even naming her 1986 memoir *Choura*.

21. Balanchine, p. 516.

22. The Zernishkovs' apartment number was 63.

23. As did Balanchine's godfather Stefanovich—a coincidence?

24. Volkov, p. 42.

25. November 9, 16, 30 (till 9 AM the next morning); December 4, 7, 14.

26. RGIA, Russian State Historical Archives, Fond 498, opis 1, del. 6528. No other boys' logbooks survive, and no girls' logbooks. Records may have been lost when RGIA, on Senate Square, closed for moving in 2002, reopening in 2008 near metro station Ladozhkaya.

27. Andrei remembered this party in a documentary film (viewed in Tbilisi); Balanchine never mentioned it.

28. Volkov, 1985, p. 42.

29. Volkov, 1985, pp. 75–76.

30. He had a fever on his birthday!

31. Twysden, p. 22.

32. Lisovskaya, p. 26

33. Volkov, 1985, pp. 62–63.
34. Each day one of the *vospitatels* filled in the logbook and signed the page. Three wrote in a cramped hand, Isaenko in a clear, rounded hand, as if he was happy in his duties.
35. The rest of the third floor was occupied by the drama day school, with older students.
36. Fomkin, pp. 76–82.
37. Fomkin, p. 78. See also Lopukhov's memoir.
38. Hall, p. 163. Grand dukes were the tsar's cousins and brothers.
39. *Russian Court Memoirs 1914–16*, by "A Russian," London: Herbert Jenkins, 1916, p. 64.
40. Apollon Balanchivadze Autobiography, Kutaisi Historical Archive, fond 23, opis 18071.
41. Tamara's personal file (*lichnoe delo*) was placed with the files of those admitted, not in the "refused" category. RGIA, Fond 498, opis 1, del. 6183.
42. Danilova, p. 42.
43. Mikhailov never knew who his father was. "He died for us within the first few days of your existence," said his mother when he asked. Mikhailov, 1966, p. 10.
44. Mikhailov, 1978, pp. 105–6.

CHAPTER FOUR

1. Krasovskaya, p. 14.
2. *Obshchii spisok ofitserskim chinam Russkoi Imperatorskoi armii: Sostavlen po 1-e yanvarya 1908 goda*, St. Petersburg: Voennaya tipografia, 1908.
3. TsGA SPb, RGIA, RGVIA.
4. *Meshchanin* was one of the *soslovia* (social estates) of the masses below the elite Table of Ranks. The others: merchant, clergy, peasant, worker, soldier, craftsman.
5. "Nixa" (1843–65), Alexander II's adored and gifted first son, died at twenty-one. His burly younger brother became Tsar Alexander III.
6. RGVIA, Moscow, Fond 2710, opis 2, dela 35, 37, 335, and Fond 400, opis 9, delo 29758, l. 699–699 ob.
7. See Krassnoff, Part I.
8. See Leshkov, Part II, section I, pp. 124 ff.
9. Diplomats George Buchanan and Maurice Paléologue have left descriptions of Tsarskoe Selo maneuvers. See also Krassnoff, pp 164–70.
10. Quotes from Lopukhov, p. 94. See also Hall, chs 3 and 4.
11. The word "junker," borrowed from Prussian army terminology, came to mean any army volunteer, of any class. Miller, p. 11.
12. Miller, pp. 88–89.
13. Later, under the conservative Alexander III, these gymnasia retrieved their former names, cadet corps.
14. Miliutin's final reform before Alexander II's 1881 assassination was universal military conscription.
15. See Steinberg's later chapters. By 1914, about half the officer corps came from classes other than the nobility.
16. TsGA SPb, Fond 1321, opis 2, l. 107.
17. Siegelbaum, 2008, pp. 8 ff.
18. See Leshkov and Krassnoff.

19. Some information about the Ivanovs came from Lidochka's two surviving cousins, Marina Zalkina and Elena Gracheva, granddaughters of Alexandra Ivanova's sister, Serafima Golubova, though they were mostly resistant to a non-Russian-born writer.

20. Almedingen, pp. 44–45. Edith Martha Almedingen, possible cousin of Balanchine's mother, left Russia for England in 1922 and later wrote memoirs and novels in English. The Ivanovs' address was 11 Srednii Prospekt, apartment 29.

21. Slonimsky, Mikhailov, Kostrovitskaya. See notes for chapters 7, 8, 9.

22. A May 1906 document entitled "A Short Description," Fond 400, RGVIA, Moscow.

23. In a 1927 limited-edition booklet about Lidochka (300 copies) published by her father after her death (Leningradskii Gublit No. 40690), Soviet art critic Gollerbach refers to Shteinberg as if readers knew him (p. 24).

24. 1904 issues of *Niva* magazine first show flags and joyous troops, then move to wounded soldiers and devastated Chinese villages. Disillusionment peaked after the Battle of Mukden in February–March 1905.

25. See also Mandelstam, pp. 88–90.

26. Vaginov's real name, Vagengeim, was Russified during WWI, as Petersburg became Petrograd. About *Bambochada*, Vaginov commented on his own title, noting that the word in Spanish means "a landscape representing banquets or drunken feasts, with grotesque figures." See Vaginov, 1931. I am indebted to Daria Khitrova's brilliant, article, "Kuzmin i smert' tantsovshchitsy," *NLO* 28 (2006), and to Yuri Tsivian for alerting me to it.

27. "I celebrate not the old world but the spectacle of its demise," said Vaginov at a hostile 1931 meeting of the Writers' Union. Barskova, p. 98.

28. Malmstad, pp. 343–44. Ivanov died of a heart attack on the street in 1929, still believing his daughter was intentionally killed.

29. The novel's level of detail has convinced several Russian scholars to treat it as a historical resource, especially Khitrova, op. cit.

30. Vaginov, p. 246.

31. Vaginov, p. 247. Along with the works of Hamsun and Ibsen, and the poems of André Chenier, Baudelaire, Akhmatova, Blok, Pushkin.

32. In life she outlasted both her daughter and husband, later inviting her sister with her two daughters and *their* daughters to share her apartment.

33. Mikhailov, Kostrovitsaya, Stukolkina, and Slonimsky.

34. On September 14, 1914, Ivanov became director of the 8th Automobile Regiment's garage: RGVIA Fond 5989, opis 1, delo 1, l. 89.

35. RGIA, St. Petersburg. Fond 498, delo 6178. In no other Theater School child's admission request have I seen a parent noting a child's birth date and exact age.

CHAPTER FIVE

1. The "kitchen stairs" connected the kitchens on all three floors. The "theater stairs" led to the second-floor theater and third-floor church.

2. Karsavina, p. 67.

3. Geidenreich founded the ballet school in Perm; Valentina Ivanova became a Soviet *caractère* dancer; Tiuntina was a Mariinsky soloist and teacher; Danilova would become a Ballet Russe prima ballerina, then a teacher at Balanchine's School of American Ballet.

4. The author visited Madame Danilova several times at home and observed these qualities.

5. See *Evterpa, Ti? Khudozhestvennye Zametki. Beesedy s artistami russkoj imigratsii,* by Mikhail Meilakh. Novoe literaturnoe obozrenie 2008.

6. RGIA, Fond 498, opis 1, delo 5916. Guardian transfer letter dated February 20, 1910.

7. *Protektsia* played a powerful role in Theater School admissions. In 1910, memoirist Lisovskaya's mother heard other mothers boast of having "a note from such and such a ballerina, and such and such a count."

8. Information about Danilova from RGIA, Fond 498, opis 1, delo 5916, her memoir, and Twysden's book.

9. Twysden, p. 21.

10. A January 1917 document lists the Theater School employees' years of employment. TsGALI, Fond 498, opis 1, delo 6355.

11. The same Smolny Institute that would in 1917 become first the Soviets' and then the Bolsheviks' headquarters.

12. Lisovskaya. pp. 21–22.

13. Their names were Anna Ludvigovna Stromilova, Olga Fedorovna Sigrist, Valentina Aleksandrovna Makedonskaya, Yulia Markovna Popova, Maria Adolfovna Enrold, and Olga Arsentievna Rogova. The Baltic Germans were the old colonizer class of the Baltic parts of the Russian Empire (Estonia, Livonia, and Courland, the last two now in Latvia).

14. Lisovskaya. P. 24

15. Volkov, p. 109.

16. Karsavina, p. 70.

17. See Catriona Kelly, "Self-Interested Giving: Bribery and Etiquette in Late Imperial Russia," in *Bribery and Blat in Russia: Negotiating Reciprocity from the Middle Ages to the 1990s,* ed. by Stephen Lovell, Alena V. Ledeneva, and Andrei Rogachevskii, London: St. Martin's Press, 2000, pp. 65–94.

18. Marius Petipa wrote that "dancers who don't have *protektsia* must wait for years to be cast whatever role in a ballet." Quoted in Rykhliakov, *Vestnik Akademii russkogo baleta im. A.Ia. Vaganovoi* no. 14.

19. Rykhliakov, ibid., p. 86.

20. Karsavina, p. 70.

21. Lisovskaya, pp. 24–25.

22. Teliakovsky invited Preobrazhenskaya to the Theater School staff on August 13, 1914, offering her a 900-ruble salary. Though never listed as regular, Preobrazhens-kaya taught Lidocha's class almost continually, from 1914 until she left Russia in 1921. RGIA, f. 498, *opis* 1, *delo* 5062, quoted in *Vestnik ARB* no. 5, p. 80.

23. Later, Savina would also sponsor Olga Spessivtseva.

24. Emil Hansen in Paris, Katti Lanner in London, Caterina Beretta in Milan. Roné, p. 26.

25. Roné, pp. 55, 97.

26. Volynsky, p. 30. For these translations and other Volynsky matters, I am deeply indebted to Stanley Rabinowitz.

27. Preobrazhenskaya's school operated till 1921; among its pupils were Alice Nikitina and Tamara Geva. Roné, p. 87.

28. The class contained fifteen first-years, including Lidochka, along with the handful of Rykhliakova's second-years who'd made the first-year cut.

29. Andreev, p. 6; Roné, p. 81.

· 254 ·

30. Nikitina, p. 19.
31. Stukolkina, quoted in Andreev, p. 6.
32. "*Tendus* provide the foundation of the technique of the leg": Roné, p. 129.
33. See Roné's ch. 9, on Preobrazhenskaya's teaching method.
34. Roné, p. 121.
35. I am greatly indebted here to talks with former NYCB soloist Zippora Karz.
36. Andreev, p. 7.
37. Balanchine later chose ballerinas almost exclusively from Preobrazhenskaya's students, in Russia and later in Paris (where she taught and he choreographed).
38. Balanchine, p. 516.
39. Balanchine, pp. 62–63.
40. Balanchine, p. 517. For ballet students watching during rehearsal, see Karsavina, p. 73.
41. Balanchine, p. 517.
42. "Legnani walked to the middle of the stage and took an undisguised preparation. The conductor, his baton raised, waited. Then a whole string of vertiginous pirouettes, marvellous in their precision and brilliant as diamond facets, worked the whole audience into ecstasies." Karsavina, p. 81.
43. The Mariinsky repertory in 1911 included about fifty-one ballets. Frame, p. 115.
44. Paléologue, Sunday, October 11 (that is, September 28), 1914.
45. He was a Fury in Meyerhold–Fokine's *Orpheus and Eurydice*, a Polovetsian Warrior in *Prince Igor*; he danced a tarantella at the Alexandrinsky (with classmate Maria Dolinskaya); he played a sprite in the Mikhailovsky's *Midsummer Night's Dream*, a student in the Alexandrinsky's *Professor Storitsyn*.
46. It's still danced today by students of the Vaganova Russian Ballet Academy, the former Theater School.
47. Borisoglebsy, M. Materialy po istorii ruskoga baleta.
48. Roné, p. 89.
49. Balanchivadze letters. See n. 23, ch. 2.
50. RGVIA, Fond 8176, opis 1, delo 3. l.1–106.
51. Balanchine quotes from Volkov, p. 60.
52. See Kostrovitskaya, Bibliography.
53. Shklovsky, p 11.
54. Danilova, pp. 44–45.

CHAPTER SIX

1. The rendition of the revolution in this and the following paragraphs comes from an array of sources including Figes, Sukhanov, Shklovsky, Wildman, etc.
2. Kostrovitskaya, see Bibliography.
3. Sukhanov, p. 5.
4. Shklovsky, p. 16.
5. Kostrovitskaya, see Bibliography.
6. Shklovsky, p. 16.
7. Slonimsky, p. 157.
8. Shklovsky, p. 14.
9. Khuchua, p. 52.
10. Hall, pp. 191–94.
11. See Sukhanov, pp. 209–11.

12. Information from Frame, p. 149; Hall, p. 188.
13. *The Russian Diary of an Englishman*, p. 79.
14. See TsGALI Fond 259, opis 2; also Frame, pp. 149–50.
15. See *Birzhevie vedomosti* (Stock Market news), which offered extensive arts coverage. The author read through the year 1917.
16. Neil V. Salzman, ed., *Russia in War and Revolution, General William V. Judson's Accounts from Petrograd, 1917–1918*, Kent, OH: Kent State University Press, 1998, pp. 39, 58. In August 1917, one ruble was worth 21 American cents; earlier, 52 cents.
17. RGIA, f. 733, *opis* 228, June 15, 1917.
18. Lisovskaya, p. 25.
19. Mikhailov, 1966, p. 106.
20. Volkov, p. 146. Even if Balanchine didn't write the letters to Lidochka, his jumping in memory from her to his small size indicates the two subjects were connected in his mind.
21. Mikhailov, 1966, p. 28.
22. Regarding Balanchivadze family letters, see n. 23, ch. 2.
23. Balanchine delighted in elegant jaunty dressing, as did Andrianov.
24. General Judson, American military attaché in the city, was begging the US government for "not less than 400 tons ordinary civilian clothing and 500 tons shoes" to be put on every American ship bound for Petrograd. Judson, p. 102.
25. See Ronald Segal, *Leon Trostky, a Biography*, New York, 1979, p. 172.
26. Andre Balanchivadze recounted those exploits so often that his children got tired of hearing them. Balanchivadze family interviews, 2006–11.

· 255 ·

CHAPTER SEVEN

1. See especially *Makers of the Russian Revolution*, ed. Georges Haupt and Jean-Jacques Marie, London: Allen & Unwin, 1974.
2. *The Diary of a Diplomat in Russia, 1917–1918*, by Louis de Robien, trans. Camilla Sykes, New York: Praeger, 1970, p. 134.
3. For quotes, see *Vospominania i vpechatlenia*, by A.V. Lunacharsky, Moscow: Sovetskaya Rossiya, 1968, and *Revolutionary Silhouettes*, by Lunacharsky, trans. and ed. Michael Glenny, New York: Hill and Wang, 1968. Also the website *Nasledie A.V. Lunacharskogo*, especially http://lunacharsky.newgod.su/lib/v-mire-muzyki/novinki-dagilevskogo-sezona.
4. Schwartz, p 12.
5. *Teatr i iskusstvo* 1917, no. 50, quoted in I.P. Khrushchevich (ed.), *Gosudarstvenny ordena Lenina akademicheskii teatr opery i baleta imeni S.M Kirova*, Leningrad: Gosudarstvennoe muzykalnoe izdatelstvo, 1957.
6. See Fitzpatrick, especially ch. 6, pp. 110 ff. Also Frame, p. 153.
7. de Robien, p. 210.
8. See Bruce Lincoln's fine book.
9. Balanchine-Taper interview, 1960.
10. Mikhailov, 1966, pp. 24–25.
11. So claims her October 1918 exit passport.
12. Danilova, p. 47.
13. Gerson, p. 91.
14. Slonimsky, p. 157. Proof of Ivanov's service in the Red Army lies in his 1922 "demobilization" document from TsGA SPb, Fond 1321, opis 2, p. 107.

15. Quoted in Lincoln, p. 90.

16. Balanchine-Taper interview, September 1961.

17. Balanchine-Taper interview, 1960.

18. Andreev, p. 26.

19. *"Goriachi, trebovatelnyi, vospriimchivyi"*: Kostrovitskaya, See Bibliography.

20. Khrushchevich, p. 23. To understand the dancers' anxiety, see Lopukhov, p. 192: "What would happen? Would the (new audience) laugh at our ballerinas, who were 'moving their legs around while half-nude?' Would they be bored, looking at these gymnastics? Would they get weary of seeing onstage princes, princesses, fairies, and evil genies?" See also Clark, pp. 100–121.

21. TsGALI, f. 259, #1–3 program. The organizers: Gerdt, Romanova, Zhukova, Leontiev, Semenov, Gavlikovsky, Kshesinsky (brother of Mathilda).

22. Actors/writers, were Kiralev, Petrov, Kobelev, Shavrov, Goreva.

23. The mature Balanchine made his own *Tarantella* in 1964, as well as many elegant jesters and clowns—stand-ins for himself?

24. Mikhailov, Slonimsky, even the critic Volynsky often mentioned Lidochka's "Mongolian" eyes.

25. Anonymous reviewer quoted in Shmakov, p.90.

26. Mikhailov, 1978, p. 13.

27. Viktor Serge, *Year One of the Russian Revolution*, trans. Peter Sedgwick, London: Pluto Press, 1992, pp. 250–81.

28. See Lincoln, pp. 131–63; Rayfield, pp. 78–79.

29. See Fitzpatrick, pp. 26–58

30. Slonimsky, pp. 13–21.

31. Lynn Mally, *Revolutionary Acts: Amateur Theater and the Soviet State, 1917–38*, Ithaca, NY: Cornell University Press, 2000, p. 33.

32. *Zhizn Iskusstva*, April 4, 1920, quoted in Rudnitsky, p. 41.

33. These can be viewed in TsGALI, Fond 259.

34. There is some disagreement about this date. Slonimsky says October 12, Mikhailov, October 19. I have found Slonimsky, a dance scholar, to be more reliable on dates.

35. Lunacharsky's speech quoted in Mikhailov, 1978, pp. 6–7; Slonimsky, pp. 13–21.

36. Drama School applicant Slonimsky saw him and asked directions from him, only learning his name later. Slonimsky, p. 14.

37. TsGA, SPb, Fond 80, inostrannyi otdel Komissariata vnutrennikh del Soyuza kommun Severnoi oblasti, opis 22, lichnye dela optantov, delo 195. Balanchivadze, Maria Nikolaevna 12.10.18.

38. Apollon Balanchivadze autobiography, Kutaisi Central Archives.

39. See Suny, Lincoln.

40. The best proof: a summer 1921 letter from Andrei Balanchivadze in Tbilisi to Maria in Petrograd.

41. On the opening page of the Theater School archive guide in TsGALI, an ironic-minded archivist wrote the school's eleven official names from 1917 to 1961.

42. TsGALI, Fond 259, opis 2, delo 17.

43. Krasovskaya, p. 9.

44. Information from Kostrovitskaya, Mikhailov, Slonimsky.

45. See Kostrovitskaya, Bibliography.

46. Mikhailov, 1966, p. 22.

47. Slonimsky, p. 158.

48. Roné, p. 85. See also *Birzhevie vedomosti*, 1917.

49. *Vek Balanchina*, p. 45.
50. Slonimsky, p. 158.
51. I thank Theater Museum staff member Elena Fedosova for pointing out Preobra-zhenskaya's choreographic skills.
52. Mikhailov, 1966, p. 51. See also Schwezoff, p. 131: "She was in a simple giton (*chiton*), she looked old, she had curved shoulders; but when she danced all this disappeared . . . she seemed to emanate the spirit of the dance, like an aureole round her."
53. Souritz, p. 44.
54. Khrushchevich, p. 23.
55. Slonimsky, p. 68.
56. Kostrovitskaya, see Bibliography.
57. Kostrovitskaya, see Bibliography.
58. Kostrovitskaya misremembered it as an Akhmatova poem.
59. Serge, p. 82.
60. Author's interview with Balanchine, 1981.
61. Danilova, p. 47.
62. Slonimsky, Kostrovitskaya, Fitzpatrick.
63. Andreev, p. 19.
64. Kostrovitskaya, see Bibliography. She mistook the film's New York for Paris.
65. See Slonimsky, pp. 129–38, and Kostrovitskaya.
66. Kostrovitskaya, see Bibliography.
67. Mikhailov, 1966, p. 23.
68. Slonimsky, 134.
69. Lopukhov, p. 99.
70. Kenez, p. 104. Even as late as 1913, Nicholas II scornfully dismissed a movie-making propaganda proposal.
71. Years later, Moscow filmmaker Viktor Bocharov discovered Shiryaev's films and made a documentary, "Belated Premiere," about him and the puppets.
72. Slonimsky, p. 142.
73. Kostrovitskaya, see Bibliography.
74. Balanchine famously called dancers of both sexes "dear." Isaenko was expelled near the end of Balanchivadze's time in the school, by a vote of the UchKom, for supposed cruelty to students. He didn't bear a grudge, but instead used to call Balanchivadze and Gusev to his bare new room to share his rations. Slonimsky, pp. 144–45.
75. Kostrovitskaya, see Bibliography.
76. Volkov, 1995, p. 293.
77. Slonimsky, see pp. 140–48.
78. Volynsky, p. 119, trans. Rabinowitz.
79. Slonimsky, pp. 164–65; Volynsky, p. 120.
80. *Ballet Review*, vol. 5, no. 3, 1975–76, p. 20.
81. Kostrovitskaya, see Bibliography.
82. The list of Balanchivadze's assigned piano pieces comes from a rough draft of Slonimsky's article on Balanchine's youth, TsGALI, Fond 157, opis 1, delo 21; a shortened version was later published in English in *Ballet Review*.
83. Balanchine-Taper interview, September 1961.
84. *Vek Balanchina*, p. 48.
85. Author is greatly indebted to talks with Zippora Karz, ex-soloist, New York City Ballet, about choreography.

86. Kostrovitskaya, see Bibliography.

87. Mikhailov, 1966, pp. 32–33.

88. Many dancers remember Balanchine demonstrating ballerina roles. Violette Verdy claimed Balanchine's Swan Queen, danced at a rehearsal, was the best she'd ever seen. Verdy Interview with the author, 2011.

89. As Balanchine himself would later do for the dancers of the New York City Ballet.

90. *The Magic Flute* information from memoirs of Mikhailov, Kostrovitskaya, Slonimsky.

91. Slonimsky, p. 160.

92. Mikhailov, 1966, p. 33.

CHAPTER EIGHT

1. The Nabokovs among them. Lincoln, pp. 448–49.

2. See Sorokin, *Leaves from a Russian Diary*, New York, Dutton, 1924.

3. Lincoln, p. 466.

4. Roné, p. 91. Preobrazhenskaya later taught in Berlin, then at Milan's La Scala (where she also choreographed), finally, for many years in Paris.

5. Roné, p. 53.

6. Lopukhov, p. 108.

7. See especially Schwezoff, pp. 97–114.

8. Examples of the former are Igor Schwezoff and Tamara Geva; of the latter, Leontina Karlovna Perm, a factory worker who began Theater School evening classes in 1921, whose daughter, Irina Kolpakova, became a Mariinsky prima ballerina.

9. Schwetzoff calls him Baron Schicksaal, but he's the same person as Miklos.

10. The address was Gagarinskaya St. #3. Schwetzoff, pp. 101–2, Kremshevskaya, pp. 37–39.

11. Teachers included Evgenia Snetkova-Vecheslova (later the Theater School youngest girls' teacher); Iosif Kshesinsky, and ex-ballroom dance teacher Gavlikovsky. See Schwezoff, p. 122.

12. The military was among government agencies sponsoring theater. See Clark, ch. 4, pp. 100–121.

13. Author interview 3/22/12 with Irina Kolpakova, Vaganova's last ballerina.

14. Krassovskaya, p. 97.

15. It was probably set to the *lezginka* in Glinka's "Ruslan and Ludmilla."

16. Quoted in Slonimsky, pp. 148–49.

17. Accounts of the NEP's beginning taken from Ball and Lincoln.

18. Quoted in Antonella Salomoni, *Lenin and the Russian Revolution*, trans. David Stryker, Northampton, MA: Interlink, 2004, p. 139.

19. Ball, pp. 16–19.

20. Schwezoff, p. 123.

21. Mikhailov, 1978, pp. 109–10.

22. Ballets performed summer 1921: *The Little Humpbacked Horse, Swan Lake, The Sleeping Beauty, Chopiniana, Paquita, Coppélia, La Halte de Cavalerie, La Fille Mal Gardée*. See weekly editions of *Zhizn Iskusstva*, summer 1921.

23. Mikhailov, 1966, p. 38.

24. The Pavlovsk casting is in *Zhizn Iskusstva*, July 1921.

25. Mikhailov, 1966, p. 41.

26. Danilova, p. 53.

27. The remaining Lopukhov child, Nikolai, refused to enter the Theater School and became an engineer.

28. Lopukhov, p. 160.
29. *Zhizn Iskusstva* was the considered the Narkompros house organ.
30. Balanchine-Taper interview, 9/20/61.
31. Lopukhov, p. 100.
32. Mikhailov, 1966, p. 238.
33. Schwezoff, p. 102.
34. Imperial uniforms remained a model for the Theater School uniforms at least until the 1960s.
35. Mikhailov, 1966, p. 35.
36. Balanchivadze family letters, see n. 23, ch. 2.
37. *Ballet Review* 1975–76, Vol. 5, No. 3, p. 48. I thank Marvin Hoshino (editor, *Ballet Review*) and Leslie Mason and Spencer Mason for generous permission to view the original Russian text (p. 82 in Russian text).
38. The Von may have been added by the nobility-fetishizing Richard Buckle, Balanchine's second biographer, who visited his brother in Tbilisi.
39. Kostrovitskaya, see Bibliography.
40. She attended Chekrygin's and Preobrazhenskaya's schools and took private lessons from ex-ballerina Sokolova.
41. Geva, p. 279.
42. Slonimsky-Lisovskaya; Gusev-Mungalova; Kostrovitskaya-Dmitriev.
43. The Zheverzheev collection became the kernel of the St. Petersburg Theater Museum, still housed on Ostrovsky Square in front of the Alexandrinsky Theater.
44. There is a discrepancy among documents pertaining to Georges's legal status at birth. Church christening records show that his parents were unmarried at their children's births but had married by 1906 when Meliton recognized the children. A copy of Georges' birth certificate, required for Theater School entrance (*Svidetelstvo No. 5055*), states that the parents were married at his birth. Meliton's marriage certificate with Maria has not been found, nor has his legal divorce from his first wife. It is possible Meliton never legally divorced his first wife or married Maria, but instead had the records falsified at a high level.
45. The March 1922 date for Georges moving to the Zheverzheevs' is a guess, based on his official Petrograd Conservatory report, in which his teacher commends his zeal in piano practice, even if he "received access to a piano of his own only in March of 1922."
46. Quoted in Naiman, p. 81.
47. See *The Woman Question*, NY, 1951, pp. 76–80.
48. Wood, p. 153, pp. 176–77; *The Woman Question*, pp. 64–87.
49. Naiman, p. 83.
50. Quoted in Naiman, p. 115.
51. Naiman, p. 136.
52. Danilova, p. 56. Choura, later a glamorous ballerina onstage and off, was possibly plainer in the early 1920s, having had no help from family. Answering the question about "Parents" on a 1921 work questionnaire, she wrote "*odinoka*," alone.
53. Quoted in Slonimsky, p. 161.
54. Slonimsky, p. 159. See also Clark, ch. 4.
55. Slonimsky, p. 162.
56. Mason, p. vii. Later, Balanchine reinforced the link between *Chaconne* and the opera when he added a prologue set to *Orfeo*'s "Dance of the Blessed Spirits."
57. Rudnitskii, p. 23, see also Clark, ch. 4.

58. A trope Konstantin Sergeev later reproduced in his 1946 production of the ballet *Cinderella*.

59. Rudnitsky., p. 61.

60. These can be seen at SPb State Theater Museum's (GMTMI) facility on 2, Graftio St. on the Petersburg Side.

61. These photos are at the St. Petersburg Theater Museum Branch at 2, Graftio St.

62. Rudnitsky, p. 17.

63. Slonimsky, p. 162.

64. Lopukhov (Slonimsky intro), p. 13.

65. Mikhailov, 1966, p. 89.

66. Kostrovitskaya, see Bibliography; see also Slonimsky, p. 160.

67. Mikhailov, 1966, p. 87.

68. Kostrovitskaya, see Bibliography.

69. Mikhailov, 1966, p. 41.

CHAPTER NINE

1. The dancers in *TanzSymphonia*: Balashov, Gusev, Balanchivadze, Danilova, Ivanova, Ivanovsky (Lavrovsky), Kirsanov, Lopukhov, Lisovskaya, Mikhailov, Pavlova, Raupenas, Svekis, Tomson, Tiuntina, Frangopulo, Kaukol.

2. Lopukhov, p. 243.

3. Schwartz, p. 62.

4. The ballet was reconstructed at Leningrad's Conservatory in the late 1990s. The author saw a lackluster performance of it, summer 2004.

5. Quoted in Lopukhov (Slonimsky Introduction), pp. 12–13.

6. Souritz, pp. 269–77, who also quotes dance historians Galina Dobrovolskaya and Arkady Sokolov-Kominsky. I am also indebted to talks with Sokolov-Kominsky.

7. Kostrovitskaya, see Bibliography.

8. Yakovlova, pp. 97–98. See also Volkov, p. 278.

9. See Stanley Rabinowitz's informative Introduction in Volynsky, pp. xvii–xliii.

10. Volynsky, p. 69, trans. Stanley Rabinowitz.

11. *Zhizn Iskusstva*, October 10, 1922.

12. Information on the entertainment scene in the early NEP came from *Zhizn Iskusstva*, 1918–1924, which the author read through on microfilm and microfiche in the NYPL Microforms Reading Room.

13. Some acts: Jean et Maria, De LaMar, Melli Scot and Bertram Tulli, Spokoiskaya and Monomakhov.

14. *Zhizn Iskusstva*, November 7, 1922.

15. *Zhizn Iskusstva*, November 14, 1922.

16. Taper-Balanchine interview, Sept. 27, 1961.

17. Slonimsky, pp. 50–51.

18. See Slonimsky, ch. 6, especially pp. 200–205.

19. Danilova, p. 57.

20. *Zhizn Iskusstva*, summer and fall, 1922.

21. Kostrovitskaya, see Bibliography.

22. Schwezoff, p. 137.

23. No one will ever quite know which steps in the Petipa classics were installed there by Lopukhov, and which were the "original" Petipa (and many of the master's ballets were already restaged versions of predecessors' works).

24. *Zhizn Iskusstva*, March 27, 1923.
25. Lopukhov, p. 202.
26. *Zhizn Iskusstva*, March 13, 1923.
27. Lopukhov, pp. 245–46.
28. I've relied for the Young Ballet's first concert especially on Kostrovitskaya, who writes vividly, remembers much that others forgot, and not intending to publish, was not constrained by a political climate that discouraged published memoirists from focusing on Balanchine's role in the Young Ballet. See Bibliography.

29. By Kostrovitskaya's recollection, Young Ballet participants from her class were "O. Mungalova, N. Mlodzinskaya, T. Mazikova, V. Faber, N. Bazarova, and me." From earlier classes: "A. Danilova, L. Ivanova, N. Stukolkina, P. Gusev, M. Mikhailov, L. Balashev, N. Efimov, M. Atrafimovich, and T. Zheverzheeva." Kostrovitskaya called Geva an "*estradnaya*" dancer but also a good classical dancer.
30. Balanchine later retained his anti-hierarchical system, often trying out young dancers in lead roles rather than casting from an unspoken seniority system.
31. This list was composed using Kostrovitskaya, Stukolkina (via Andreev), a Young Ballet poster dated June 1, 1923, and the Balanchine Foundation's Catalogue.
32. It's now a bank.
33. Danilova, Eliseeva, Ivanova, Kostrovitskaya, Lisovskaya, Mlodzinskaya, Mungalova, Nikitina, Stukolkina, Tiuntina, Balanchivadze, Balashev, Gusev, Efimov, Kirsanov, Lavrovsky, Mikhailov.
34. Facts from Slonimsky and Kostrovitskaya.
35. As in *Swan Lake*, Act IV?

CHAPTER TEN

1. For this idea I thank astute dance scholar Tim Scholl.
2. Mikhailov must mean Olga Spessivtseva and Viktor Semenov. This is possibly also when Georges's avant-garde *Enigma* pas de deux was danced with Lidochka.
3. Mikhailov, p. 238.
4. Kostrovitskaya, see Bibliography.
5. Rudnitsky, p. 54, 140–42.
6. See Schwartz, p. 46. This "equality in the eyes of art" was carried by Balanchine to his own New York City Ballet. No stars, only ensemble.
7. Mikhailov, 1966, pp. 238–39.
8. The picture is labeled "young members of the Ak-Ballet," but most were also Young Ballet members.
9. *Egyptian Nights* was a version of Fokine's 1910 Diaghilev hit *Cleopatra*.
10. *Zhizn Iskusstva*, late October 1923. "I value this young artist, making a career with demonstrable success from the very beginning . . . Statuesque figure, everything long, placement of the head, neck—everything grows and blooms. But in *Egyptian Nights* this artist's appearance doesn't reward either herself or the public. Let's admit it: a naked body isn't pretty on the stage."
11. Danilova, p. 56.
12. Slonimsky, pp. 163–65.
13. *Zhizn Iskusstva*, June 1923.
14. Mikhailov, 1978, p. 117.
15. Kostrovitskaya, see Bibliography.
16. Slonimsky, p. 172.

17. Slonimsky, p. 176.

18. Mikhailov, 1978, p. 117.

19. These memories come from Kostrovitskaya, Slonimsky, and Mikailov, in that order. The quote is from Mikhailov, 1978, p. 117.

20. Kostrovitskaya, see Bibliography.

21. See Slonimsky, pp. 183–88.

22. Mikhailov, 1978, p. 116.

23. Slonimsky, p. 164.

24. Ibid., p. 164.

25. Quoted in Slonimsky, p. 177.

26. Ibid., p. 164.

27. Mikhailov, 1966, p. 239. Only eight "Clubs" were listed in *Ves Leningrad*, 1925 under "casinos," but one was an auto club and two were trade clubs, leaving five: Casino, the Trocadero, the Vladimirsky, and two called "Elektroloto."

28. Both quotes from Mikhailov, 1966, pp. 240–41.

29. *Zhizn Iskusstva*, NYPL, tk

30. Slonimsky, pp. 176–79. The 1927 booklet "Lidiia Ivanova" lists her roles at the back: 27 classical roles and 21 concert numbers. See Bibliography.

31. The paintings from the Theater Museum on Graftio St. where a pair of Lidochka's rose-colored toe shoes can also be found. Inside one shoe a former curator penciled "poor Lidiia Ivanova."

32. Kostrovitskaya, see Bibliography. Mikhailov, 1978, pp. 119–20.

33. Conversation with Lidochka's cousin Yelena Gracheva, and with singer-artist Platon Shvets.

34. Thank you to filmmaker Lucy Kostelanetz and Professor Yuri Tsvian of the University of Chicago for help locating this film, and much else.

35. Quoted in Slonimsky, pp. 185–86.

36. The address was #12 on both streets.

37. Now the Cheka Museum.

38. Naiman, esp. ch. 1.

39. See Slonimsky, ch. 6, pp. 189–220.

40. Information from *St. Petersburg Moussorgsky State Academic Opera and Ballet Theatre*, vol. 2, pp. 12–13, courtesy of Arkady Sokolov-Kaminsky, and from the website of the theater, now once again the Mikhailovsky.

41. *St. Petersburg Moussorgsky*, etc., pp. 13–14. See also reviews in *Zhizn Iskusstva*.

42. *St. Petersburg Moussorgsky*, etc., pp. 13–15.

43. *Zhizn Iskusstva*, Oct. 9, 1923.

44. *Zhizn Iskusstva*, December 1923. Historian Natalia Lebina writes that prostitution became the most prominent emblem of the NEP era. Quoted in Barskova, p. 165.

45. In a 2006 concert in St. Petersburg's Anna Akhmatova Museum, the beautiful, carnival-flavored music from Kuzmin's *Eugen Neschastny* was played.

46. Quoted in *Vek Balanchina*, p. 85.

47. *Zhizn Iskusstva*, Dec. 25, 1923.

48. TsGALI, Fond 298, opis 2, dok. 153. For money clarification, see History Learning Site, The NEP.

49. Geva, p. 296.

50. *Ves Leningrad*, 1925.

51. Rayfield, p. 124.

52. Sherikh, p. 20, quoting *Krasnaya Gazeta*, Jan. 24, 1924.

53. Rayfield, pp. 89–91.
54. Kostrovitskaya, see Bibliography.
55. See "Lidiia Ivanova," Bibliography.
56. Pushkinsky Dom, Rukopisnoe otdelenie, Zoshchenko file.
57. Balanchine-Taper interview, March 9, 1962.
58. Documents in Harvard Houghton Library, Balanchine Archive.
59. Geva, p. 314.
60. Several witnesses, including Balanchine, say she was a good swimmer; only Slonimsky writes that she couldn't swim (censorship?). Her father, who took her to the beach in Terioki and gave her lessons in everything, would have taught her to swim.
61. See John E. Malmstad, "The Mystery of Iniquity: Kuzmin's 'Temnye ulitsy rozhdajut temnye mysli,'" *Slavic Review* Vol. 34, No. 1 (1975), p. 53.

CHAPTER ELEVEN

1. I owe much to Professor Daria Khitrova's earlier examination of the facts of Lidia's death, *"Kuzmin i smert tantsovshchitsy,"* NLO 2006 N78. Also to an article by Igor Khaabarov in *Soviet Ballet*, No. 3, May–June 1988, pp. 46–49, generously shared by Daria Pavlova.
2. *Zhizn Iskusstva*, July 1, 1924.
3. *Krasnaya Gazeta*, evening edition, June 18, 1924.
4. Benois, p. 750.
5. Ibid., p. 761.
6. This 4-page article, called "Tainy ee tragicheskoj gibeli", was reprinted in *Soviet Balet* No. 3, 1988. See n. 1 above.
7. For a discussion of the meaning of "real people" and "marginality" for young NEP radicals, see Barskova, pp. 200–216.
8. Vaginov, pp. 296–97.
9. See Elena Fedosova's fine article in the album *Olga Spessivtseva*, pp. 42–43.
10. Translation, John Malmstad, *Slavic Review*, Vol. 34, No. 1, p. 47.
11. Danilova, p. 61.
12. Volkov, pp. 146–47.
13. For another narrative of Lidochka's death, see Sherikh, pp. 155–63.
14. Heartfelt thanks to Daria Khitrova for unearthing it. TsGALI SPb, Fond 260, opis 3, delo 811.
15. Gerson, pp. 227–29.
16. Ibid., pp. 227–28.
17. See especially Rayfield, 2004, and Sheila Fitzpatrick, 1992, Introduction.
18. Rayfield, 2004, p. 83.
19. Alexander Tarasov-Rodionov, *Chocolate*, trans. Charles Malamuth (Garden City, NY: Doubleday, Doran & Co., 1932; repr. Westport, CT: Hyperion Press, 1973). See also Viktor Serge's novel, *A Conquered City*, trans. Richard Greeman (Garden City, NY: Doubleday, 1975).
20. Malmstad, *Slavic Review* (see n. 10 above), p. 53.
21. Coincidentally, in the same issue is an announcement of the premiere of *Apollo* with Diaghilev's Ballets Russes.
22. Information from Lidia Pavlova *lichnoe delo*, TsGALI SPb, Fond 260, opis 3, delo 1346.
23. Danilova, p. 62.

24. Ibid., p. 62.

25. Ibid., pp. 64–69.

26. Taper, p. 84.

27. Diaghilev visited Russia last in 1913–14, but after 1917 he still dreamed of returning. See Scheijen, pp. 214–19 ff.

28. Author's interview with Balanchine, 1980.

29. St. Petersburg's Tauride St. is especially rich in atlantes and caryatids. It runs between the Balanchivadzes' Suvorovsky Prospekt apartment and the Tauride Garden, where the Balanchivadze children played.

30. I am grateful to many colleagues' discussion of the ballets, notably Arlene Croce, Laura Jacobs, and Nancy Goldner, whose two books discuss the ballets individually. For *Apollo* and Balanchine's quote about "family relations," see Goldner 2008, p. 6.

31. She alternated in the role with Alice Nikitina, the favorite of Diaghilev's contributor Lord Rothermere.

32. Taper, p. 153.

33. Ibid., p. 156.

34. Ruthana Boris, in *Reading Dance*, ed. Robert Gottlieb, New York, 2008, pp. 1063–69, suggests that Serenade's opening pose was connected in Balanchine's mind with the Nazi salute, which he altered to ward off evil.

35. Balanchine quoted in Goldner, 2008, p. 24.

36. Danilova quoted in Mason, p. 7.

37. Quoted in Malmstad, p. 51. See n. viii above. This inscription was kindly shown me by Jerry and Helen Polynsky, who helped re-translate it.

38. Lidochka was pictured in her own cartoon in a *Zhizn Iskusstva* issue dated March, 1924, as Estrella in Fokine's *Carnaval*. Georges got one too, in April; it showed him wearing a beret and artist's smock, kneeling, holding a screaming miniature ballerina upside-down.

39. Balanchine-Taper interview, 1961.

40. Reynolds, p. 242.

41. Even if earlier and later *Mozartianas* are different, a chain of memory stretches back through the *Mozartiana* ballerinas, first Toumanova, then Danilova, then Suzanne Farrell. Lynn Garafola's observation to author. And the dancer who first danced the *Gigue* was Christopher d'Amboise, son of Jacques d'Amboise, who often danced "for" Balanchine in his own ballets.

42. Mikhailov, 1966, pp. 54–55.

43. Kostrovitskaya, see Bibliography.

Bibliography

PRIMARY SOURCES

Almedingen, Edith Martha. *I Remember St. Petersburg*. London: Longmans Young, 1969.

Andreev, Alexei. "Balerina iz dinastii krepostnykh." Unpublished manuscript about Nina Stukolkina. Academy of Russian Ballet, Fond 18, delo 3.

Baedeker, Karl. *Russia: A Handbook for Travelers (A Facsimile of the Original 1914 Edition)*. New York: Arno Press, 1971.

Balanchine, George. *Balanchine's New Complete Stories of the Great Ballets*. Edited by Francis Mason. New York: Doubleday, 1954.

Balashov, Evgenii A. *Karelskii peresheek: Zemlia neizvedannaia*. St. Petersburg, Novoe Vremya, 2006, especially Vol. 3, Kuolemajärvi–Kanneljärvi.

Benua (Benois), Aleksandr. *Dnevnik. 1918-1924*. Moscow: Zakharov, 2010.

Danilova, Alexandra. *Choura: The Memoirs of Alexandra Danilova*. New York: Knopf, 1986.

Fokine, Mikhail. *Memoirs of a Ballet Master*. Translated by Vitale Fokine. Boston: Little, Brown, 1961.

Geva, Tamara. *Split Seconds: A Remembrance*. New York: Harper & Row, 1972

Karsavina, Tamara. *Theatre Street*. New York: E. P. Dutton, 1931.

Khuchua, Pavel. *Meliton Balanchivadze*. Tbilisi: Zarya Vostoka, 1952.

Kostrovitskaya, Vera. Personal archive in TsGALI. In these letters and articles she tells multiple versions of events. Documents consulted include Fond 151, opis 1, delo 26; Fond 154, opis 1, delo 20; Fond 157, opis 1, dela 20, 21, 45, 95.

Krassnoff, General P. N. *From Double Eagle to Red Flag*. New York: Duffield and Co., 1928.

Kshesinskaya, Matilda. *Dancing in Petersburg: The Memoirs of Mathilde Kschessinska*. Translated by Arnold Haskell. New York: Da Capo Press, 1977.

Le Clercq, Tanaquil. *The Ballet Cook Book*. New York: Stein and Day, 1966.

Leshkov, Denis. *Parter i kartser* [Parterre and barracks]. Moscow: Molodaia gvardiia, 2004.

Lisovskaya, Natalia Leonidovna. "Vospominaniia o Petrogradskom teatralnom uchilishche." *Vestnik Akademii Russkogo baleta* No. 4 (1995): 18–26.

Lopukhov, Fedor. *Shestdesiat let v balete: Vospominania i zapiski baletmeistera*. Moscow: Iskusstvo, 1966.

Mandelstam, Osip. *The Noise of Time*. Translated by Clarence Brown. Evanston, IL: Northwestern University Press, 2002.

Mason, Francis. *I Remember Balanchine: Recollections of the Ballet Master by Those Who Knew Him*. New York: Doubleday, 1991.

Mikhailov, Mikhail. *Molodye gody leningradskogo baleta*. Leningrad: Iskusstvo, 1978.

Mikhailov, Mikhail. *Zhizn v balete*. Edited by David Zolotnitsky. Leningrad: Iskusstvo, 1966.

Nabokov, Vladimir. *Speak, Memory*. New York: Putnam, 1966.

Nikitina, Alice. *Nikitina by Herself*. London: Wingate, 1959.

Paleologue, Maurice. *An Ambassador's Memoirs*. New York: George H. Doran, 1923; reprinted New York: Octagon, 1972.

Pleshcheev, Alexander. *Nash balet (1673–1899)*. St. Petersburg: A. Benke, 1899; reprinted St. Petersburg: Planeta muzyki, 2009.

Serge, Victor. *Memoirs of a Revolutionary*. Translated by Peter Sedgwick. New York: New York Review Books, 2012.

Shklovsky, Viktor. *A Sentimental Journey*. Translated by Richard Sheldon. Ithaca, NY: Cornell University Press, 1970, rev. ed. 1984.

Schwezoff, Igor. *Borzoi*. London: Hodder and Stoughton, 1935.

Slonimsky, Yuri. *Chudesnoe bylo riadom s nami: Zametki o petrogradskom balete 20-x godov*. Leningrad: Sovetskii kompozitor, 1984.

Sorokin, Pitirim, *Leaves from a Russian Diary*, New York, E. P. Dutton, 1924.

Sollertinsky, Ivan. *Stati o balete*. Leningrad: Muzyka, 1973.

Sukhanov, N. N. *The Russian Revolution*. Translated by Joel Carmichael. New York: Harper, 1962.

Vaginov, Konstantin. *Bambochada*. Leningrad: Izdatelstvo Pisatelei, 1931.

Volynsky, Akim. *Ballet's Magic Kingdom*. Edited and translated by Stanley J. Rabinowitz. New Haven, CT: Yale University Press, 2008.

Yastrebtsev, Vasily Vasilievich. *Reminiscences of Rimsky-Korsakov*. Edited and translated by Florence Jonas. New York: Columbia University Press, 1985.

SECONDARY SOURCES

Alston, Patrick L. *Education and the State in Tsarist Russia*. Stanford, CA: Stanford University Press, 1969.

Ball, Alan M. *Russia's Last Capitalists: The Nepmen, 1921–1929*. Berkeley: University of California Press, 1987.

Barskova, Polina. "Enchanted by the Spectacle of Death: Forms of the End in Leningrad Culture (1917–1934)." PhD diss., University of California, Berkeley, 2006.

Bater, James H. *St. Petersburg: Industrialization and Change*. London: E. Arnold, 1976.

Bindig, Susan F. "Dancing in Harlequin's World." PhD diss., New York University, 1998.

Chamberlain, Lesley. *Lenin's Private War: The Voyage of the Philosophy Steamer and the Exile of the Intelligentsia*. New York: St Martin's Press, 2006.

Clark, Katerina. *Peterburg, Crucible of Cultural Revolution*. Cambridge, US: Harvard University Press, 1995.

Deliukin, Leonid, and Vladimir Levtov, eds. *Sankt-Peterburgskii Gosudarstvennyi akademicheskii teatr opery i baleta imeni M.P. Musorgskogo*. St. Petersburg: LIK, 2001.

Fedosova, E.M., S.V. Laletin, and V. Golovitser. *Olga Spesivtseva*. Saint Petersburg: Art Deko, 2009.

Figes, Orlando. *A People's Tragedy, The Russian Revolution, 1891–1924*. New York: Penguin Books, 1996.

Fitzpatrick, Sheila. *The Commissariat of Enlightenment*. Cambridge: Cambridge University Press, 1970.

Fomkin, Alexei. *Dva veka "teatralnoi" tserkvi*. St. Petersburg: Akademiia russkogo baleta im. A. IA. Vaganovoi, 2003.

Frame, Murray. *The St. Petersburg Imperial Theaters: Stage and State in Revolutionary Russia, 1900–1920*. Jefferson, NC: McFarland, 2000.

Garafola, Lynn. *Diaghilev's Ballets Russes*. New York: Oxford University Press, 1989.

Goldner, Nancy. *Balanchine Variations*. Gainesville: University Press of Florida, 2008.

Goldner, Nancy. *More Balanchine Variations*. Gainesville: University Press of Florida, 2011.

Gottlieb, Robert. *George Balanchine, the Ballet Maker*. New York: HarperCollins, 2004.

Green, Martin, and John Swam. *The Triumph of Pierrot: The Commedia dell'Arte and the Modern Imagination*. University Park: Pennsylvania State University Press, 1986.

Hall, Coryne. *Imperial Dancer: Mathilde Kschessinska and the Romanovs*. Stroud, UK: Sutton, 2005.

Kelly, Catriona. *Children's World: Growing up in Russia, 1890–1991*. New Haven, CT: Yale University Press, 2007.

Kenez, Peter. *The Birth of the Propaganda State: Soviet Methods of Mass Mobilization, 1917–1929*. Cambridge: Cambridge University Press, 1985.

Khuchua, Pavel. *Meliton Balanchivadze*. Tbilisi: Zarya Vostoka, 1952.

Krasovskaya, Vera. *Vaganova: A Dance Journey from Petersburg to Leningrad*. Translated by Vera Siegel. Gainesville: University Press of Florida, 2005.

Kremshevskaya, Galina D. *Agrippina Iakovlevna Vaganova*. Leningrad: Iskusstvo, 1981.

Levenkov, Oleg. *Dzhordzh Balanchin, Ch. 1* [George Balanchine, Part 1]. Perm, Russia: Knizhnyi mir, 2007.

Levitin, Grigorii M. *Tatiana Georgievna Bruni*. Moscow: Khudozhnik RSFSR, 1986.

Lincoln, W. Bruce. *Red Victory: A History of the Russian Civil War*. New York: Simon and Schuster, 1989.

Lovell, Stephen. *Summerfolk: A History of the Dacha, 1710–2000*. Ithaca, NY: Cornell University Press, 2003.

Malmstad, John. *Mikhail Kuzmin: A Life in Art*. Cambridge, MA: Harvard University Press, 1999.

Maryinsky Theater, et al. *Vek Balanchina–The Balanchine Century, 1904–2004*. St. Petersburg: Aurora Design, 2004.

Marx, Karl, Friedrich Engels, V. I. Lenin, and I. V. Stalin. *The Woman Question*. New York: International Publishers, 1951.

McKean, Robert B. *St. Petersburg between the Revolutions: Workers and Revolutionaries, June 1907–February 1917*. New Haven, CT: Yale University Press, 1990.

Miller, Forrestt A. *Dmitrii Miliutin and the Reform Era in Russia*. Nashville, TN: Vanderbilt University Press, 1968.

O'Connor, Timothy Edward. *The Politics of Soviet Culture: Anatolii Lunacharskii*. Ann Arbor, MI: UMI Research Press, 1983.

Naiman, Eric. *Sex in Public: The Incarnation of Early Soviet Ideology*. Princeton, NJ: Princeton University Press, 1997.

Rayfield, Donald. *The Literature of Georgia: A History*. London: Garnett Press, 2010.

Rayfield, Donald. *Stalin and His Hangmen*. London: Viking, 2004.

Reynolds, Nancy. *Repertory in Review: 40 Years of the New York City Ballet*. New York: Dial Press, 1977.

Roné, Elvira. *Olga Preobrazhenskaya: A Portrait*. Translated by Fernau Hall. New York: M. Dekker, 1978.

Rudnitsky, Konstantin. *Russian and Soviet Theater 1905–1932*. Translated by Roxane Permar. Edited by Dr. Lesley Milne. London: Thames and Hudson, 1988.

Rykhliakov, Vadim. "M.I. Petipa in the Life and Art of the Ballerina V. T. Rykhliakova." ARB *Vestnik*, No. 2 (22), 2009.

Scheijen, Sjeng. *Diaghilev: A Life*. New York: Oxford University Press, 2009.

Scholl, Tim. *From Petipa to Balanchine*. New York: Routledge, 1994

Scholl, Tim. *Sleeping Beauty, A Legend in Progress*. New Haven, CT: Yale University Press, 2004.

Schwarz, Boris. *Music and Musical Life in Soviet Russia 1917–1970*. New York: W. W. Norton, 1972.

Sherikh, Dmitrii Yu. *1924: Iz Petrograda v Leningrad*. Moscow: MiM-Delta, 2004.

Shmakov, Gennady. *The Great Russian Dancers*. New York: Knopf, 1984.

Siegelbaum, Lewis H. *Soviet State and Society between Revolutions, 1918–1929*. Cambridge: Cambridge University Press, 1992.

Siegelbaum, Lewis H. *Cars for Comrades: The Life of the Soviet Automobile*. Ithaca, NY: Cornell University Press, 2008.

Souritz, Elizabeth. *Soviet Choreographers in the 1920s*. Translated by Lynn Visson. Edited, with additional translation, by Sally Banes. Durham, NC: Duke University Press, 1990.

Steinberg, John W. *All the Tsar's Men: Russia's General Staff and the Fate of the Empire, 1898–1914*. Washington, DC: Woodrow Wilson Center Press, 2010.

Suny, Ronald Grigor. *The Making of the Georgian Nation*. 2d ed. Bloomington: Indiana University Press, 1994.

Taper, Bernard. *Balanchine: A Biography*. Berkeley: University of California Press, 1984.

Twysden, A. E. *Alexandra Danilova*. New York: Kamin Dance Publishers, 1947.

Volkov, Solomon. *Balanchine's Tchaikovsky: Interviews with George Balanchine*. New York: Simon and Schuster, 1985.

Volkov, Solomon. *St. Petersburg: A Cultural History*. Translated by Antonina W. Bouis. New York: Free Press, 1995.

Wachtel, Andrew Baruch. *Plays of Expectations: Intertextual Relations in Russian Twentieth-Century Drama*. Seattle: University of Washington Press, 2006.

Wildman, Allan K. *The End of the Russian Imperial Army*. Princeton: Princeton University Press, 1980.

Wood, Elizabeth A. *The Baba and the Comrade: Gender and Politics in Revolutionary Russia*. Bloomington: Indiana University Press, 1997.

Wortman, Richard S. *Scenarios of Power, Myth and Ceremony in Russian Monarchy*, Volume Two. Princeton: Princeton University Press, 2000.

Yakovleva, Yulia. *Mariinskii teatr: Balet XX vek*. Moscow: Novoe Literaturnoe Obozrenie, 2005.

Index

· 270 ·

· 279 ·